CW01023314

# Making Strategic Leaders

# Making Strategic Leaders

Narendra Laljani

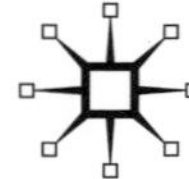



First published 2009 by
PALGRAVE MACMILLAN

Palgrave Macmillan in the UK is an imprint of Macmillan Publishers Limited, registered in England, company number 785998, of Houndmills, Basingstoke, Hampshire RG21 6XS.

Palgrave Macmillan in the US is a division of St Martin's Press LLC, 175 Fifth Avenue, New York, NY 10010.

Palgrave Macmillan is the global academic imprint of the above companies and has companies and representatives throughout the world.

Palgrave® and Macmillan® are registered trademarks in the United States, the United Kingdom, Europe and other countries

ISBN-13: 978-0-230-57749-7 hardback

This book is printed on paper suitable for recycling and made from fully managed and sustained forest sources. Logging, pulping and manufacturing processes are expected to conform to the environmental regulations of the country of origin.

A catalogue record for this book is available from the British Library.

A catalogue record for this book is available from the Library of Congress.

10 9 8 7 6 5 4 3 2 1
18 17 16 15 14 13 12 11 10 09

Printed and bound in Great Britain by
CPI Antony Rowe, Chippenham and Eastbourne

*For*
*Mangho and Shanta Laljani*
*and with an eye to the future,*
*for Milan*

# Contents

# List of Figures and Tables

## Figures



## Tables

# Acknowledgements

A large number of people gave generously with their time and ideas while I was developing the thinking that underpins this work. I would particularly like to express my gratitude to Prof. Cliff Bowman, Dr. Catherine Bailey, and Dr. Veronique Ambrosini – all at Cranfield University – for their guidance and support.

I am also thankful to Prof. Joe Nellis, Prof. Mark Jenkins, and Prof. Kim James at Cranfield, Prof. Veronica Hope-Hailey at City University, Dr. Eddie Blass at the University of Hertfordshire, and Prof. Henry Mintzberg at McGill University, for their encouragement and always insightful comments.

At Ashridge, I am indebted to Bob Stilliard, Fiona Dent, Kai Peters, James Moncrieff, Steve Watson, Albert Zandvoort, Phil Hodgson, Stefan Wills, Elaine Stedman, Gabriele Silver, Peter Silver, and Sarah Graves for their support and assistance.

I would also like to acknowledge the contribution of the various interviewees at different stages of the research who offered their candid reflections on their roles, the leadership challenges they faced, and their formative development experiences. For obvious reasons, their identities have been anonymized.

This study also builds on the work of numerous distinguished scholars. Every effort has been made to cite them appropriately and secure copyright permission where required. If any inadvertent omissions have occurred I will be happy to remedy these at the earliest opportunity.

On a more personal note, this book evolved over several years. The start of the research that informs it coincided with the arrival of my son, Milan, and frequently competed with his needs and interests. This balancing act – which I hope Milan will agree some day that I got mostly right – would not have been possible without the support of my wife, Karin. Thank you.

# Introduction

Following 15 years in managerial roles in industry, I took to an academic and consulting career in 1995. In this incarnation, my early work was anchored in the teaching of strategy, and strategic analysis in particular. Both the content and style of my teaching were greatly influenced by my own educational experience as an MBA student in the late 1970s. I had been taught to believe that managers planned, organized, directed, and controlled: a seemingly elegant and linear process. Curiously, leadership did not get much attention in that curriculum.

At Ashridge, my audiences were mainly made up of executives on short management development programmes. Although they had a bias for action and practice, they appeared to find analytical frameworks seductive. I often wondered if I was colluding with their needs for simplicity in a complex world. At the back of my mind was the Bill Gates question, posed to me by an MBA student: *are you suggesting that Bill Gates did a strategic analysis of the software industry when he was building Microsoft?*

For some time, then, I nursed a sense of unease about my professional practice. Perhaps there was more to strategy than analysis, more to leader effectiveness than a vision and self-awareness, and more to development than a high-impact classroom experience. I perceived a gap between the reality of the world of the strategic leader and common leadership development interventions, and as I inquired further I realized that I was not alone. This gap became the primary motivation for this research.

This study unites the domains of strategy and leadership, and offers an integrated perspective on the dimensions, development, and deployment of strategic leader capability. The research was carried out in three phases. In the first, a conceptual framework was developed based on four key dimensions of capability: judgement, the strategic conversation, contextual mastery, and behavioural complexity. In the second phase, empirical findings from in-depth qualitative interviews with individuals in strategic leadership roles corroborated and enriched the framework; highlighted the importance of informal learning; and emphasized the role of mentors and stretch assignments as formative development processes. In addition, critical reflection, through either informal or formal processes, was found to play an important "sense-making" and developmental role. In the third phase, action research involving two formal leader development interventions was undertaken with the objective of developing strategic leader capability while deliberately managing the influential development processes identified.

The results indicated that while strategic leader capability can be learned, and that key development processes can be simulated with varying degrees of success, positive performance outcomes also require high self-efficacy. Based on these findings, this study presents a model which links together strategic leadership capability, major development processes, self-efficacy, context, and performance outcomes. These insights into strategic leader performance and development have significant practical implications for individuals, organizations, and the leader development industry. I believe the research also raises numerous interesting questions that merit further inquiry.

# 1
# From Classroom to Boardroom: A Gap in Knowledge and Practice

## The problem

This book documents a journey of discovery based on three thematically linked research projects. While the details of these are reported in the following chapters, the background on the issue or "problem" that motivated this study, an overview of the research questions, and the accompanying research methodology are discussed here.

There has been a substantial increase in management training and development spend, particularly in Europe and the USA, over the last ten years. The global executive education market is now estimated to be worth over $12–14 billion, with business schools accounting for just over a quarter of this. In the UK alone, there are several hundred business schools, consulting firms, and training organizations competing in this market. This reflects the widespread appreciation in organizations of the need to invest in the development of people, and also the opportunity to use development interventions as an instrument of organizational change.

Paradoxically, this growth has been accompanied by increasing disquiet and debate about the effectiveness and impact of business schools and management and leadership development interventions, both in the lay media as well as in the research community. One example is symptomatic: a widely cited study by AACSB (the Association to Advance Collegiate Schools of Business) found that management graduates thought that the ability to communicate effectively with another person was the single most useful skill in their career, but that only 6% of business schools were even "moderately effective" in teaching that skill (*The Economist*, 2002).

Other common criticisms levelled at business schools include the arguments that learning outcomes are respected more in theory than in practice; that major business innovations are emanating from business itself rather than business schools; and that business schools have lost their edge in producing the kind of research that truly improves the practice of business (Schleede, 2002).

Wilmott argues that management development "does little to develop the capacity to learn how to understand the complexities of management practice or to respond to new challenges" (1994: 110), whilst Williams laments the use of "pretentious American psycho-babble" in development interventions (1996: 3). Using a socio-psychological perspective of client organizations, Clarke (1999: 38) describes management development as a game of "meaningless outcomes". It has also been asserted that within the academic community itself, other than in a handful of subjects, there is no basis for what sound learning means in many disciplines (Frost and Fukami, 1997).

The field of strategy – this author's professional area of interest – offers a case in point. The desire to improve strategic capability is high on the wish list of individuals and organizations investing in or participating in management development interventions. For example, a University of Michigan survey of "Pressing Problems" faced by executives identifies three strategy "hot buttons" viz. strategic thinking, staying ahead of the competition, and aligning vision, strategy and behaviour as among the top ten challenges faced by executives (Lippert, 2001). However, in responding to these needs, it is this author's belief that the teaching of strategy continues to be characterized by significant limitations, and that management development interventions aimed at improving the ability of individuals to "strategize" suffer from a potential disconnect between classroom concepts and workplace reality. This gap is best epitomized in a quandary expressed by a professor of strategic management: "there is a trade-off between how much analysis you do and how much reality" (Bongiorno, 1993: 3).

A study which examined how members of the Academy of Management teach business policy or strategic management, discovered that such courses focused primarily on analysing the strengths and weaknesses of the firm, identifying strategy alternatives, and determining the firm's goals and objectives and that "recent empirical and theoretical advances had not found their way into the classroom" (Alexander et al, 1986: 342). Although this finding is somewhat dated, continuing evidence, as well as this author's personal experience, suggests that, in the main, little has changed. For example, the prevalent teaching of strategy has been described as "the mindless application of technique" in which strategy is "equated with analytical decision making" (Mintzberg and Lampel, 2001: 2). It is clear that although strategy theory has moved away from an emphasis on analytical frameworks and techniques; pedagogy has not. Strategy coursework has largely remained focused on how to plan and analyse in highly artificial contexts, and "the outcome has often been to programme students with a laundry list of techniques" (Liedtka and Rosenblum, 1998: 286). In general, current practice in teaching and management development in the area of strategy appears to be largely oriented towards "strategy as planning". This is but one of many strategy-making modes, and arguably one that is not closest to reality.

The domain of leadership is also not immune from such criticisms. For example, Allio (2005: 1072) argues that "organisations continue to embrace the myth that they can develop leaders by investing in leadership training programmes – in a day, week, or year – and the dubious proposition of all suppliers is that an intensive educational experience can raise consciousness, change behaviour, and transform managers into leaders. Those who graduate from strategy or leadership programmes acquire a new vocabulary and literacy, and this may allow them to act with greater authority. Essentially they give participants a cognitive experience, but do not teach how to lead".

In a similar vein, Conger and Fulmer (2003: 78) observe that leadership development as traditionally practised focuses on one-off events, and "participants often return to the office energised and enthused, only to be stifled by the reality of corporate life". Similar scepticism is found within the client and practitioner community, with apparent post-programme behaviour changes often dismissed with the stereotypical comment "he must have been on a training programme, give him a few days, he'll be back to normal".

Client perspectives on what constitutes development are also noteworthy – in one study, most of the executives surveyed regarded development as simply a function of training programmes (Handfield-Jones, 2000). In other words, clients often focus on the development event rather than the learning process and outcomes. The limitations of such a perspective are highlighted by Tichy (2002: 161) who argues that "80% of leadership development comes on the job and through life experiences. Formal development has the potential to deliver only about 20% of the knowledge and capabilities needed". Despite this, there is an entire industry – made up, *inter alia*, of business schools, corporate universities, and learning and development consultancies – dedicated to improving and leveraging the latter 20%.

While much of value is no doubt achieved through formal learning, this apparent contradiction of increasing investment for doubtful return suggests that closer attention needs to be paid to the relationship between the realities of the managerial world and the management and leadership development industries, and this underlines the need for new approaches to learning and development. These issues constitute a gap in knowledge and practice, and serve as the motivation for this study.

## Research overview

### Purpose

The overall purpose of this research is to enhance and support the development, and as a result, the performance of individuals in "strategic leader" roles. In order to maintain a distinction between the individual leader, as opposed to the collective or organizational leadership process, the term "strategic leader" is used throughout this study.

The goal is to produce knowledge for action, which is a defining characteristic of applied research. In particular, a "practice perspective" (Whittington, 2003) is followed, in which the concern is principally for the performance of practitioners, and only indirectly for the performance of the organization as a whole.

In this study, a key choice has therefore been made to focus on the individual within an organizational context, rather than on the organization itself. Although organizational routines and team dynamics also affect strategic outcomes, the individual's ability to understand, interpret, work within, or shape these variables may be viewed as part of the capability of the individual. It is also suggested that groups and organizations are made up of individuals, and therefore both thought and action originate within the individual and in interactions between individuals. Additionally, the research is driven by the desire to improve the effectiveness of learning and development interventions, most of which occur at the level of the individual.

Another important boundary decision in this research has been to examine the strategic leader role at the apex of the organization, as this author's professional work is primarily concerned with the development of individuals for such roles.

### Objectives

The specific questions around which this research is structured are as follows:

1. What are the dimensions of strategic leader capability?
2. What are the processes by which individuals in strategic leader roles acquire or develop these capabilities?

3. Can the influential development processes be deliberately managed, and if so, with what effects?

Based on these, this study aims to develop a theoretical framework about strategic leader capability and its development. In this context, the term theory is being used to denote functionality i.e. patterns of relationships and explanatory schemes, or a "heuristic device for organising what we know, or think we know, at a particular time about some more or less explicitly posed question or issue" (Inkeles, 1964: 28). In line with an idea widely attributed to Weick (1979), the intention is to present a "workable version of reality". In the process of developing the theoretical framework, this author has been guided by the tests of theory suggested by Hjelle and Ziegler (1981), which are:

1. *Verifiability*: the concepts must be clearly and explicitly defined and logically related to one another, and must lend themselves to verification by independent investigators
2. *Heuristic value*: the theory must stimulate further research
3. *Internal consistency*: the theory should not contradict itself, and must account for things in an internally consistent way within a given set of assumptions
4. *Parsimony*: the number of concepts required to explain events within its domain must be economical. The law of parsimony, also known as Occam's Razor, states that the preferred explanation is the one that demands the fewest number of concepts
5. *Comprehensiveness*: the range and diversity of phenomena encompassed by a theory must be comprehensive, as opposed to a narrow, more circumscribed theory
6. *Functional significance*: the theory must be useful in helping people to understand relevant human behaviour.

In order to explore, describe, and understand strategic leader capability, a qualitative research strategy (Blaikie, 2000) has been followed, implying that the findings may have "theory generalizability" but not "data generalizability" (Johnson and Harris, 2002: 109). Such an approach is consistent with the philosophical stance which underpins this research, and which is explored in the following section.

## Philosophical orientation

Perceptions of knowledge and the process of knowledge creation are influenced by underpinning philosophical attitudes. A philosophical orientation may be characterized as a belief system or worldview that guides the researcher, based on assumptions about ontology i.e. a view on the nature of reality, and epistemology i.e. a view on how we know the reality. Varying amalgams of opposing ontological and epistemological perspectives result in a diversity of philosophical positions (Chia, 2002).

This study eschews the notion of an external and objective reality which is independent of human experience and which can be accessed in a detached manner. By contrast, this author has assumed that the phenomena under study are socially constructed and based on perceptions and experiences of individuals, and that the narrative constructed by a researcher in this domain is not neutral, and is in fact also shaped by the interests and direct involvement of the researcher. Best described as constructivism, the implications of this philosophical orientation are that while appropriate for an inquiry aimed at improving understanding of phenomena, knowledge is shaped by the coalescence of individual accounts, and is subject to continuous revision. This encourages humility in claims made in the representation of reality, and encourages reflexivity on the part of the researcher. The key considerations in assessing the quality of knowledge and progress in its accumulation are authenticity, and increasing sophistication (Guba and Lincoln, 1998).

**Approach**

Phase I commenced with the premise that there was a need to improve our understanding of the implications of various strategic and leadership processes for the capability and skill sets of the individual. The identification of the elements of strategic leader capability at the level of the individual therefore formed the starting point for the research, and this phase was exploratory in nature. Since strategic leader capability did not lend itself to direct observation, its nature and function had to be first imagined and modelled, and then evidence for its existence sought. Phase I was therefore a conceptual inquiry based on a critical review across several domains of literature. The inquiry was shaped by conversations with an informal panel of experts, and support for the findings was secured via two focus groups. Phase I culminated in a conceptual framework of strategic leader capability.

The purpose of Phase II was to explore strategic leader capability and its development from the perspective of individuals in strategic leader roles. Twenty-five individuals in strategic leader roles were interviewed. In order to "stay open to surprise", a deliberate decision was taken to go into Phase II, to the extent feasible, on a "theory and expectation free basis" (Johnson and Harris, 2002: 110). In other words, while this author obviously could not be an "empty vessel", attention was paid to the potential for bias brought about by the author's prior experiences. The intention was to be conscious of, and suppress, preconceived notions; to be mindful of emerging questions, constructs, and relationships; and to remain faithful to the voices of the interviewees. This phase resulted in corroboration and enrichment of the conceptual findings of Phase I, and led to an empirically adjusted framework. Phase II also surfaced an unexpected pattern in influential development processes.

Recognizing the shortcomings in current practice, and armed with an initial stance shaped by "working hypotheses" generated from Phases I and II, Phase III sought to improve strategic leader development practice in "live" settings. This author was directly involved in designing, carrying out, and evaluating the outcomes of two strategic leader development interventions. This action research phase yielded new perspectives on leader development and the deployment of strategic leader capability, as well as provoking ideas for future development strategies.

A brief overview of the approach and methodology adopted across the three phases, and the outcomes, is shown in Table 1.1.

Chapters 2 to 6 provide details of the three research projects undertaken in the three phases referred to in Table 1.1. Finally, Chapter 7 provides:

- a "stock-taking" of the key findings
- an attempt to weave the findings into a new theoretical framework
- a review of the theoretical contribution made by this research
- an exploration of the implications for practice
- a discussion of the limitations of this study and the possibilities for further research.

**Table 1.1** Overview of the Research

| | Phase I | Phase II | Phase III |
|---|---|---|---|
| **Purpose** | A conceptual framework of strategic leader capability | Patterns in the dimensions and development of strategic leader capability | Developing strategic leaders: a new synthesis |
| **Approach** | Conceptual | Empirical | Action research, empirical, and conceptual |
| **Methodology** | Inter-disciplinary literature review guided by expert panel, and testing "face validity" of findings via two focus groups | In-depth qualitative interviews with 25 individuals in strategic leader roles | Engagement with the development literature, and the design, delivery and review of two longitudinal strategic leader development interventions involving 20 executives |
| **Outcomes** | Conceptual framework with four key dimensions of strategic leader capability: engagement with strategic paradoxes, understanding and challenging context, the ability to conduct a strategic conversation, and cognitive and behavioural complexity | Support for and adjustment of the conceptual framework, and identification of patterns in leader development: mentors, stretch assignments, and reflection and networking | An integrated perspective of the development processes, and the role of self-efficacy in leader development and deployment of capability |

# 2
# The Strategic Leader

## Introduction to Phase I

The purpose of the first phase of this study was to explore the make-up of strategic leader capability at the level of the individual as a basis for further research.

A key objective of this phase of the research was to examine existing literature in order to develop an enhanced understanding of the constituents of strategic leader capability, the processes by which strategic leader capability is exercised, the contextual considerations in this process, and implications for the effectiveness of individuals in strategic leader roles.

Phase I also forms a basis for the subsequent research in Phases II and III, which addresses the questions: what are the formative development processes that contribute to the acquisition of strategic leader capability, and how can strategic leader capability be developed most effectively?

The principal ideas developed in the course of Phase I are discussed in Chapters 2 and 3. Beginning with a brief note on *Methodology*, the rest of this chapter provides a broad appreciation of the multi-faceted nature of strategy and strategic processes in reality, which is the context within which strategic leadership is exercised, and which strategic leaders must engage with. This represents an essential starting point for understanding the capability required by individuals in strategic leader roles.

In particular, *Perspectives on strategy and the strategic process* examines the range and complexity of strategic processes that individuals in strategic roles must contend with.

*The strategic leader* focuses on the roles that individuals play in strategy and the strategic process, and indicates the manner in which the capability of individuals in strategic leader roles may be an important contributor to organizational success.

*Key themes* briefly summarizes the preceding discussion about strategy and the roles of individuals.

With this background, Chapter 3 thereafter examines the dimensions of strategic leader capability at a more granular level.

## Methodology

An inter-disciplinary literature review, based on initial suggestions made by an informal panel of experts drawn from academia and consulting, was the basis of Phase I. For details of the experts, see Appendix 1(a). The experts not only provided their own point of view and, where possible, sanity checks on emergent findings, but also drew attention to relevant prior research.

In early consultations with the panel, it became clear that the strategic management literature did not, in itself, provide complete answers to the questions about strategic leader capability under consideration. In order to develop a more comprehensive and coherent view, it was necessary to synthesize insights gained from multi-disciplinary streams of literature such as strategy, leadership, organization theory, and psychology. These represented broad fields of inquiry – which often overlapped – rather than discrete domains, and were chosen in consultation with the expert panel.

Reflective immersion in, and a critical review of these domains was undertaken. In the process, over 200 scholarly articles in these domains were examined. The papers were selected in order to embrace a diversity of perspectives and points of view, and to cast a net wide enough to minimize the chances of a relevant concept being missed. Recurrent themes and patterns were identified, until no additional constructs seemed to emerge.

The conclusions from this phase of the research were also discussed and tested with two focus groups – conducted by an independent facilitator – composed of representatives of the leadership development and managerial communities.

Lastly, this author's personal experience of more than 25 years in both general management and management development roles (the latter has included strategy development and implementation workshops with over 2,500 senior managers) inevitably also influenced some of the observations made in this study. This entailed a process of critical reflection, in which the author questioned his previously held assumptions, and re-evaluated prior experience, in the light of new learning gained during the course of this research.

While the ensuing discussion will develop all the key concepts and ideas further, some working definitions may be useful at this stage:

*Strategy*: a pattern in a stream of actions and decisions that shapes the future of an organization (after Mintzberg, 1978)

*Strategic Process*: how strategies are formed and implemented (Chakravarthy and White, 2002)

*Strategic Leader Role*: a role with the opportunity and empowerment to influence the strategic process and outcomes, commonly found at or near the apex of the organization

*Strategic Leader Capability*: the ability to think and act strategically in a manner most appropriate to a given context

Underpinning this, a view has been taken that capability is the ability to create resources or make them more valuable or sustainable. Capabilities therefore include tacit knowledge, skills, abilities, and routines (Miller et al, 2002) as well as judgement, perspective, and energy (Christensen and Donovan, 1999).

## Perspectives on strategy and the strategic process

### Strategy

Thanks to its multi-dimensional and situational nature, strategy has been defined in a variety of ways, but often with the common theme of a deliberate and conscious set of guidelines that determine actions into the future. This is typified by Chandler's view of strategy as "the determination of the basic long term goals and objectives of the enterprise, and the adoption of courses of action and the allocation of resources necessary for carrying out these goals" (1962: 13). On the other hand, in alternative views, strategy has been defined as "good luck rationalized in hindsight" (de Bono, 1984: 143) and "a more or less explicit articulation of the firm's theory... about its achievements" (Burgelman, 1983a: 66).

Mintzberg (1978) observes that strategy is commonly viewed as (a) explicit (b) developed consciously and purposefully, and (c) made in advance of the specific decisions, i.e. strategy as plan. Mintzberg (1978) labels the deliberate and conscious plan as "intended strategy".

Intended strategies that do not get realized can be described as unrealized strategies, and realized strategies that were never intended may be called emergent strategies. Additionally, there are other relationships between intended and realized strategies, e.g. intended strategies that get over realized, emergent strategies that get formalized as deliberate ones, and intended strategies that change form and become, in part, emergent. According to Mintzberg, strategy in general and realized strategy in particular, can be defined as a "pattern in a stream of decisions" (1978: 935). In other words, when a sequence of decisions in some area exhibits a consistency over time, a strategy will be considered to have formed. This perspective enables us to consider strategy as intended, as well as having evolved or emerged. The strategy maker may formulate a strategy through a conscious process, or a strategy may form gradually, perhaps unintentionally. Research on strategy *formation* – as distinct from formulation – can then focus on a tangible phenomenon, the decision stream. Strategies therefore become observed patterns in such decision streams.

This decision-based view of strategy appears to have wide support. Frederickson (1983) points out that while not all organizations have formal plans, they all make strategic decisions. Clearly, however, not all decisions are strategic. Eisenhardt and Zbaracki (1992) define a strategic decision as one that is important, in terms of the actions taken, the resources committed, and the precedents set. Chaffee (1985: 89) suggests that organizations use strategy to deal with changing environments. Because change brings novel combinations of circumstances to the organization, the substance of strategy remains "unstructured, un-programmed, non-routine, and non-repetitive". Strategic decisions are therefore related to the environment and are non-routine, and are also considered to be important enough to affect the overall welfare of the organization.

## The strategic process

The strategic process may usefully be distinguished from the content of strategy.

Frederickson (1984) defined strategic process as a pattern of organization behaviour that is visible to executive level members and postulates that the characteristics of that process tend to be consistent across decisions that are clearly perceived as strategic i.e. there is an assumption of consistency. Hart and Banbury (1994) argue that strategy-making can be conceptualized as a key process requiring purposeful design. Most recently, Chakravarthy and White (2002: 182) have simplified several of these views of strategic process into "how strategies are formed and implemented".

Chakravarthy and White (2002) observe that while strategy content researchers describe "attractive destinations", or the *what*; the getting there, or "the journey", is the preoccupation of strategy process researchers concerned with *how* strategies are formed and implemented. While recognizing the dangers of a disconnect between the journey and the destination, they suggest that the complexity of the strategy process frustrates efforts to establish explicit linkages, although it may be intuitively self-evident that good strategies result from good strategic processes. Chakravarthy and White (2002) contend that the strategic process is concerned with improving, consolidating, and changing the firm's strategic position, and that "the strategic process must bridge the artificial divide between strategy formation and implementation" (2002: 184). Underlining the importance of including implementation in the strategic process, Pettigrew (interviewed in Starkey, 2002) takes the view that the process has two parts – choice and change – and highlights that strategic decision-making and implementation are therefore inextricably intertwined.

Although Hannan and Freeman (1989) suggest that strategic decision processes matter little in the face of external constraints and environmental determinism, most researchers do not share this view. Dean and Sharfman (1996) observe that the argument that strategic processes matter rests on two assumptions. Firstly, different processes lead to different choices. While this may seem intuitively obvious, it should be seen in the light of the observation that environmental constraints play a role in determining choices and thus reduce the importance of choice processes. However, some managers make very poor strategic choices, with devastating consequences for their firms, while others in very similar circumstances make much better choices for their firms. Secondly, different choices lead to different outcomes. Once again, external forces also influence outcomes, but it is unlikely that the influence of external forces eliminates the impact of strategic choice on effectiveness, as it is hard to imagine a situation in which all potential choices will be equally successful or unsuccessful.

## Strategic process typologies

As Hart (1992) observes, a range of strategic process archetypes have been developed by numerous researchers. As a result, our understanding of strategic process has become more finely-grained over the years.

The foundations of strategic process theory lie in the well-known rational model, which calls for comprehensive and exhaustive analysis prior to a decision. The rational model applied to strategy suggests systematic environment analysis, assessment of internal strengths and weaknesses, explicit goal setting, evaluation of alternative courses of action, and the development of a comprehensive plan to achieve the goals. Organizationally, this usually calls for a formal planning system.

However, behavioural theory has challenged the assumptions of rationality that underpin the planning approach. Nutt (1984) observes that managers do not use the normative methods for good decision-making prescribed by scholars. Most decision processes are solution centred – an approach that restricts innovation – with a limited number of alternatives considered, and a perpetuation of biases. Hart (1992) emphasizes that individuals and organizations can only achieve bounded rationality. Heuristics and biases in human judgement result in many departures from optimality.

The motivational assumptions inherent in rational strategy-making processes are also questionable. Also, at an organizational level, strategic assumptions and frames of reference can predispose firms to act in certain ways. Independent assumptions about organizational intention and changing roles can result in a "garbage can model" of strategic choice in which strategy emerges out of "organised anarchy" (Cohen et al, 1972). Eisenhardt and Zbaracki (1992), reflecting on rationality in strategic decision-making, conclude that people are rational, but that rationality is bounded such that power wins battles of choice, and chance affects the course of strategic decision-making. Further, although there is a long-standing view of rationality versus bounded rationality as a continuum, rationality is more multi-dimensional. Decision-makers are rational in some ways but not in others. Strategic decision-making is therefore best described as an interweaving of boundedly rational political and social processes.

Mintzberg (1978) accelerated the developing scepticism of the traditional view of the strategic process by identifying three modes of strategy-making: planning, adaptive, and entrepreneurial. The planning mode represented the dominant view at that time. In the tradition of management science and bureaucratic theory, it describes the process as highly ordered, neatly integrated, with strategies explicated on schedule by a purposeful organization. The adaptive mode is described as a process in which many decision-makers with conflicting goals bargain among themselves to produce a stream of incremental, disjointed decisions. In the entrepreneurial mode, a powerful leader takes bold, risky decisions towards the vision of the organization's future. A compelling argument is also made that in addition to the limitations derived from bounded rationality, there are other significant problems with the planning mode. The dichotomy between strategy formulator and implementer appears to be based on two questionable assumptions: first, that the formulator is fully informed about the environment and the organization's capabilities, or at least as well informed as the implementer; and second, that the environment is sufficiently stable, or at least predictable, to ensure that there would be no need for reformulation during implementation. Mintzberg and Waters (1985) subsequently refined this work and suggested that deliberate and emergent strategies may be conceived as two ends of a continuum along which real world strategy processes lie. Along this continuum, various other types of strategy may be found: planned, entrepreneurial, ideological, umbrella, process, unconnected, consensus, and imposed.

Mintzberg and Lampel (1999) identified ten different strategy process schools, which may be divided into three prescriptive and seven descriptive categories. This work represents the most comprehensive, most nuanced, and most contemporary view of strategy-making, and therefore merits further description here:

*Prescriptive schools*

1. Design
   In this perspective, which dates back to the 1960s, "senior management formulates clear, simple, and unique strategies in a deliberate process of conscious thought, which is neither formally analytical nor informally intuitive". The design school continues to influence the teaching and practice of strategy even today.
2. Planning
   This school makes assumptions similar to the design school, but significantly, adds the notion that "the process is not just cerebral, but also a formal one that consists of distinct stages, checklists, and techniques. The formalization results in staff planners replacing senior managers as the key players".
3. Positioning
   In this view, heavily influenced by industrial organization economics, the essence of strategy is a choice of generic positions selected through rigorous industry analysis. It is suggested that the apparent veneer of "science" has resulted in a burgeoning strategy consulting industry based on the positioning school.

*Descriptive schools*

4. Entrepreneurial
   This school is centred on the chief executive, and is underpinned by the idea that the strategy process is anchored not in precise plans, but in the vision or broad perspective of a forceful leader.
5. Cognitive
   This school is based on psychology, and puts the mental process e.g. "cognitive frames, models, maps, and concepts" used by individuals and groups to construct strategy in their minds at the centre of the strategy process.
6. Learning
   The most significant of the descriptive schools, learning describes a process in which "strategies are emergent, found throughout the organization", and action may precede the plan. "Formulation and implementation therefore intertwine".
7. Power
   In this school, strategy-making is essentially a political process, and strategies are negotiated through persuasion and coalition-building.
8. Cultural
   While the focus of the power school is self-interest, the cultural school focuses on common interest, and views strategy as a social process rooted in organization culture.
9. Environmental
   Strategy is essentially shaped in response to the demands of the environment, with the organization having limited freedom to manoeuvre.
10. Configuration
    This is an integrative school that visualizes organizations as configurations i.e. "coherent clusters of characteristics and behaviours", and integrates the points of view of the other schools. Each configuration therefore has its own unique place.

Mintzberg and Lampel acknowledge that while the prescriptive schools are clear and consistent, making the dissemination and adoption of their ideas into practice easier, the descriptive schools are fuller and richer, but are untidy, and "can end up in tangled confusion, generating many contingencies and multiple perspectives that stymie application" (1999: 29). Mintzberg and Lampel (1999) also leave open the possibility that some or many of the schools could represent different stages of the same strategy process. For example, data that is analysed in the positioning school could feed into the cognitive school that focuses on the mind of the strategist, and into the planning school which looks ahead to program the strategy created.

Nine of the ten schools may usefully be recast along the deliberate–emergent and prescriptive–descriptive axes, as shown in Figure 2.1. The configuration school – a descriptive one – has been omitted, as it suggests that unique configurations of the other schools may be discernible by context.

It may be noted that the labels of prescriptive and descriptive are not mutually exclusive. Indeed in a discussion with this author, Mintzberg has suggested that planning has some descriptive elements and conversely, learning has some prescriptive elements. However, it is this author's contention that each school has a discernible centre of gravity along the prescriptive–descriptive axis.

Other sense-making devices for the plethora of strategic processes have also been suggested. Miller (1989) suggests that strategic processes may be characterized by the inherent degree of rationality, interaction, and assertiveness. *Rationality* may be evaluated on a scale of high or low information processing; *interaction* on a scale of a high or low degree of politicking, bargaining, and consensus building; and *assertiveness* on the

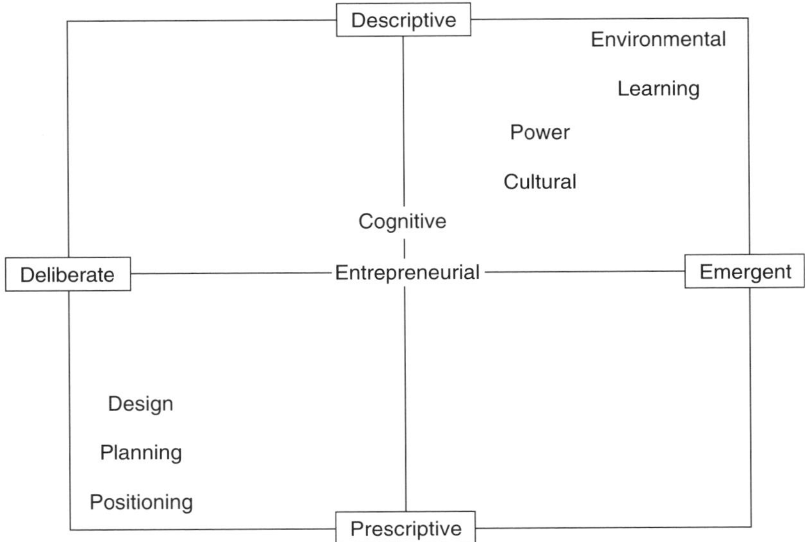


*Figure 2.1* Re-casting the Strategy Schools

levels of risk-taking and the degree to which decisions are made reactively or proactively.

In a similar vein, Hart and Banbury (1994) observe that three recurrent variables may be used to differentiate the various perspectives: *rationality*, or the extent to which the strategic process can or should be comprehensive, exhaustive and analytical in approach; *involvement*, that is to say, the extent and type of involvement of organization members in the strategy-making process; and *vision*, or the role of top managers in the strategic process and the extent to which leaders can proactively articulate a clear strategic vision and motivate organizational members to adopt it.

An assessment of the literature therefore suggests that as strategy process theory has evolved away from an exclusive dependence on the rational model, it has also moved away from prescription to description, with obvious implications for management practice. In effect, as our understanding of the reality of the strategy process has improved, advice to managers on ways and means in which they can develop their ability to make and execute strategy has not kept pace. At the same time, the teaching of strategy has remained anchored largely in the design, planning, and positioning schools, i.e. the prescriptive schools.

## Bridging the planning/learning divide

The polarities of the various strategic process schools are perhaps best epitomized by Ansoff (1979), an advocate of planning, and Mintzberg, an advocate of learning. The same dichotomy is reflected in Hart's rational and transactive modes, and in Frederickson's synoptic and incremental modes.

Clearly, each extreme carries potential risks. For instance, Bonn (2001) identified the lack of strategic thinking as a major problem in organizations, regardless of whether the organization had a formalized strategic planning system or used a non-formalized approach. In formal systems, the problem was "getting carried away by detail and losing strategic perspective". On the other hand, in companies without a formalized system, the challenge was to "get decision makers to think in strategic rather than operational terms" (Bonn, 2001: 63).

Alongside, and perhaps influenced by, decades of research on the correlation between planning and performance, which have yielded inconsistent findings, there has been scepticism about the value of formal planning. Brews and Hunt (1999) question such a general condemnation, and contend that far from being the antithesis of learning, formal planning may be the necessary precursor to successful learning. Both are necessary, and neither is sufficient. In their view, dissatisfaction with formal planning has surfaced the practices to be avoided in planning, rather than providing support for the proposition that the remedy for bad planning is no planning. In fact, the remedy for bad planning is good planning, which includes learning and incrementalism within its ambit. Though plans should be specific, they must also be flexible, especially in unstable environments. Once formed, firms must be prepared to rework plans incrementally as plans proceed. Additionally, the planning capabilities of the firm can and do improve over time. In other words, "firms must both learn to plan and plan to learn" (Brews and Hunt, 1999: 889).

**The strategic process: A dynamic view**

A key implication of the diversity and simultaneity of strategic processes is that organizations cannot be neatly shoehorned into a strategic process type. Strategy-making in reality in most organizations is likely to be a mixture of various concurrent processes. Hart and Banbury (1994: 265) contend that "high performance firms were simultaneously planful and incremental, directive and participative, controlling and empowering, visionary and detailed". Purity of process therefore appears to be much less important than the nurturing of multiple, competing and complementary processes of strategy-making deep within the organization.

Quinn (1980) has also highlighted the multiple facets of the strategic process in reality, and observed that "successful managers acted logically and incrementally to improve the quality of information used in key decisions, to overcome the personal and political pressures resisting change...and to build the organizational awareness, understanding, and psychological commitment essential to effective strategies". Interestingly, implementation does not have to wait for the strategy to be fully evolved, and "by the time the strategies began to crystallize, pieces of them were already being implemented. Through the very processes they used to formulate their strategies, these executives had built sufficient organizational momentum and identity with the strategies to make them flow towards flexible and successful implementation" (Quinn, 1980: 17). Strategy formulation is therefore a continuously evolving analytical–political consensus forming process with neither a finite beginning nor a definite end. "The total process was anything but linear. It was a groping, cyclical process that often circled back on itself, with frequent interruptions and delays". This model of strategy-making is akin to "fermentation in biochemistry rather than an industrial assembly line" (Quinn, 1980: 13).

One important implication of such a plurality of processes is that the individual in strategy requires multiple competencies. For example, Stumpf and Mullen (1991: 53) suggest that understanding, accepting, and feeling comfortable with a strategy process that is "messy, non-linear, and iterative, and which involves discovery" is critical to the ability of effective strategic leaders.

Building on previous work by Mintzberg (1978, 1983), Moncrieff (1999) offers a model of strategy as a dynamic process, which involves the formation of strategic intent, the alignment of action with intent, and the response to emerging issues as well as the learning which is deeply implicated in all three. This model is displayed in Figure 2.2.

This model suggests that most deliberate strategies are, at best, intended strategies. Some elements of the strategic intent fall away unrealized (for example, due to an under-estimation of the challenge involved, or the resources required) while managers attempt to implement it. Meanwhile, the organization may have a "strategy in action" which may be divorced from the strategic intent. The "strategy in action" may be the outcome of habit, misunderstandings, or behaviours induced by personal preferences, peer pressure, or institutional mechanisms such as measures of performance. A key task for the manager therefore is to align the "strategy in action" with strategic intent. Meanwhile, in a dynamic environment, events bubble up to the surface of the organization – these may be unfore-

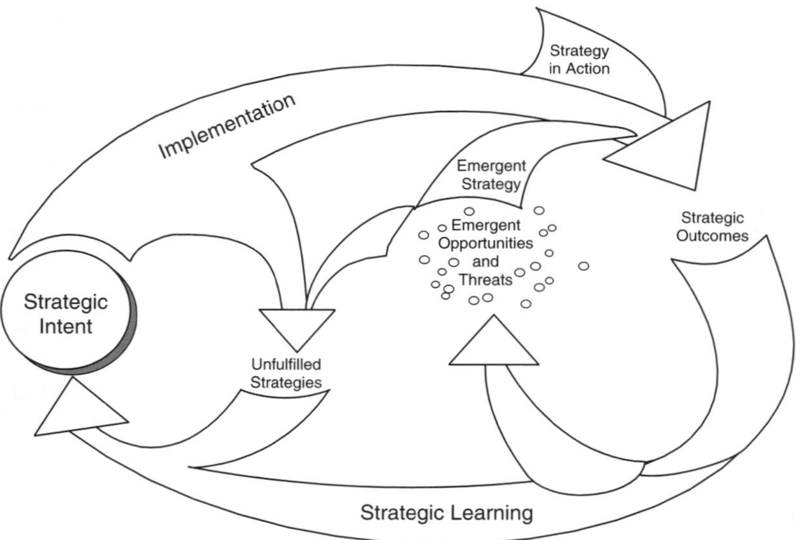


*Figure 2.2* A View of Strategy as a Dynamic Process

*Source*: From "Is Strategy Making a Difference?", by Moncrieff, J. in *Long Range Planning*, Vol. 32, No. 2, copyright © 1999, reproduced with permission of Elsevier Limited.

seen competitive actions, opportunities, or threats. Agility and flexibility is required to leverage these emergent strategies. The resulting strategic outcomes may therefore be very different from the original strategic intent. This creates a strategic learning opportunity for both the content and process of strategy, which in turn impacts the strategic intent. The strategic process is therefore a dynamic one, which must embrace deliberate strategies, strategies in action, emergent strategies, and strategic learning.

In summary, strategy in reality may be characterized as the outcome of messy, non-linear, and iterative process that are far removed from early theory as well as from commonplace and simplistic prescriptions. While strategy may be planned, it is often emergent, and effective strategy-making therefore requires a synthesis of both planning and learning. Strategies are shaped by both rational as well as social and political organizational processes. Although strategy is contextual, most organizations display a mixture of concurrent strategic processes.

The implications of strategy and the strategic process in reality for the individual in a strategic leader role are explored in the next section.

## The strategic leader

Why does individual strategic leader capability matter? Both the resource-based view of the firm and the strategic leadership perspective offer useful and complementary insights.

### Resource-based view

Hart (1992) observed that firms that demonstrate high strategic process capacity might be expected to perform well on more performance dimensions than single mode or less process capable organizations. Several researchers have advocated explicitly the desirability of combining different modes of strategy-making either sequentially or simultaneously. For example, Chaffee (1985) suggests that there might be a hierarchy of strategy-making types, where each successive level incorporates those that are less complex, and that firms accumulate strategic process skills over time.

This is consistent with the resource-based view of the firm (Barney, 1991) which holds that superior profit can be earned by leveraging resources that are valuable, rare, imperfectly imitable, and non-substitutable. It may be appropriate to think of firms possessing different combinations or levels of strategic processes and capabilities, and a competitive advantage may be secured from multiple competencies that are difficult to identify or replicate. Building on this theme, Hart and Banbury (1994) suggest that firms able to accumulate and develop several different process skills into a complex strategy-making "capability" might thus be expected to outperform less process capable organizations. In their research, Hart and Banbury (1994) concluded that capability counts, and that high capability is robust, i.e. higher levels of strategy-making process capability facilitate superior performance in a wide variety of settings and situations, and that strategy-making processes are significant predictors of firm performance.

Support for the importance of strategic process capability also comes from Eisenhardt and Martin (2000) who contend that both theoretical and empirical research into the sources of enduring competitive advantage has begun to point to organizational capabilities as being much more critical than product-market positions or tactics. Strategy-making is therefore a potential "dynamic capability" (Teece et al, 1997) through which managers pool their various business, functional, and personal expertise to make the choices that shape the major strategic moves of the firm.

While the previous points of view have tended to examine capability at the level of the organization, some researchers have bridged the organizational and individual levels. For instance, Castanias and Helfat (1991) suggest that superior managerial skills are rare and difficult to imitate resources which are internal to the firm, and which may be key to the firm's acquisition and maintenance of sustainable competitive advantage. In other words, the managerial ability to strategize effectively may, in itself, be a source of competitive advantage.

### Strategic leadership perspective

The strategic leadership perspective focuses even more closely on the individual. Numerous studies have recognized effective strategic leadership as a key asset, as well as an aspiration, for the firm. For example, a Korn Ferry study (1989), which was based on interviews with 1,500 leading business executives in 20 countries, determined that the CEO (Chief Executive Officer) of the future would be a "person of vision and a master strategist capable of winning battles even before they begin". Korn Ferry also suggested that the best CEOs would excel in several areas, chief amongst which were strategy formulation and implementation. In the same vein, Davids (1995: 58) cites a survey of 1,450 executives from 12 global corporations around the world, which found that the ability to "articulate a tangible vision, values, and strategy" for the firm was the most important of over 20 competencies considered to be crucial skills for global leaders in the future. Tait (1996) also reports that the most important key qualities of leadership were found to be "long term strategic thinking", "seeing the wood for the trees", the "big picture outlook" or "helicopter vision".

Ireland and Hitt (1999: 43) suggest that strategic leadership may be defined as a person's ability to "anticipate, envision, maintain flexibility, think strategically, and work with others to initiate changes that will create a viable future for the organisation". They identify the components of strategic leadership as vision, exploiting and maintaining core competencies, developing human capital, sustaining an effective organization culture, emphasizing ethical practices, and establishing balanced organizational controls. Ireland and Hitt (1999) go on to observe that when strategic leadership processes are difficult for competitors to understand and hence to imitate, the firm has created a competitive advantage.

Rowe (2001) offers a somewhat broader definition of strategic leadership, and defines it as the ability to influence others to make decisions that enhance the long-term viability of the organization, while at the same time maintaining its short-term financial stability. This idea, which is consistent with the idea of strategic paradoxes that will be developed in Chapter 3, is displayed in Figure 2.3. In this view, strategic leadership is a synergistic combination of visionary leadership which is future-oriented

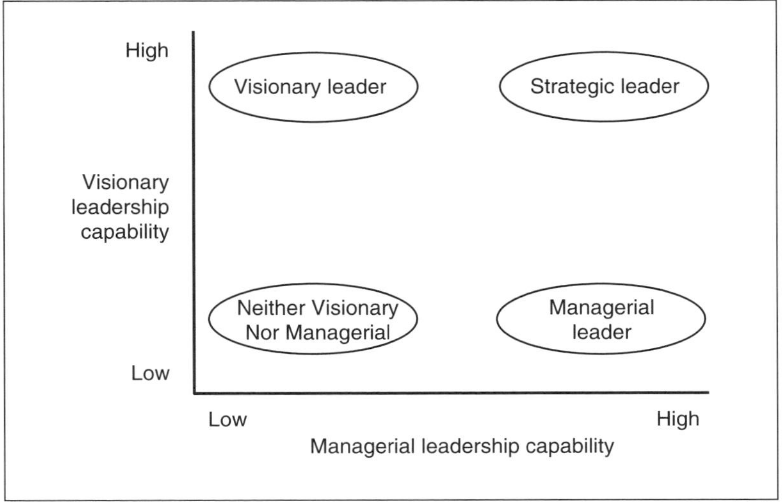


*Figure 2.3* Managerial, Visionary and Strategic Leadership

*Source*: From "Creating Wealth in Organizations: The Role of Strategic Leadership", by Rowe, G.W. in *Academy of Management Executive*, Vol. 15, No. 1, copyright © 2001 by Academy of Management (NY). Reproduced with permission of Academy of Management (NY) via Copyright Clearance Center.

and concerned with risk-taking, and managerial leadership, which is concerned with stability and preservation of the existing order.

Rowe (2001) suggests that the exercise of strategic leadership is a contributor to organizational wealth creation. Since the development of sustainable competitive advantage is the universal objective for all commercial organizations, being able to exercise strategic leadership in a competitively superior manner facilitates the firm's efforts to earn superior returns on its investment.

**Roles in the strategic process**

Clearly, not all leaders play a strategic role, and not all strategists are leaders. Who is the strategic leader? What are we to make of the roles of various individuals in shaping strategic choices in an organization? Reflecting on these issues has helped shape the scope of this study.

In this research, a choice has been made to focus on individuals who by virtue of their roles have the opportunity and empowerment to influence the strategic outcomes of the organization. Such roles are most commonly associated with executives at the apex of the organization or business, because of their broad perspective as well as their power and influence.

The role of strategic leaders is central to strategic choice, and the influence of leaders over strategic decision-making is well recognized – strategic leaders shape, orchestrate, or facilitate it.

Child (1972) argues that the strategic choices exercised by dominant coalitions of top managers are central to organizations. Developing this thinking further into the "upper echelons" perspective, Hambrick and Mason (1984) argue not only that top executives matter, but that organizations also become a reflection of their top managers, and that strategic choices and performance levels can be partially predicted by managerial background and characteristics. Managers act on the basis of their incomplete, filtered, and highly stylized understanding of their situations. In order to understand why organizations do things the way they do, and why they perform the way they do, we must understand the values, motives, and biases of the top team. Demographic characteristics – such as tenure, functional background, education etc – could be seen as partial indicators of psychological properties and executive dispositions. Despite the limited, imprecise, and surrogate nature of demographics, Hambrick (1984) contends that a number of highly significant associations between executive profiles and organizational outcomes can be observed. In the same vein, Bowman and Daniels (1995) suggest that managers' belief structures are derived from their experience, and report evidence of functional bias in managers' perceptions of strategic priorities.

Although strategy-making has traditionally been envisioned as the province of top managers – particularly in the rational model – this view has given way to the increasing involvement of other organizational members. Difficulties with strategy implementation, and an increased rate of environmental change, are often cited as the reason for such wider involvement (Hart and Banbury, 1994). The previous discussion on emergent strategy also suggests that an unduly narrow view of the strategist can be unhelpful. The consensus is that strategy-making can no longer be limited conceptually to the CEO or the top management team, and that strategy-making is an organization wide phenomenon. Liedtka and Rosenblum (1996) argue for the widespread diffusion of strategy-making capabilities in individuals throughout the organization. This relies upon a combination of requisite abilities as well as the empowerment to act. Similarly, Wall and Wall (1995: 18) point out that "once considered the exclusive province of senior management, strategy is now becoming everybody's business".

Ireland and Hitt (1999) observe that substantial numbers of chief executive officers have traditionally adopted the notion that strategic leadership responsibilities are theirs alone. As a result of the significant choices available to the CEO as the firm's key strategic leader, this individual often worked as a solitary figure when shaping the future of the firm. Isolated from those being led, the firm's key strategic leader commanded the organization primarily through top down directives. Particularly when these choices resulted in financial success for the company, the key strategic leader was recognized widely as the "corporate Hercules". Senge (1992) also describes this historical isolation between strategic leaders and those they led. Ireland and Hitt (1999) contend that this worked in an era of relative stability and predictability and conditions of manageable amounts of uncertainty and ambiguity. However, conditions associated with the global competitive landscape (shorter product life cycles, accelerating rates and types of change, the explosion of data and the need to convert it to useable information) prevent single individuals from having all the insights necessary to chart a firm's direction. It may therefore be argued that having strategic leadership centred on a single person or a few people at the top of a hierarchical pyramid is increasingly counterproductive. Insightful top managers recognize that it is impossible for them to have all the answers, and are willing to learn along with others.

Consequently, the "great group" theory, as opposed to the "great man" theory, has gained prominence (Ireland and Hitt, 1999). In this perspective, strategic leadership is distributed among diverse individuals who share the responsibility to create a viable future for the firm. Combinations or collaborations of organizational citizens functioning successfully have been labelled "great groups" by Ireland and Hitt (1999: 46). These collaborations feature managers with significant profit and loss responsibilities, internal networkers who "move about the organization spreading and fostering commitment to new ideas and practices" and others with intellectual capital that stimulate the development and or leveraging of knowledge (Bennis, 1992). Consistent leadership between and among all of the "great groups" in the firm fosters innovative strategic thinking, and rapid acceptance of organizational change.

By contrast, Floyd and Wooldridge (1992, 1994) offer a "middle management perspective" with their finding that certain middle management behaviours are crucial to developing organizational capability. Floyd and Wooldridge suggest that it is easy to exaggerate the significance of top management, and to ignore the less prominent influence of middle management initiative or inertia. Further, involvement in the formation of strategy by middle managers is associated with improved organizational performance. Specifically, consensus among middle managers does not impact organizational performance, but involvement does. The implication is that top managers must encourage middle managers to think strategically, that the involvement of middle managers must be substantive, and that this is best achieved in settings where individuals are given the freedom to critically examine strategic decisions.

Ericson et al (2001) suggest that the role of the strategist varies from one organization to another, and is sometimes invisible (the "strategist as analyst"), sometimes very conspicuous (the "strategist as visionary"), and sometimes a gestalt (the "coalition as strategist"). Similarly, Mintzberg et al (1998) contend that the strategic role is contingent upon the strategic process dominant in an organization. For example, in the design school of strategic process, the chief executive officer is the strategist, whereas in the power school of strategic process, anyone with power may play a strategic role.

Other research also makes it clear that executives and managers can assume a variety of postures and roles. For instance, Bourgeois and Brodwin (1984) suggest that the role played by top managers can range from that of a "commander", where strategy is consciously formulated at the top and issued to the rest of the organization, to what might be called the "sponsor" where strategy emerges from below and is merely recognized and approved from the top. Similarly, the complementary role played by managers can range from "good soldier", where members execute the plans formulated by top management, to "entrepreneur", where they are expected to behave autonomously and pursue new initiatives.

Floyd and Lane (2000) present a distillation of previous research findings in the form of ten specific roles that top, middle, and operating management perform in the strategic process. These are displayed in Table 2.1. Each of the ten roles involves processing information and taking action that facilitates change. It should be noted, however, that there are overlaps across the roles, and also that the definition of top, middle, and operating management varies considerably across organizational settings.

**Table 2.1** Roles in the Strategic Process

| Roles | Behaviours | Documenting Studies |
|---|---|---|
| *Top management* | | |
| Ratifying | Articulate strategic intent<br>Monitor<br>Endorse and support | Hamel and Prahalad (1989)<br>Burgelman (1983a)<br>Hart (1992) |
| Recognizing | Recognize strategic potential<br>Set strategic direction<br>Empower and enable | Burgelman (1991)<br>Mintzberg (1983)<br>Hart (1992) |
| Directing | Plan<br>Deploy resources<br>Command | Ansoff (1987)<br>Schendel and Hofer (1979)<br>Bourgeois and Brodwin (1984) |
| *Middle management* | | |
| Championing | Nurture and advocate<br>Champion<br>Present alternatives to top management | Bower (1970)<br>Burgelman (1983a, b; 1991)<br>Wooldridge and Floyd (1990) |
| Synthesizing | Categorize issues<br>Sell issues to top management<br>Blend strategic and hands-on information<br>Synthesize | Dutton and Jackson (1987)<br>Dutton and Ashford (1993)<br>Nonaka (1988)<br>Floyd and Wooldridge (1992) |
| Facilitating | Nourish adaptability and shelter activity<br>Share information<br>Guide adaptation<br>Facilitate learning | Bower (1970)<br>Mintzberg (1978)<br>Chakravarthy (1982) |

**Table 2.1** Roles in the Strategic Process – *continued*

| Roles | Behaviours | Documenting Studies |
|---|---|---|
| *Middle management (continued)* | | |
| Implementing | Implement<br>Revise and adjust<br>Motivate and inspire<br>Coach | Schendel and Hofer (1979)<br>Nutt (1987)<br>Hart (1992)<br>Quinn (1980) |
| *Operating management* | | |
| Experimenting | Learn and improve<br>Link technical ability and need<br>Initiate autonomous initiatives | Argyris and Schón (1978)<br>Burgelman (1983a, b)<br>Burgelman (1991)<br>Hart (1992) |
| Adjusting | Experiment and take risks<br>Respond to the challenge | Hart (1992) |
| Conforming | Be a good soldier<br>Follow the system | Bourgeois and Brodwin (1984)<br>Hart (1992) |

*Source*: From "Strategizing Throughout the Organization: Managing Role Conflict in Strategic Renewal", by Floyd, Steven W. and Lane, Peter J. in *Academy of Management Review*, Vol. 25, No. 1, copyright © 2000 by Academy of Management (NY). Reproduced with permission of Academy of Management (NY) via Copyright Clearance Center.

With this background, and in relation to Table 2.1, this research focuses on individuals who would qualify as members of the top management team, and who would be expected to demonstrate a wide range of strategic leader behaviours.

## Key themes

A review of the strategy process literature suggests that strategic outcomes are shaped by highly complex organizational processes. Interestingly, while perspectives on the strategic process abound, advice to leaders and managers does not.

Against this backdrop, numerous strategic roles exist within organizations, bounded by the opportunity and empowerment to influence the strategic process. By definition, all strategic roles are potentially organization-wide in their consequences, and shape the long-term rather than the short-term future of the organization. In particular, the capability of strategic leaders – most commonly found at or near the apex of the organization – is an important potential contributor to organizational success. The nature of this capability is explored further in Chapter 3, which begins by developing the idea that given the messy reality of strategy and the strategic process, individuals in strategic leader roles must think and act in appropriate ways that serve to shape both organizational direction and change.

# 3
# Strategic Leader Capability: A Conceptual Framework

## Thinking and acting strategically

A key stance adopted in this study is that strategic leader capability consists of both strategic thinking, and acting strategically.

Strategic thinking has variously been defined as identifying different ways for people to attain their organizational objectives and determining what actions are needed to get them in the position they want to be in (Stumpf and Mullen, 1991), a method for finding a vision and obtaining perpetual invigoration for that vision (Pellegrino and Carbo, 2001), the prelude to designing an organization's future (Zabriskie and Huellmantel, 1991), a combination of analytical thinking and mental elasticity used to gain competitive advantage (Ohmae, 1982), or the thought mechanism that can be used to generate strategic options (Bandarowski, 1985).

According to O'Shannassy (2002: 55) strategic thinking has also been characterized as being made up of "a clear mental picture of the complete system of value creation", identifying problems, "hypotheses or propositions for investigation with an understanding of the wider business context", using both intuition and analysis, "an intuitive understanding of the future direction of the organization, a clear statement of the organization's strategic intent", as well as a consideration of the past, present, and future of the organization, i.e. its history, ethos, cultural legacy etc.

The variation in these definitions illustrates the ambiguous and unstructured nature of strategic thinking. There is no single formula, and hence managers need to develop flexibility in their problem-solving style. Wilson (1998: 511) argues that "innovative strategies do not emerge from sterile analysis and number-crunching; they come from new insights and intuitive hunches. Equally clear, however, is the fact that intuition, if it is to be strategically helpful, must be grounded in facts." In a similar vein, O'Shannassy (2002: 56) has suggested that strategic thinking is a "combination of generative, creative, synthetic, and divergent thought processes, as well as a rational, analytical, and convergent approach to problem solving", and that "thinking and action can be intertwined or linear depending on the strategy context confronting the organisation".

In other words, strategy formulation and implementation can take place sequentially – in either direction – or concurrently. It could even be argued that "analysis is execution and implementation is formulation" (Weick, 2001) and hence the dichotomy between thinking and acting is artificial. This point of view is visually depicted in Figure 3.1, which suggests that, just as thinking may inform action, so too may action inform thinking. Thinking and acting make up an oscillating process, which may be described as strategizing. Thinking surfaces choices and possibilities, and gets things moving. As individuals take actions, new discoveries are made, and this triggers further thinking about what needs to be understood more and what should be done next. As Weick (2001) puts it, "action clarifies meaning".

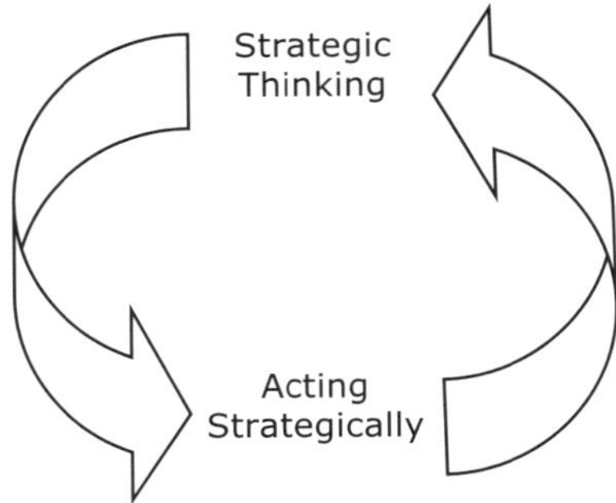


*Figure 3.1* "Strategic Thinking" and "Acting Strategically"

This view is also consistent with the approach of Cummings and Wilson (2003), who suggest that thinking strategically is about offering a language by which complex options can be understood, communicated, bounced around and debated, thereby enabling a group to focus in order to learn about themselves and what they want to achieve, and locate themselves in relation to their environment. Acting strategically is about getting people beyond indecision so as to begin the process of mapping and taking a course.

In other words, abstract thinking alone is not sufficient. As Drucker (1974: 128) has pointed out, "the best plan is only good intentions, until it degenerates into work". Both conditions – of thinking and acting – must be met.

## Orientation and animation, direction and action

The outcomes of strategic thinking and acting strategically are vision, aspirations, direction, or a conceptualization of the future of the business i.e. orientation, as well as actions that change the status quo and move the organization forward i.e. animation. Both these domains have been well researched by scholars such as Cummings and Wilson (2003), who offer an interesting interaction between orientation and animation, which is visually depicted in Figure 3.2.

In convoluted planning procedures, managers can develop an unhealthy obsession with numbers, analyses, and reports, and can become bogged down in "paralysis by analysis" (Langley, 1995). Cummings and Wilson (2003) characterize this as an extreme focus on orientation – all plotting and planning and no animation or action. Conversely, Langley suggests ill-conceived and arbitrary decisions can result in all "extinction by instinct". As Cummings and Wilson put it, all animation and no orientation results in chaos. Further, in this author's own experience, low orientation and low animation may be symptomatic of an organization locked in

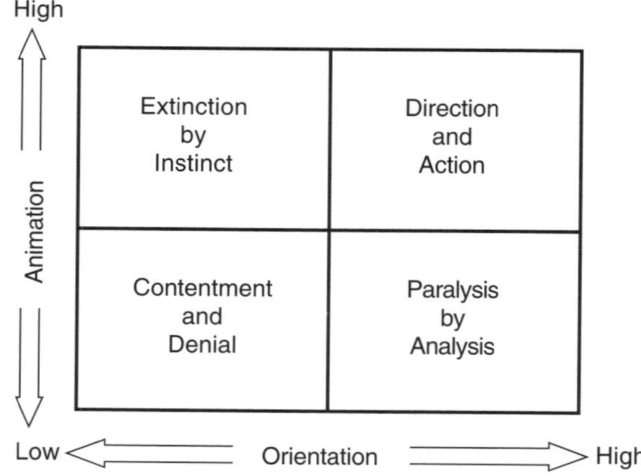


*Figure 3.2* Strategy as Orientation and Animation

"contentment and denial". Good strategy therefore animates and orients, and provides both a sense of direction and action.

The strategic process therefore deals both with cognitive issues and motivational issues. The strategy-making process involves new ways of thinking that are translated into new ways of behaving, and these in turn affect ways of thinking.

Although the term thinking conjures up an image of detached and rational analysis, such a view is unduly limiting. It should be emphasized that cognition is not just a "mentalistic phenomenon" (Brocklesby and Cummings, 2003), but rather cognition is an integral part of our everyday mindful and unmindful activities. Although we notice deliberate, intentional analysis, the way we deal with the world is a subconscious process embodied in our actions. Brocklesby and Cummings argue that natural skills, guidance and encouragement, practice, trial and error, and repetition of success all create a "coupling" between mind and action, so that we can feel, anticipate, or act without conscious thought.

One element that gets to the heart of being strategic is vision (Orndoff, 2002). A vision is closely aligned with future directed goals, and represents how one wants the future to be. A vision is also a stretch towards something better, and gives people the inspiration and understanding needed to act. Various other definitions of purpose or vision have also been offered. Bennis (1998: 3) describes it as "providing people with a bridge to the future". Ireland and Hitt (1999: 48) take the view that vision "allows a company to focus its learning efforts in order to increase its competitive advantage". Visions that facilitate development of this type of focus make sense to all organizational citizens but are still within the bounds of possibility, are understood easily, and create a cultural glue that allows individuals and teams to share knowledge and develop commonality of purpose. Employees are then challenged to take determined actions that will help the firm achieve its objectives. Bonn (2001) suggests that a genuine vision conveys a sense of direction and provides the focus for all activities within the organization. Fernandez and Hogan (2002) deliberately use the word aspirations instead of vision because, in their view, setting direction for an organization involves much more than just a cognitive exercise: setting direction also has a strong component of emotion.

As Hart and Quinn (1993) point out, the view of the leader as a dynamic vision setter has been well developed in management and organization theory as well as sociology and political science (Conger and Kanungo, 1987, 1988). Bennis and Nanus (1985) emphasize not only the importance of a clear and compelling vision but also the need for consistency and clarity on the part of the leader. Similarly, Kotter (1982) and Tichy and Devanna (1986) stress not only the creation of a new vision but also the necessity of institutionalizing the new vision through personal example and organizational design. Indeed, it is suggested that without a challenging core mission and a set of values understood by all employees, the best technical and economic strategy will go unrealized. In an overall sense, theory and research in this domain emphasize three roles for the strategic leader:

1. Recognizing the need for departure from the status quo
2. Creating and articulating a compelling vision or "agenda for change", and
3. Institutionalizing the vision through consistent personal example and organizational structure, processes, and systems.

Evidence for the importance of a clear and compelling vision has also been provided by Collins and Porras (1998), who argue that visionary companies outperform non-visionary ones. Leaders in visionary companies place a strong emphasis on building an organization that has a deep understanding of its purpose and of its core values. Collins and Porras also found that the authenticity and consistency with which the vision is translated into everything that the organization does is more important than the content of the vision. Similarly, Tait (1996) suggests that in order to mobilize people into action, the vision must be communicated in a clear and compelling way, and that in this process, credibility matters more than eloquence. Developing a genuine vision and building it into the very fabric of the organization must therefore be a central element of the work of strategic leaders. As Bonn (2001) emphasizes, a vision that is shared throughout the organization fosters commitment rather than compliance, and creates a sense of commonality that permeates the whole organization. It inspires people's imagination and provides a focus for employees to contribute in ways that make the most of their talents and expertise. Vandermerwe and Vandermerwe (1991) contend that vision must become the focus and direction for everything and everyone. People must use it to differentiate the behaviours and activities that are important from those that are not. The vision must be shared and owned by key people. The change leader must not only support it, but also promote it and be actually seen to be "living" it on a daily basis.

Providing a sense of direction is not exclusively about the future. History, culture, and identity are also crucial shapers of strategic thought and action. Direction is therefore also about the subtle processes of linking the past, present, and future (Pettigrew, 2003). Shaping strategic direction is closely intertwined with strategic change.

Strategic change may be described as "non-routine, non-incremental, and discontinuous, and altering the overall organization" (Tichy, 1983: 16), and requires discontinuous thinking, and "looking at everything in a new way" (Handy, 1989: 19). Strategic change commences with "strategic discomfort" (Vandermerwe and Vandermerwe, 1991: 176), which can be used to unfreeze existing ways of doing things. Some threat or opportunity must be depicted and communicated in a way that leaves no doubt in the minds of key people that strategic change is necessary.

"Activating" a strategy (Vandermerwe and Vandermerwe, 1991) entails energizing, empowering, and mobilizing people, setting priorities, articulating new performance criteria, and monitoring and updating the strategy. Often this involves handpicking key people, and sending strong signals about what is important, for example, through structure changes, or setting up of key projects. In this process, the personal skills that strategic change leaders need can be identified as being persuasive, winning people over, and having the ability to inspire; being facilitative, conducting, orchestrating, co-ordinating; having a consistency in message and behaviour; being visible and identified as a rallying point; and having integrity.

In summary, there is widespread agreement in the literature that strategic thinking and acting strategically are at the heart of strategic capability, and are fundamentally concerned with both organizational direction and change. This involves cognitive and behavioural processes, which may be tightly and inextricably coupled.

Against this backdrop, what is it that individuals in strategic leader roles must do? What are the key challenges they face, and what determines their effectiveness? A critical and iterative review of the literature that is pertinent to an understanding of strategic leader capability has yielded four distinct but inter-connected dimensions that are recurrent, and which coalesce to form what may be identified as strategic leader capability.

These four dimensions are: engagement with strategic paradoxes, cognitive and behavioural complexity, the ability to conduct a strategic conversation, and contextual challenges and their resolution. The dimensions are not mutually exclusive but are inter-dependent, and taken together, offer a conceptual and integrative framework of strategic leader capability. These dimensions are explored further in the following five sections:

*Strategic paradoxes* suggests that the exercise of judgement about a range of significant strategic paradoxes is a crucial dimension of strategic leader capability.

*Cognitive and behavioural complexity* examines these two concepts as key determinants of the effectiveness of individuals in strategic leader roles.

*The strategic conversation* explores the need for the strategic leader to be able to conduct a "strategic conversation" at multiple levels.

*Contextual challenges* argues that the work of strategic leaders is contextual, and that every context poses both interpretive and inertial challenges that must be mastered.

*A conceptual framework of strategic leader capability* brings these four dimensions (strategic paradoxes and the judgement they call for, the strategic conversation, contextual challenges, and cognitive and behavioural complexity) together, and offers a conceptual framework of strategic leader capability, as well as a commentary on the possible relationships between these constructs.

## Strategic paradoxes

Numerous strategy and organization researchers have pointed to the significant paradoxes that managers must work with in the formation and execution of strategy. Paradoxes are not problems that must be solved, but rather opposing positions that must be held meaningfully at the same time.

Lawrence and Lorsch (1986) highlighted this issue by identifying the need to manage within the "loose-tight" paradox, or the need both to give parts of the organization freedom (differentiation) and to pull them together (integration). Hart and Banbury (1994) argue that high performance requires mastery of seemingly contradictory skills. Mintzberg and Quinn (1996) emphasize the need to reconcile change and continuity. As pattern recognizer the manager has to be able to sense when to exploit established strategies, and when to encourage new strains to displace the old.

Jonas et al (1990: 40) found that effective executives must "simultaneously embody the status quo and question it". As the custodian of the firm's history the chief executive officer must act as a force for stability. However, the leader must also challenge norms, ask frame-breaking questions, and play the maverick to stimulate innovation. Bourgeois and Eisenhardt (1988) uncovered similar combinations of paradoxical conditions in their study of strategic decision processes in "high velocity" environments. They found that executive leadership in such firms required not only the articulation of a broad vision and bold commitments of resources, but also the ability to maintain flexibility and empower people throughout the organization to take risks and challenge the status quo. The paradoxical nature of executive leadership is also captured by Itami's (1987) concept of "dynamic fit" which states that the role of top management in today's world is both to create and destroy balance. Senior management must send consistent messages and align strategy with structure but must never allow the organization to settle into complacency. Complexity theorists add a paradox of organizational control for business leaders, where less is more (Sonsino, 2002). Shaw (2002: 70) observes that "being constructive of the future involves an everyday paradox of subversion".

In the same vein, organizing and learning are also paradoxical and essentially antithetical processes. To learn is to disorganize and increase variety. To organize is to forget and reduce variety (Weick and Westley, 1996).

Effective executive leadership would therefore appear to require a range of skills which seem on the surface to be mutually exclusive: an ability to focus on broad visions for the future while also providing critical evaluation of present plans; to create a sense of excitement and challenge while also focusing on getting the job done today; to purposefully seek organizational alignment and to retain organizational agility; to maintain stability and to prepare for change; to have a deliberate strategy and to allow the emergence of strategies; to know the business and at the same time be able to examine it as an outsider; and to work within the context but also challenge the context. Strategic leaders must paradoxically be reflective yet adventurous; they must have good plans prepared but at the same time be ready to forego those plans (Cummings, 1995). Managers must seek cultural cohesiveness within the organization, but avoid stultifying conformity (Pascale, 1999). Strong values or a coherent, close knit social system, or a company's well synchronized operating system or "organizational fit" are therefore all "double edged swords". The paradox that a strength can also be a weakness (for example, a strong organizational culture can result in an organization becoming incestuous and myopic) has also been described as The Icarus Paradox (Miller, 1990).

The centrality of paradoxes in modern managerial life has led one observer to describe them as "inevitable, endemic, and perpetual" (Handy, 1994: 12).

What are the implications for strategy? Legge (2003) suggests that strategy is about reconciling these paradoxical demands, for example, for pattern and consistency, as well as the freedom to be both unpredictable and creative. In other words, strategizing is a sense-making activity in a world of paradoxes. It may also be noted that the inevitable internal tensions generated by paradoxes should not be viewed as pathologies; instead, the constructive tension generated by them should be thought of as a source of dynamism and renewal (Hardy, 1994).

Pascale (1990) observes that paradoxes are made up of "contending opposites" which have to be tackled on a "both/and" basis, rather than an "either/or" basis, and that there is no middle point, or "golden mean". The dynamic synthesis between contending opposites is the engine of organizational self-renewal. This is because paradoxes help to disturb the equilibrium, and "a social system that fosters disequilibrium i.e. encourages variation and embraces contrary points of view, has a greater chance of knowing itself, thanks to continually re-examining its assumptions and juggling its internal tensions" (Pascale, 1990: 109). According to this reasoning, issues that have commonly been regarded as hardship or chronic sources of aggravation for managers are, in fact, drivers of organizational vitality.

Lewis (2000) defines paradox as having three characteristics. First, a paradox may denote a variety of contradictory yet interwoven elements, for example perspectives, demands, interests, or practices. Second, paradoxes are constructed. As managers attempt to make sense of an increasingly ambiguous and changing world, they frequently simplify reality into polarized either/or distinctions that conceal complex interrelationships. Third, paradoxes become apparent through self or social reflection or interaction that reveals the seemingly absurd or irrational coexistence of opposites. In other words, paradoxical tensions are perceptual: cognitively or socially constructed polarities that mask the simultaneity of conflicting truths. Unlike dilemmas, paradoxes signify two sides of the same coin.

Managers need to recognize, become comfortable with, and even profit from paradoxical tensions that have enlightening potential (Lewis, 2000). This involves critically examining assumptions to construct a more accommodating perception of opposites, developing a more complicated repertoire of understandings and behaviours that better reflect organizational intricacies, and the exercise of judgement.

Strategic paradoxes, and the exercise of judgement they call for, are characteristic of much of the work of forming and executing strategy, and several key strategic paradoxes have been identified in this research. For leaders, the challenge is not so much to make choices, but rather to transcend the paradox and synthesize contending opposites. The ability to work with strategic paradoxes is therefore directly linked to cognitive and behavioural complexity, a construct that is explored further in the next section.

## Cognitive and behavioural complexity

Despite the increasing prominence of leadership as a domain of study, Hart and Quinn (1993) point out that views regarding the characteristics and behaviours of effective leaders remain deeply divided. On the one hand, effective leaders are portrayed as visionary, innovative, dynamic, charismatic, transformational, participative, empowering, and motivating (McGregor, 1966; Likert, 1967; Zaleznik, 1977; Burns, 1978; Tichy and Devanna, 1986; Block, 1987; Conger and Kanungo, 1987, 1988). On the other hand, successful leaders are also described as powerful, assertive, decisive, expert, analytical, stable, consistent, and demanding (Katz, 1974; Shetty and Perry, 1976; Kotter, 1982; Ohmae, 1982; Levinson and Rosenthal, 1984; Bennis and Nanus, 1985; Nulty, 1989). Any seminal overview of leadership, such as that by Bass (1981), reveals a confusing array of leadership theories and models.

Many researchers have asserted that effective leadership requires the mastery of apparently contradictory or paradoxical capabilities. Leaders must be simultaneously decisive and reflective, offer a high level vision and also attend to detail, make bold moves as well as incremental adjustments, and have a performance as well as a people orientation (Mitroff, 1983; Bourgeois and Eisenhardt, 1988; Quinn and Cameron, 1988). Quinn et al (1990: 14) observe that "for managers, the world keeps changing... from hour to hour, day to day, and week to week. The strategies that are effective in one situation are not necessarily effective in another. Even worse, the strategies that were effective yesterday may not be effective in the same situation today".

Consequently, high performing managers possess higher levels of cognitive complexity, and are able to utilize multiple frames of reference in dealing with problems (Streufert and Swezey, 1986; Shrivastava and Schneider, 1984). Furthermore, there is evidence to suggest that leadership effectiveness demands not only complex thought processes, but also behavioural complexity i.e. the ability to play out a wide range of roles in the interpersonal and organizational arena.

Goleman (2000) cites a large-scale empirical research project undertaken by the consulting firm Hay/McBer, which found six different effective leadership styles. The styles, taken individually, appear to have a direct and unique impact on the working atmosphere of a company, division, or team, and in turn, on its financial performance, with organizational climate being an intervening variable. More importantly, the research indicates that leaders with the best results do not rely on one leadership style; they use most of them in a given week, seamlessly and in different measure, depending upon the business situation. The six leadership styles are portrayed in Table 3.1. This study suggests that leaders who have mastered four or more styles – especially the authoritative, democratic, affiliative, and coaching styles – deliver the best organizational climate and business performance.

Others who have taken multi-dimensional views of leadership have also noted the paradoxical nature and the conflicting demands of the top manager's job. Drucker (1974: 616) summarized this by observing that top management requires simultaneously "a thought man, an action man, a people man, and a front man". Mintzberg (1973), in a landmark study of five chief executive officers, identified ten roles of executive leadership. In a significant observation, Mintzberg states that the ten roles form a gestalt, or an integrated whole, and that leadership effectiveness hinges on the execution of all of the roles simultaneously.

A "theoretically integrated" model of executive leadership roles is offered by Quinn (1988) and Quinn et al (1996: 16). This uses a "Competing Values Framework" (CVF) to highlight the various roles – some conflicting and some complementary – required for managerial effectiveness in complex environments.

The elements in the CVF carry paradoxical orientations on key dimensions of effective management. Organizations need to be adaptable and flexible, and at the same time stable and controlled. Similarly, organizations need an external focus, but must also attend to internal processes. Each quadrant has different organizational characteristics and outcomes, described as human relations (with a focus on the development of people); open systems (with a focus on growth, expansion, change); rational goal (with an emphasis on planning and goal setting); and internal process (with a bias for stability and continuity and a focus on processes and routines). Within the four-quadrant model, eight leadership roles may be found. This framework is displayed in Figure 3.3.

**Table 3.1** Overview of Six Leadership Styles

| | Coercive | Authoritative | Affiliative | Democratic | Pacesetting | Coaching |
|---|---|---|---|---|---|---|
| The leader's *modus operandi* | Demands immediate compliance | Mobilisers people towards a vision | Creates harmony and builds emotional bonds | Forges consensus through participation | Sets high standards for performance | Develops people for the future |
| The style in a phrase | "Do what I tell you" | "Come with me" | "People come first" | "What do you think" | "Do as I do, now" | "Try this" |
| Underlying emotional intelligence competencies | Drive to achieve, initiative, self-control | Self-confidence, empathy, change catalyst | Empathy, building relationships | Collaboration, team leadership, communication | Conscientiousness, drive for achievement, initiative | Developing others, empathy, self-awareness |
| When the style works best | In a crisis, to kick start a turnaround or with problem employees | When change requires a new vision, or when a clear direction is needed | To heal rifts in a team or to motivate people during stressful circumstances | To build buy-in or consensus, or to get input from valuable employees | To get quick results from a highly motivated and competent team | To help an employee improve performance or develop long-term strengths |
| Overall impact on climate | Negative | Most strongly positive | Positive | Positive | Negative | Positive |

*Source*: Reprinted by permission of Harvard Business Review from *Leadership that Gets Results* by Daniel Goleman, March–April 2000. 

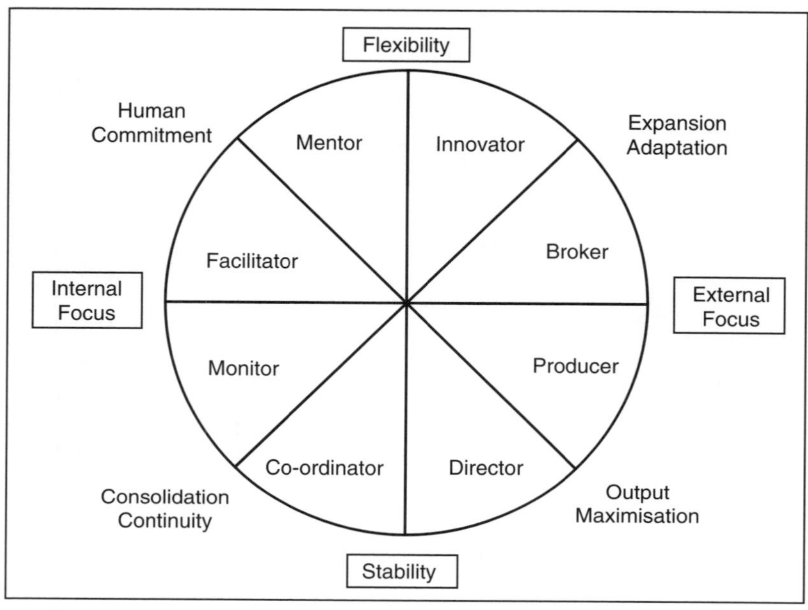


*Figure 3.3* The Competing Values Framework

*Source*: From *Becoming a Master Manager: A Competency Framework*, 2nd Edition, by Robert E. Quinn, Sue R. Faerman, Michael P. Thompson and Michael McGrath, copyright © 1996 by the authors. Reproduced with permission of John Wiley & Sons, Inc.

Building on the work of Quinn et al (1996), Vilkinas and Cartan (2001) identify a range of behaviours associated with each of the leadership roles in the Competing Values Framework, and these are displayed in Table 3.2.

A key proposition underlying the Competing Values Framework is that the simultaneous use of multiple roles by executives is associated with high performance on several dimensions. Quinn et al (1996) suggest that the model is not static, and that the CVF is explanatory of a very dynamic process involving managers moving very quickly from one quadrant to another, perhaps on an incident by incident basis. The CVF therefore underlines the idea that managers must be able to deploy a diverse repertoire of skills in response to rapidly changing circumstances. Effective managers must be elastic in their behaviour, in that they must be able to operate comfortably in all quadrants. Further, managers who are effective across a range of roles achieve higher levels of performance relative to others who are not. This does not mean that high performers can arbitrarily move from one firm or industry context

**Table 3.2** Leadership Roles in the Competing Values Framework

| Role | Description |
|---|---|
| Innovator | Continually searches for innovation and improvements<br>Solves problems in a creative way<br>Envisions needed changes |
| Broker | Exerts upward influence<br>Acquires needed resources<br>External focus |
| Producer | Gets the work done<br>Customer focus<br>Achievement orientation |
| Director | Provides direction<br>Clarifies priorities<br>Communicates unit's goals |
| Co-ordinator | Co-ordinates activities<br>Schedules<br>Brings sense of order to workplace |
| Monitor | Monitors progress<br>Collects information<br>Holds regular reviews |
| Facilitator | Builds teams<br>Facilitates consensus<br>Manages conflict |
| Mentor | Develops staff<br>Listens empathetically<br>Treats each staff member in a caring way |

*Source*: From "The Behavioural Control Room for Managers: The Integrator Role", by Tricia Vilkinas and Greg Cartan, in *Leadership and Organization Development Journal*, Vol. 22, No. 4, copyright © 2001, reproduced with permission of Emerald Group Publishing Limited; all rights reserved.

to another, but it does suggest that behavioural complexity is a universally valued attribute. The capacity to balance competing demands and play multiple roles at a high level pre-supposes lengthy experience, hard work, and the development of knowledge and relationships over a long period, and this has a developmental implication.

Ireland and Hitt (1999) suggest that the four competing demands which all managers face are: innovation i.e. the future positioning of the organization in terms of strategic direction, products, and service; commitment i.e. the development and motivation of people and the maintenance of a distinctive identity and value system; efficiency i.e. the management of ongoing operations and the critical evaluation of alternative projects and programs; and performance i.e. the execution of plans and the achievement of results in the marketplace. The four corresponding executive leadership roles are: a vision setter who provides a sense of mission; a motivator who manages meaning and translates the vision into a cause worth fighting for; the analyser who provides efficient management of the internal operating system and integrates functional perspectives; and the task master who focuses on performance and results with a "hands on" role, getting the job done today.

To paraphrase Vilkinas and Cartan (2001: 177), the various roles are not discrete entities, and therefore managers are not required to be "4-role or 8-role schizophrenics". Moving across the roles with facility and assurance requires managers to have the ability to read their environment in order to determine which role must be adopted, as well as the ability to exercise the behaviours inherent in the chosen role. In other words, there is an additional managerial role, which may be thought of as an integrator role. The integrator aligns appropriate managerial behaviour with need. Such a role is, in effect, a "behavioural control room". According to Vilkinas and Cartan (2001), the integrator role requires an effective manager to possess a high degree of external awareness and self awareness, and be both a "critical observer" and a "reflective learner". The manager must critically observe and interpret the changing environment on an ongoing basis; possess refined self-diagnostic skills in order to provide an accurate analysis of personal strengths and limitations and the individual's impact on that environment; and must have the capacity to learn from and adapt to the environment based on previous experiences.

In summary, therefore, there is significant evidence to suggest that effective leaders deploy high levels of both cognitive (i.e. seeing and understanding) and behavioural (i.e. doing) complexity.

## Cognitive complexity: A closer look

In the managerial cognition perspective, managers are assumed to be "information workers" (McCall and Kaplan, 1985) i.e. they spend their time absorbing, processing, and disseminating information about issues, opportunities, and problems. The challenge is that such work is complex and ambiguous, and managers must find their way through a relentless and often bewildering flow of information. Individuals meet such challenges by employing "knowledge structures" to facilitate information processing and decision-making. A knowledge structure may be defined as a mental template that enables individuals to give recognition, form, and meaning to an environment. However, while these knowledge structures may transform complex environments into manageable ones through a process of cognitive simplification (Simon, 1993), they may also blind strategy makers, for example, to important changes in their business environments, and compromise their ability to make sound strategic decisions (Walsh, 1995).

Pellegrino and Carbo (2001) examined strategic thinking from an individual perspective, and in particular, the role of cognitive simplification tools, and highlighted that many simplification techniques become dangerous when applied to strategic issues and problems because they apply a simple structure to an unstructured situation. This has also been stated by other researchers such as Duhaime and Schwenk (1985) and DeKluyver (2000). Stumpf (1989) suggests that the greater an individual's personal need for structure, the more likely the reliance on cognitive simplification techniques to create that missing structure.

What are the implications for managers? "Complicate yourselves" is the advice Weick offers to managers (1979: 261). Weick suggests that managers need to be able to see and understand organizational and behavioural events from several perspectives, rather than a single one. They need, for example, to understand that organizational problems may have several types of causes, and they need to be able to determine the causes responsible for specific problems.

Weick contends that most people perceive and interpret events from narrow frames of reference. Yet many situations are sufficiently complex to be amenable to a wide variety of interpretations and understandings: no single and complete definition of the situation exists. Having a narrow framework for understanding therefore often results in ineffective managerial behaviour. In order to be effective, managers must develop their ability to generate several alternative interpretations and understandings of organizational events so that the "variety" in their frames of reference is equivalent to the variety in the situation and the variety of others' perceptions – a principle consistent with the law of requisite variety (Ashby, 1952). Only such equivalent variety will enable managers to register accurately the complex nature of many of the events they face, as well as to choose actions most suited for dealing with particular problems. More complicated understanding will result in better understanding of organizational problems, so that the manager is likely to be more effective in addressing them.

With this background, cognitive complexity may be defined as a continuum, with simplistic categorization and evaluation of information representing low-level thinking, and the ability to generate theoretical frameworks that organize complex events and relationships making up high-level or complex thinking (McDaniel and Lawrence, 1990). There is general agreement that individuals utilize a varying number of constructs to perceive and evaluate their environment. Individuals with low complexity, therefore, are characterized as having categorical black and white perceptions as well as relatively few, but rigid, rules of integration. On the other hand, individuals who are relatively complex are characterized as perceiving more differences in their environment, more likely to view others in ambivalent terms, and better able to assimilate contradictory cues (Larson and Rowland, 1974).

Theories of cognitive complexity suggest that people who are more cognitively complex are more capable than others of applying such multiple perspectives.

According to Wang and Chan (1995), the concept of cognitive complexity, which has been extensively researched by cognitive psychologists over the last four decades, includes two primary components: differentiation, which refers to the number of dimensions used by individuals to perceive organizational stimuli; and integration, which refers to the complexity of rules used by individuals in organizing the differentiated dimensions. Cognitively simple individuals tend to perceive stimuli in simple and minimally differentiated terms, and to apply fixed rules for organizing stimuli (Schroeder, 1971). By contrast, cognitively complex individuals perceive multiple dimensions in stimuli, and apply more complex rules to interpret them (Bartunek and Louis, 1988).

An example of the need for cognitive complexity is cited by Bartlett and Ghoshal (1989: 212) while discussing the challenges of managing a transnational company: "It has more to do with developing managers than designing structures and procedures. Diverse roles and dispersed operations must be held together by a management mindset that understands the need for multiple strategic capabilities, views problems and opportunities from both global and local perspectives, and is willing to interact with other openly and flexibly… the task is not to build a sophisticated structure, but to create a matrix in the minds of managers".

Research evidence suggests that in complex situations, cognitive complexity leads to more accurate perceptions as well as more effective behaviours. Cognitive complexity correlates positively with tolerance for ambiguity, assumption of a leadership role, and prediction accuracy (Streufert et al, 1968). People with a higher level of cognitive complexity are more capable of taking the perspective of others (Triandis, 1977), they tend to be less prejudiced (Gardiner, 1972), more likely to make moral judgements on the basis of principle and reciprocal role taking (Kohlberg,

1969), and to be better able to resolve conflicts co-operatively (Eiseman, 1978). A more cognitively complex individual will have a greater ability to: (a) perceive and define the situation, (b) establish and organize a frame of reference concerning the other's behaviour, and (c) proceed with the analysis and elaboration of the situation encountered (Porter and Inks, 2000).

Wang and Chan (1995: 35) cite a number of empirical studies which identify four characteristics of cognitively complex individuals. Such individuals attend to broader ranges of information as well as search for more information (Tuckman, 1967), spend more time in interpreting information (Dollinger, 1984), and thus have a more accurate perception of the complexity of the environment (Streufert and Driver, 1965).

It should be noted, however, that an individual could be cognitively complex in one domain and cognitively simple in another, depending upon his knowledge and experience in that domain (Gardner and Schoen, 1962). In other words, context is an important consideration.

The cognitive complexity of an organization's leaders profoundly affects the quality of their own and other organization members' responses to events, and more importantly, to the dynamics that ensue. Increasing organizational leaders' levels of complexity therefore has the potential for significant ripple effects through other parts of the organization.

Stumpf and Mullen (1991) assert that experiences that destroy the sense of structure and predictability in a person's life improve the ability to think strategically. Events may make things go from clear and defined, to unstructured and ambiguous. Such experiences force people to re-evaluate, and expand their structures and their thinking. They must face alternatives and possibilities they would otherwise not want to examine. In other words, the strategic thinker is an individual who does not need to rely heavily on cognitive simplification. A strategic thinker is a person with a low personal need for structure.

In summary, a number of theoretical arguments and empirical studies coalesce around the premise that managers with high cognitive complexity are likely to attend to and search for information from a broader range of sources, and are thus better able to understand the implications of dynamic, complicated, and ambiguous information.

Just as thinking and acting are tightly coupled, it may be argued that cognitive complexity is closely related to behavioural complexity.

**Behavioural complexity: A closer look**

The concept of behavioural complexity (Hooijberg and Quinn, 1992; Denison et al, 1995) is used to refer to the need for managers to perform a wide array of leadership functions in the organizational arena. In contrast to other approaches to leadership research, behavioural complexity reflects the idea that managers who perform multiple leadership functions, and tailor the performance of these functions to the demands of their organizational role set, will be more effective than managers who perform only one leadership function and who do not vary the performance of their leadership functions.

The behavioural complexity construct has at its core the idea that managers have to manage a network of relationships with people. As the size and differentiation of the manager's network grows, so does the potential for paradox and contradiction. The ability of the leader to match his/her behavioural repertoire to the demands of the situation thus becomes his/her distinctive competence. Like cognitive complexity, the concept of behavioural complexity is best understood in conjunction with the idea of requisite variety (Ashby, 1952). Behavioural complexity therefore results in a simple definition of effective leadership as the ability to perform multiple roles and behaviours that correspond to the requisite variety implied by a particular organizational or environmental context (Denison et al, 1995).

Behavioural complexity does not imply an extreme form of situationalism. Rather than defining an infinite set of contingencies, behavioural complexity suggests the development of a portfolio of leadership functions that allow a leader to respond to complex demands.

Hooijberg (1996) distinguishes two dimensions of behavioural complexity: behavioural repertoire and behavioural differentiation. The concept of behavioural repertoire refers to the portfolio of leadership functions a manager can perform. However, managers need more than the ability to perform multiple leadership functions, they also need to be able to discern when and in which situations to perform these leadership functions. The concept of behavioural differentiation refers to the extent to which a manager varies the performance of the leadership functions depending on the demands of the organizational situation.

### *Behavioural repertoire*

A key premise is that the broader a manager's behavioural repertoire, the more likely it is that the manager can respond appropriately to the demands of the environment. The need for a broad behavioural repertoire becomes especially important as managerial jobs become more complex.

The notion of the repertoire is also found elsewhere. Yukl (1989) distinguishes at least 11 leadership roles. Most researchers argue that managers need to perform a range of leadership roles depending, for example, on the nature of the task at hand, the skills and other characteristics of their subordinates and colleagues, and the culture of the organization.

There is some evidence that supports the idea that managers who perform multiple leadership functions are more effective than those who do not (Mintzberg, 1973). Various other researchers (Quinn, 1988; Quinn et al, 1991; Hart and Quinn, 1993; Denison et al, 1995) have found that managers who balance competing leadership functions well tend to perform more successfully than managers who focus myopically upon a specific leadership function. Blake and Mouton (1964) also suggest that managers who perform both people oriented and task oriented leadership functions would be more effective than managers who emphasized either one substantially more than the other.

*Behavioural differentiation*

Being an effective leader across a range of situations and time horizons requires of managers not only "the ability to perceive the needs and goals of a constituency but also the ability to adjust one's personal approach to group action accordingly" (Kenny and Zaccaro, 1983: 678). The concept of behavioural differentiation refers to the ability of managers to perform the behavioural functions they have in their repertoire in an adaptive and discerning way, depending upon the organizational situation.

For example, managers who can be directive and authoritarian, as well as use persuasion in promoting their ideas, are more likely to be effective than managers who can only be directive and authoritarian.

Several researchers have emphasized the ability and willingness to learn as an important pre-requisite for the ability to be effective in a behaviourally complex manner. In addition to Vilkinas and Cartan (2001), the need for heightened and more accurate environmental and self-awareness is also stressed by Covey (1991), Bennis (1992), and Kouzes and Posner (1995).

Eisenhardt and Martin (2000) suggest that repeated practice is an important learning mechanism for the development of a dynamic capability. Practice helps people to understand processes more effectively and so develop more effective routines. The codification of experience into technology and formal procedures makes that experience easier to apply, and accelerates the building of routines. Mistakes also play a role in the evolution of dynamic capabilities. Interestingly, according to Eisenhardt and Martin (2000) small losses, rather than major successes or failures, contribute to effective learning. Success often fails to engage managers' attention sufficiently so that they may learn from their experience. By contrast, learning from major failures may be blocked by defence mechanisms. Pacing of experience – or the rate at which experiences unfold – also impacts development of capabilities. Experience that comes too fast can overwhelm managers, leading to an inability to transform it into meaningful or actionable learning. Infrequent experience can result in forgetting what was learned previously, and therefore little knowledge accumulation.

In summary, effective leadership seems to require a balancing and mastery of seemingly contradictory capabilities, and effective leaders not only think multi-dimensionally but are also able to execute multiple roles simultaneously. High-performing strategic leaders demonstrate high levels of cognitive and behavioural complexity, deployed in a highly integrated and complementary way in the strategic process. The implications of strategy-making processes for individuals in leader roles are considered in further detail in the next section.

## The strategic conversation

Strategy-making may be conceptualized as the outcome of an interactive process, which unfolds as a "conversation" in the organization.

Manning (2002: 36) suggests that the strategic conversation is "both an ongoing event and a product, mostly occurs implicitly rather than explicitly, and is the central and most important executive tool".

Liedtka and Rosenblum (1996) argue that the ability to conduct strategic conversations is a key skill, and suggest that using a metaphor of strategy-making as conversation conveys an inclusive "give and take image" which enables scrutiny and inclusion of different players, viewpoints, and processes.

The strategic conversation may be thought of as a process of sensing changes in the external and internal environments, generating options, provoking ideas and innovation, shaping strategy, inspiring action, and learning from what happens, and sharing that experience.

The idea of the conversation is anchored in a view of the organization as a social system, and the conversation may be visualized as occurring at three distinct levels.

Firstly, conversations occur between individuals. Liedtka and Rosenblum (1996: 148) argue that "it is through conversation that organizations come to co-create the shared meaning behind the strategy". Managers who are not party to these conversations may lack an understanding of the context and rationale for the strategic choices that have been made, and may be confused and de-motivated as a result. This, in turn, may undermine the energy needed to accomplish change. It is not sufficient merely to be told of the logic of the decisions, because different managers have different cognitive frames that process what they are told differently. Widening participation in the strategic conversation also potentially enhances the quality of the strategic choices themselves, not just their execution. Managers who do not share the same cognitive frames are more likely to question the invisible or unarticulated assumptions underpinning the perspectives of others. Such questioning of assumptions is a critical step in the kind of dialogue that is essential for generating better, more innovative solutions. Thus a strategy that is co-created within an inclusive conversation is more likely to reflect a more complex and multi-faceted view of reality.

Secondly, conversations may be said to occur between events or local environments and individuals. Echoing the notion of emergent strategy, as individuals act, or choose not to act, the consequences of their choices "talk back".

Thirdly, there is a conscious or sub-conscious reflective conversation within the individual.

These three conversations together may be visualized as the strategy-making process. These metaphorical conversations are concurrent rather than sequential; each shapes the others; and they flow back and forth in iterative and unpredictable ways. These conversations occur simultaneously throughout the organization on an ongoing basis. When aggregated at an institutional level, a dominant pattern may emerge. This not only helps to reshape and refine strategic intent, it also serves to build commitment. As Liedtka and Rosenblum (1996: 148) put it, "these strategic conversations are the interactions through which choices at all levels get made, tested, and the rationales behind them developed".

Similar "conversational" perspectives are implicit in Shaw's work (2002) in which it is suggested that conversation in organizations means participating in evolving events when there is little clear foresight, and hindsight is not yet available. Grundy and Wensley (1999: 327) assert that strategic decision-making often occurs as a "continuous stream of discussion without producing specific, tangible decisions, and which generates strategy incrementally rather than as a holistic plan". Similarly, Quinn's (1980) notion of logical incrementalism is underpinned by a desire to tap the talents and psychological drives of the whole organization, in order to create cohesion, and to generate identity with the emerging strategy. In this perspective, executives may be able to predict the broad direction, but not the precise nature of the ultimate strategy that will result. Accordingly, it makes sense for top managers to focus on developing a broad strategic direction, allowing the details to emerge over time. Quinn suggests that rather than seeking the rational and comprehensive ideal, leaders must work to create a general sense of purpose and direction that will guide the actions taken by organization members.

Building a widely distributed strategic process requires strategic thinking at the individual level as well as the ability to use this as input into a larger conversation whose outcome is coherent at the organizational level. Strategy-making that operates at these two levels creates what may be called a "meta-capability" that enhances the ability of a business to remain competitive over time – meta capabilities being the kinds of skills and knowledge that underlie the process of capability-building itself (Liedtka and Rosenblum, 1996).

Although the strategic conversation is not elemental, a few significant patterns that can be discerned are the exploration of mental models; synthesizing learning, creativity, and analysis; and navigating the social and political dynamics of the organization. Figure 3.4, which is based on Moncrieff (1999), and adapted in a discussion between Moncrieff and the author, offers a useful organizing scheme.

It should be emphasized that the boundaries between these various activities are very blurred. As Quinn suggests (1980: 3), executives man-

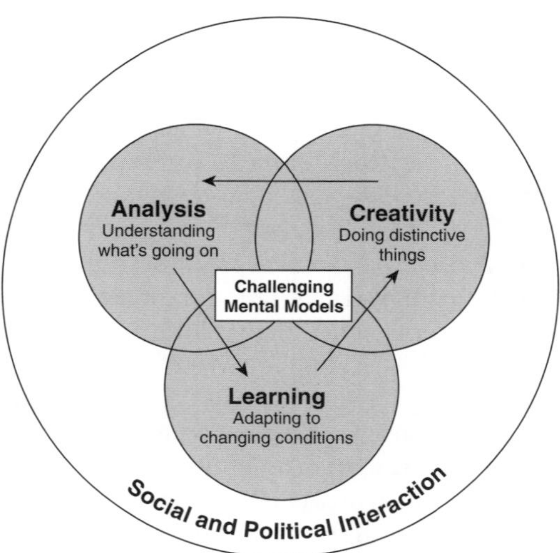


*Figure 3.4* The Strategic Conversation

aging strategic change "artfully blend formal analysis, behavioural techniques, and power politics to bring about cohesive, step by step movement towards ends which are initially broadly conceived, but which are then constantly refined and reshaped as new information appears".

These themes are developed further in the following sections titled Exploring mental models, Learning, Creativity, Analysis, and Social and political interaction.

*Exploring mental models*

In their study of organizational renewal and decline, Barr et al (1992: 15) propose that the cognitive processes of "noticing and constructing meaning" offer important insights into the phenomenon of organizational evolution. Schwenk (1988) identifies several relationships between cognition and the strategic decision process, such as cognitive heuristics and biases, which result in assumptions and cognitive maps, which in turn shape decision-making. Kiesler and Sproull (1982: 548) suggest that "a crucial component of managerial behaviour in rapidly changing environments is problem sensing, or the cognitive processes of noticing and constructing meaning about environmental change so that organizations can take action". A key problem, as noted by Simon (1993), is that individuals have limited data processing capabilities, yet these limited capabilities must be used to make sense of vast amounts of ambiguous data. To make sense of the world, managers often rely on simplified representations in the form of mental models.

Mental models consist of concepts and relationships an individual uses to understand various situations or environments. The mental models of managers determine which environmental signals and stimuli get attention and which are ignored, as well as their interpretation. Mental models help individuals cope with an overabundance of stimuli, but strongly held mental models may lead managers to overlook important environmental changes. Mental models can cause problems in three ways: (a) they determine what information will receive attention, (b) the stimuli gaining attention tend to be interpreted in relation to the individual's current mental model, and (c) mental models shape the actions taken in response to the stimuli. Just as mental models selectively limit the information used, mental models also limit the range of alternative solutions to the issues that have been identified. On the whole, the persistence of mental models that are no longer appropriate would explain why organizational decline is often a downward spiral, despite an abundance of managerial talent and available cues as to the trouble ahead (Johnson, 1988).

Barr et al (1992) propose that organizational renewal requires managers to change their mental models in response to environmental changes. In particular, managers may need to alter their cause and effect understandings of the environment, and the means by which data are interpreted. Mental models that can no longer accommodate or explain occurrences in the environment must be altered and new understandings of the environment must be developed.

Senge (1990) has described mental models as deeply ingrained assumptions, generalizations, and images that influence how we understand the world and how we take action. Managers may be unaware of such models, which usually remain tacit; yet they have a strong influence on individual and organizational behaviour. Mental models may also be thought of as "routines" or "assumptions and beliefs". Bowman (1994) suggests that routines are the way things get done in an organization. They can be highly emergent in nature, taking the form of generally accepted and understood ways of working that have never been explicitly agreed or even discussed. Implicit routines can exercise an insidious and profound influence on behaviour. It requires a great deal of challenging reflection to uncover these embedded behaviours and routines. Crafting good strategies requires breaking out of these routine ways of thinking. The ability to understand, articulate, scrutinize, and challenge prevalent mental models, assumptions, and core beliefs is therefore crucial for the development of unique strategies. As a result, Pascale (1990) emphasizes the role of unleashing contention in the strategic process.

Organizational renewal therefore hinges on learning, a process that necessarily requires and results in additions to or changes in mental models, routines, or assumptions and beliefs.

### *Learning*

Learning can be conceptualized in many ways, two of which are particularly relevant for this study. Single loop learning is reflected in changes in behaviour rather than changes in understanding. This results in incremental modifications or minor adjustments to existing interpretations. By contrast, double loop learning (Argyris and Schon, 1996: 21) involves a restructuring of the individual's mental models and results in a significant change in understanding, and may be described as "learning that results in a change in the values of theory in use, as well as its strategies and assumptions".

One influential way of characterizing this process is in terms of unfreezing, change, and refreezing (Lewin, 1947). During unfreezing, old beliefs are discarded to make way for new understandings, and this is sometimes also described as unlearning. Once old beliefs are unlearned, new understandings about the environment can be achieved, often via experimentation. In the final phase, changes in mental models are solidified, new belief structures become frozen as they are supported by the occurrence of anticipated events. Double loop learning therefore involves unlearning, or the deletion of concepts and prior associations, and the addition of new concepts and associations.

The learning dimension of the strategic conversation is well recognized. Croom and Batchelor (1997) point out that any strategic change is the outcome of a learning process, which can be categorized along four dimensions: (a) the nature of the challenge and whether it is a complex or simple problem, (b) the extent to which the learning outcome will be different from previous strategies, (c) the extent to which the environment is predictable and it is known *a priori* how to respond, and (d) the idiosyncrasy of the knowledge base on which the strategy is founded i.e. can ideas and approaches used elsewhere be employed, or will dedicated skills and knowledge need to be acquired.

Shrivastava and Grant (1985) also postulate that strategic decision processes have a relationship with a critical related process, namely organizational learning, which may be defined as the autonomous capacity of organizations to create, share, and use strategic information about themselves and their environments for decision-making. Decision-makers cope with uncertainty by searching for, acquiring, and then using relevant information. These activities may be institutionalized in organizational learning processes, which shape the organization's knowledge base about action-outcome relationships and the influence of the environment upon these relationships. To the extent that strategy formation draws upon this knowledge base, strategy is influenced by learning processes. Managers therefore need to design and develop learning systems that support strategic decision processes within their organization.

Strategic learning includes learning from past successes and failures, learning from analogues elsewhere inside and outside the organization, as well as learning about markets, customers, competitors, technologies, and so on. Thompson (1996) suggests that important elements of organizational learning include tracking events in the marketplace, choosing responses, and monitoring outcomes; making sure that all important information from the questioning and learning is disseminated effectively; and adopting policies and procedures to better guide future decisions. In this process, a high degree of discernment or judgement is involved. Vickers (1965) has identified three types of judgement. Reality judgements of "what is" include strategic awareness of the organization and its environment based on perceptions, interpretation, and meaning systems. Action judgements, or "what to do about it", involve deciding what to do about perceived issues. Lastly, value judgements require evaluating expected and desired results and outcomes from a particular decision. It is suggested that such judgement cannot be taught, it comes from experience.

Mintzberg (1973) observes that learning requires the ability to detect emerging patterns and help them take shape, and not to preconceive strategies but rather to recognize their emergence elsewhere in the organization and intervene when appropriate. This includes shaping the climate within which a wide variety of strategies can grow. In complex organizations this may mean building flexible structures, hiring creative people, defining broad umbrella strategies, and watching for patterns that emerge. Pascale (1996: 89), another proponent of strategy as learning, observes that "there is a widespread tendency to overlook the process by which organizations experiment, adapt, and learn. We tend to impute coherence and purposive rationality to events when the opposite may be closer to the truth. How an organization deals with miscalculation, mistakes, and serendipitous events outside its field of vision is often crucial to success over time. In reality, corporate direction evolves from an incremental adjustment to unfolding events".

The exploration of mental models and learning are both intimately connected with creativity, and the search for novel solutions.

### *Creativity*

Bonn (2001: 66) observes that "strategy is about ideas and the development of novel solutions to create competitive advantage. Strategists must therefore search for new approaches and envision better ways of doing things". A prerequisite for this is creativity, and in particular, the ability to question prevalent concepts and perceptions, and to recombine or make connections between seemingly unconnected issues.

Creative thinking refers to "how people approach problems and solutions – their capacity to put existing ideas together in new combinations" (Amabile, 1998: 79). This involves challenging the "tyranny of the given" by questioning prevailing beliefs or mental models in the organization. De Bono (1996) argues that the creative process also involves the selection and development of ideas – a good strategic leader is able to recognize the potential of a new idea at a very early stage. In other words, the strategic leader need not be an originator of ideas, but must have the ability to evaluate the potential of the ideas of others.

Creative ideas must be married with a deep and integrated understanding of the business. Bonn (2001) suggests that this requires an understanding of how different problems and issues are connected with one another, how they influence one another, and what effect a solution in one particular area would have on other areas. This requires a detachment from the minutiae of day to day operational problems, and an ability to see the overall pattern.

Senge (1990: 43) describes this ability as systems thinking and contends that "we must look beyond personalities and events; we must look into the underlying structures which shape individual actions and create the conditions where certain types of events become likely". Mintzberg (1989) believes that to know the business is not intellectual knowledge, nor is it analytical reports or abstracted facts and figures, but personal knowledge and intimate understanding.

*Analysis*

In the process of developing an understanding of a business, Simon (1993) highlights the importance of attempting to anticipate the future. This means sensing and interpreting unusual features in the environment that may affect the firm significantly in the future, and determining at what point in time they should be attended to and dealt with. Using the metaphor of the human body, Simon goes on to argue that it is no accident that the eyes and ears are located on the surface of the body and not in its interior. Intelligence requires constant contact with the relevant environments. From a complexity theory perspective, Stacey (1996) argues that managers need to be sensitive to interactions across different parts of the organization, and need to understand how managerial actions and resulting feedback combine to shape organizational outcomes over time.

While the use of systematic analysis to aid understanding of the organization and its environment is well documented (Porter, 1980; Ansoff, 1987). Grundy and Wensley (1999) point out that strategic decision-making is at best a part rational process, which entails careful evaluation of decision alternatives only in exceptional cases. Similarly, Langley (1990) researched the use of formal analysis in strategic decisions and concluded that strategic decision-making is rarely fully encompassed within a comprehensive analytic process, and that formal analysis is used in an incremental way in decisions. Formal analysis is also used for a variety of purposes in organizations, and the way in which it is used varies from one organization to another. Principally, there are three patterns of use: (a) analysis is used for substantive input to decisions, to control implementation, and to ensure convergence towards action; (b) analysis is a key tool of persuasion and verification in the negotiating process between levels of the hierarchy concerning actions to be taken; and (c) analysis is used in an unproductive way as people stake out contradictory positions, and attempt to gain time in an atmosphere of indecision and divergence. In effect, formal analysis is used not just for decision-making, but also as a social and political tool.

*Social and political interaction*

Moncrieff (1999) observes that strategy formation usually involves a group of people, with real issues at stake, so it can be subject to the social dynamics of the group, and the political dynamics of the organization. Kisfalvi (2000) emphasizes that individuals do not come to the strategic process as empty vessels; they inevitably bring their deeply rooted personal preferences and prejudices with them. During strategy formation, these personal issues can become intertwined with organizational issues. As a result, some strategic issues, because they may be particularly meaningful to key individuals in positions of power or influence, may gain prominence on the firm's strategic agenda. Pettigrew (in an interview with Starkey, 2002: 22) has highlighted that organizational change processes can be seen as an elaborate influence and communication process. Big changes unscramble the resource system of organizations so "people feel their empires are going to be dissolved – this releases a lot of political energy. Power, politics, and change are bedfellows". Strategy-making can therefore become a battle of ideas where coalition forming and bargaining are crucial human processes that shape outcomes (Pettigrew, 2003). This view is echoed by Butcher and Clarke (2001) who observe that although politics is often viewed as made up of divisive self-interest and personal agendas, it is in fact the essence of organizations. Because organizations cannot be places of unity, politics is a legitimate managerial activity, and managers must be "constructive politicians". Eisenhardt and Zbaracki (1992) suggest that some sources of conflict are more beneficial than others, and there is perhaps an optimal level of conflict that adds to decision quality. A key task for strategic decision-makers is to gain the benefits of constructive social and political interaction in the organization without the costs of conflict.

In essence, strategy-making may be visualized as unfolding in the organization through a set of metaphorical as well as literal conversations. Although these conversations are not elemental, they include the exploration of mental models; synthesizing learning, creativity, and analysis;

and navigating the social and political dynamics of the organization. The ability to conduct a strategic conversation is therefore a key strategic leader skill, but one which may be bounded by context. The strategic challenges inherent in every unique context are examined further in the next section.

## Contextual challenges

Although it may be argued that strategic thinking and behaviour is generic, it appears that context could be a significant variable. There are a variety of important concepts of organization – strategy, the leader, process, structure, systems, culture, power, and style – which combine to form the contexts of organizations. In effect, a context is a type of situation wherein particular structures, relationships, processes, and competitive settings can be found (Mintzberg and Quinn, 1996). Most organizations fit one context or another, but none ever does so perfectly – the world is too nuanced for that. Many organizations do not fit any single context at all.

Chakravarthy and White (2002) suggest that context has a direct influence on the strategic decision and action premises that guide a firm's strategy, and that there is a dynamic relationship between strategy and context. Not only must we understand the context; we must also understand how the context itself may be changed. They go on to suggest that there is an internal organizational context (for example, purpose and culture) as well as an external business context (for example, competitive setting and life cycle).

Numerous other contextual models have been suggested, such as strategic orientation (Miles and Snow, 1978), organization type (Mintzberg, 1981), the 7-S (Peters and Waterman, 1982), life cycle (Miller, 1989), and culture webs (Johnson, 1993). In all cases, the context appears to influence the identification of strategic issues, the paradoxes to be worked through, the nature of the strategic conversation, the pacing of strategic change, and the appropriateness of the behaviours of leaders.

Even the very nature of what may be considered a strategic decision is context dependent. As Mintzberg (1979: 60) asserts, "no type of decision is inherently strategic; decisions are strategic only in context. The introduction of a new product is a major event in a brewery, but hardly worth mentioning in a toy company".

Croom and Batchelor (1997) observe that the types of learning required in an organization are variable and context dependent. In a calm environment, simple changes may take place without any radical rethinking of the way the organization operates i.e. adaptive or single loop learning may suffice. In turbulent times, a fundamental shift in the way the organization thinks and operates may be required i.e. generative or double loop learning may become essential.

Similarly, the pacing of strategic change is contingent upon the situation (Vandermerwe and Vandermerwe, 1991). For instance, in a crisis, the performance decline may be immediate and of such severity that a rapid completion of the change process may be vital. A reactive mode, in which an event has just begun to cause a problem, and hence more time is usually available to get the needed results, may be more appropriate in other situations. In yet another setting, when some future event is likely to be potentially problematic, the change process may be anticipatory. Although crisis-driven change is the easiest to handle, waiting for a crisis is obviously potentially dangerous.

Miller (1989: 6) offers a corporate life cycle model of strategic leadership behaviours, as displayed in Figure 3.5, in which the vertical axis shows "the health of the culture as measured by its ability to create and maintain wealth" and the horizontal axis represents "the maturing of the corporation over time".

The leadership styles that dominate various stages of the life cycle, as proposed by Miller (1989), are described in Table 3.3.

While the universal applicability of this point of view is clearly debatable, the variety in the leadership styles described in Table 3.3, and their variation across the organizational life cycle, reinforce the construct of behavioural complexity discussed earlier.

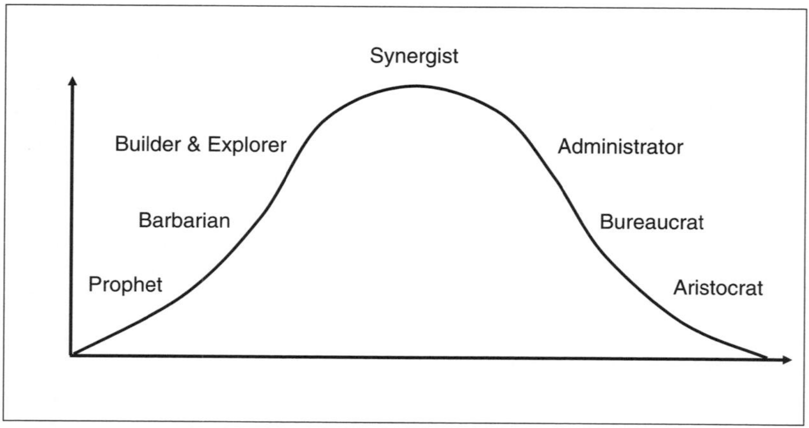


*Figure 3.5* A Life Cycle Model of Strategic Leadership

*Source*: From *Barbarians to Bureaucrats* by Lawrence M. Miller, copyright © 1989 by Lawrence M. Miller. Used by permission of Crown Publishers, a division of Random House, Inc.

**Table 3.3** Leadership at Different Life Cycle Stages

| Leadership Style | Description |
|---|---|
| Prophet | Visionary who creates the breakthrough |
| Barbarian | Leader of crisis and conquest, commands organisation into rapid growth |
| Builder/Explorer | Developer of specialised skills and structures, shifts emphasis from command to collaboration |
| Administrator | Creator of integrating systems and structures, shifts focus from expansion to security |
| Bureaucrat | Imposer of tight controls |
| Aristocrat | Inheritor of wealth, often causes rebellion and disintegration |
| Synergist | Maintains balance, continues forward motion by unifying and appreciating the diverse contribution of the Prophet, Barbarian, Builder, Explorer, and Administrator |

*Source*: From *Barbarians to Bureaucrats* by Lawrence M. Miller, copyright © 1989 by Lawrence M. Miller. Used by permission of Crown Publishers, a division of Random House, Inc.

Numerous organizational configurations are offered by Mintzberg (1979, 1981, 1989) and each resulting context has implications for the strategic process. A sample derived from Mintzberg, is displayed in Table 3.4:

**Table 3.4** A Typology of Organizational Contexts

| | Entrepreneurial | Bureaucracy | Professional | Adhocracy |
|---|---|---|---|---|
| Environment | Start-up, crisis, turnaround | Mature | Stable but complex | Dynamic change and complex technologies |
| Focus | Simple innovation | Standardization of outputs | Performance | Complex innovation |
| Strategic Process | Specific individual | Deliberate planning | Interactive, collective | Emergent |
| Sources of Power | Ownership | Hierarchy | Expertise | Ideas, coalitions |
| Key Skills | Vision | Analysis and programming | Consensus building | Championing, leading teams of experts |

## The interpretive and inertial challenge

Whichever contextual frame is adopted, the key issue appears to be the extent to which the context poses both an interpretive and an inertial challenge.

The interpretive challenge involves the interpretation of strategic issues. Strategic issues are trends, developments, and dilemmas that affect an organization as a whole and its position in the environment (Egelhoff, 1982). Issues include opportunities, threats, and problems. They are often ill structured and ambiguous and require an interpretation effort (Daft and Weick, 1984).

Exploring the link between organizational context and interpretation, Daft and Weick (1984) suggest that the information from an environment that top managers attend to and the meaning they attach to that information are, in part, functions of frameworks embodied in organization level contextual factors. These frameworks or "modes of interpretation" will affect which situations and events managers will attend to, which they will ignore, and which they will perceive as having a strategic impact on their organization.

Even when exposed to identical stimuli, top managers in different organizations often construct different interpretations of the same strategic issue. Such interpretations differ because they are subjective constructs (Wildavsky, 1979), or *a priori* theories, beliefs, structures, and procedures about the issues (Hall, 1984). Past actions are stored in a "retained set" of organizational knowledge consisting of the memories of organizational members, archival records, and organizational structures. This retained set provides frameworks for deciding what data to attend to and how to interpret the data. Both the cognitive processes of the organization's members and the contextual features of the organization embody these frameworks.

Previous work by Bower (1970) and Burgelman (1983b) has also emphasized the importance of the strategic and structural context of an organization in managing and implementing strategic decisions. A key finding is that if top managers want to alter their interpretation of their environment, and the range of variables they consider in interpretation efforts, they need to deliberately manage the way in which the information is gathered, processed, and communicated. A change in information processing capacity may alter the conceptual lenses used, and consequently the range of possible actions available. This has implications for how strategy is formulated over time. "People choose variations and interpret results within the frameworks of their current beliefs and vested interests, so misperceptions not only persist, they accumulate" (Starbuck, 1983: 100). Altering the strategic or structural context in which interpretations persist may be one way to interrupt this positive feedback loop, and thereby facilitate strategic change.

This perspective is also corroborated by Eisenhardt (1989), who takes the view that top management teams with a high level of participation in strategic decision-making and a well developed ability to access and analyse information, have a sense of mastery and control over strategic decisions as well as an ability to increase the range of variables to be considered.

Johnson (1988) proposes an "organizational action" view of strategy formation in which strategy is best seen as the product of the political, cognitive, and cultural fabric of the organization. In this view, a key driver of strategic thinking is the set of assumptions and beliefs taken for granted by managers, and held relatively in common through the organization. This set of assumptions and generalized beliefs about an organization and the way it is, or should be, makes up a paradigm. Since it is taken for granted, it may be difficult to surface or identify as a coherent statement. The paradigm is closely related to the dominant organizational routines, which in turn play a substantial part in shaping strategy in the business. Specifically, the paradigm plays a central role in the interpretation of environmental stimuli and the configuration of organizationally relevant strategic responses. Johnson (1988) argues that the paradigm is preserved and legitimized in a "cultural web" of organizational action in terms of myths, rituals, symbols, control systems, and formal and informal power structures that support and provide relevance to core beliefs. The key implication is that this organizational context may constrain individual ability to think and act. Ideological heterogeneity in management systems, deliberate assumption surfacing and challenging devices, and active involvement of "outsiders" with lesser adherence to the organizational culture or paradigm therefore become important elements of an effective strategic process.

Along the same lines, Starbuck (1983) argues that "strategic decision-making can be non-adaptive because behaviours get programmed through spontaneous habits, professional norms, education, training, precedents, traditions, rituals, as well as through formalized procedures".

Apart from the interpretive challenge, a context also presents an inertial problem. Many organizations do not adapt effectively to changes in their environments. Although strategic drift can occur for various reasons, Hambrick et al (1993) focus on organizational inertia as an underlying phenomenon, and observe that many organizations have difficulty changing at the same rate as their environments. Inertial pressures can come from many quarters such as: sunk investment in specialized assets, bureaucratic control, internal political and cultural restraints, and external restrictions (Hannan and Freeman, 1989). In addition, a great deal of the normative thinking on strategy implementation suggests that employee resistance to change is another principal source of inertia.

Mental models also influence how leaders view their contexts. Evidence exists that top executives themselves are often not open minded about change, and remain committed to the status quo thanks to a psychological adherence to "industry recipes" (Spender, 1989). Hambrick et al (1993) found that "industry tenure" shapes psychological adherence to industry recipes, and this in turn drives a belief in the enduring correctness of current policies. Membership in an industry inserts a person into a social setting in which actions, contexts, and outcomes are subjected to a shared interpretation (Burrell and Morgan, 1979). Those individuals who have participated in this "social construction of reality" for the longest time are most convinced of its correctness. In fact they may have difficulty in even conceiving alternative logics. "Industry wisdom" may have some beneficial effects, but taken to an extreme it reduces management's open mindedness towards change. While there may be some situations where industry recipes provide solutions that are superior to those produced by executive teams with extra-industry experience, in general, top management teams composed of a mixture of individuals, some with long industry tenure and some with short industry tenure, may be best able to adapt to an environment that simultaneously has elements of continuity and change. Left unchallenged, industry wisdom may accumulate about the ideal profile of different sub-classes of firms within the industry (e.g. regional airlines, generic pharmaceutical producers) to such an extent that the "chosen" strategies are nothing more than "scripts" for an organization's widely accepted role in the industry.

Another key finding by Hambrick et al (1993) is that industry tenure as a source of inertia has a stronger effect in high discretion industries, possibly because in situations of greater ambiguity and uncertainty executives grasp onto industry strategic recipes as a way of dealing with or reducing that uncertainty. High performance also strengthens the effect. The researchers also affirm a well known human tendency: incumbent CEOs tend to believe that their eventual successors should be just like them.

Frederickson (1986) adds an organizational perspective by asserting that the relationship between structure and strategy is reciprocal. Structure can have a profound and deterministic effect on strategy.

Organizations that differ in their dominant structure (centralization, formalization, complexity dimensions) are likely to make strategic decisions using very different processes. Certain structures can perpetuate certain types of strategic behaviour. For example, in an international company, an organization structure built around national operating companies (with local measures of performance and rewards) may persistently generate "local" rather than "global" strategic behaviours.

Frederickson and Iaquinto (1989) also suggest that strategic decision processes are likely to exhibit considerable inertia, resisting all but modest change. This feature can also be described as momentum, or simply habit.

A major emergent theme is that all strategy is contextual. The context influences the understanding of what is strategic, the nature of the strategic conversation and the strategic paradoxes, and strategic leadership behaviours. Each context offers unique interpretive and inertial challenges, which may inhibit the ability to think and act. Not only do strategic leaders need to understand context, they must also understand how to change the context.

## A conceptual framework of strategic leader capability

The major themes in the preceding discussion merit repetition, and may now be drawn together as follows.

A review of the strategy process literature suggests that strategic outcomes are shaped by highly complex organizational processes. Interestingly, while perspectives on the strategic process abound, advice to leaders and managers does not.

Numerous strategic roles exist within organizations, bounded by the opportunity and empowerment to influence the strategic process. By definition, all strategic roles are potentially organization-wide in their consequences, and shape the long-term rather than the short-term future of the organization. In particular, this research focuses on the capability of strategic leaders – most commonly found at or near the apex of the organization – as an important potential contributor to organizational success.

There is widespread agreement that strategic thinking and acting strategically in a manner most appropriate to a given context is at the heart of strategic leader capability, and that this is fundamentally concerned with both organizational direction and change. This involves both cognitive and behavioural processes, which may be tightly and inextricably coupled.

Against this backdrop, the four dimensions of strategic leader capability may be identified as:

**Engagement with Strategic Paradoxes**
Strategic paradoxes, and the exercise of judgement that they call for, are characteristic of much of the work of forming and executing strategy. Several key strategic paradoxes which must be engaged with have been identified. The challenge of paradoxes is not so much to make choices, but rather to transcend the paradox and synthesize contending opposites.

**Cognitive and Behavioural Complexity**
Effective strategic leadership requires a balancing and mastery of seemingly contradictory capabilities, and effective leaders not only think multi-dimensionally but are also able to execute multiple roles simultaneously. High-performing strategic leaders demonstrate high levels of cognitive and behavioural complexity, deployed in a highly integrated and complementary way.

**Ability to Conduct a Strategic Conversation**
Strategy-making may be visualized as unfolding in the organization through metaphorical strategic conversations. Although these conversations are not elemental, they include the exploration of mental models, synthesizing learning, creativity, and analysis, and navigating the social and political dynamics of the organization. The ability to conduct a strategic conversation is a key strategic leader skill.

**Understanding and Challenging Context**
All strategy is contextual. The context influences the understanding of what is strategic, the nature of the strategic conversation and stra-tegic paradoxes, and strategic leader behaviours. Each context offers unique interpretive and inertial challenges, which may inhibit the ability to think and act. Not only do strategic leaders need to understand context, they must also understand how to change the context.

Taken together, these four constructs make up a conceptual framework of individual strategic capability as depicted in Figure 3.6.

The previous discussion in this study has not yielded explicit linkages across the four constructs, however it may be conjectured that all the constructs are related to one another, resulting in six possible interactive relationships.

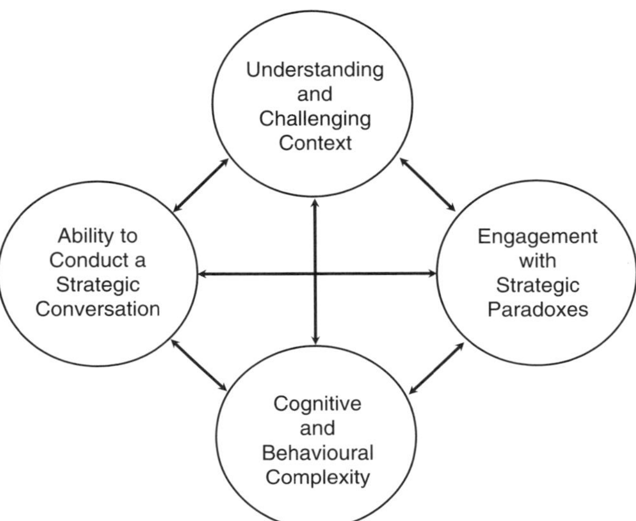


*Figure 3.6* A Conceptual Framework of Strategic Leader Capability

1. *The relationship between strategic conversation and contextual challenges*: the nature of the strategic conversation is greatly influenced by the nature of the context. For example, in a highly capital intensive industry with a stable environment, the conversation may focus largely on analysis. On the other hand, in a business with short product life cycles in an entrepreneurial setting, the conversation may focus more on creativity. The strategic conversation may also influence the context. For example, a conversation that challenges existing mental models or assumptions and beliefs in a robust way may result in a re-framing of strategic issues in such a way that the inertial or interpretive challenges inherent in the context may be overcome.
2. *The relationship between strategic conversation and engagement with strategic paradoxes*: a robust strategic conversation is likely to assist in identifying and transcending the critical strategic paradoxes. Equally, the manner in which the paradoxes are worked through, and strategic leadership judgement exercised, and the resulting outcomes, represent strategic learning that will influence the strategic conversation.
3. *The relationship between cognitive and behavioural complexity and the strategic conversation*: high levels of cognitive and behavioural complexity will result in a more meaningful strategic conversation, and the cumulative experience of diverse and numerous strategic

conversations will enhance the cognitive and behavioural complexity of the individual.

4. *The relationship between cognitive and behavioural complexity and engagement with strategic paradoxes*: high levels of cognitive and behavioural complexity will result in a greater ability to transcend strategic paradoxes, and the learning from the manner in which the paradoxes are worked through and strategic leadership judgement exercised, and the resulting outcomes, will enhance the cognitive and behavioural complexity of the individual.
5. *The relationship between contextual challenges and engagement with strategic paradoxes*: the context is likely to determine the nature of the paradoxes that need to be worked through. For example, in a professional organization such as a university the primary organizational paradox may be one of balancing organizational alignment with individual autonomy, whereas in an innovative organization the paradoxical tension may primarily be between a planned strategy and the need to sponsor emergence. At the same time, the judgement exercised over the paradoxes may affect the context. A failure to balance alignment and autonomy in the university, for instance, may worsen the inertial challenge embedded in the organization. On the other hand, success in transcending strategic paradoxes may serve to revitalize the context, reducing the interpretive and inertial challenges.
6. *The relationship between contextual challenges and cognitive and behavioural complexity:* a high degree of interpretive and inertial challenge in the context will require a high degree of cognitive and behavioural complexity from the individual attempting to bring about strategic change in such a setting. For example, in a organization characterized by conflicting and seemingly irreconcilable functional perspectives and political strife, the strategic leader will be required to deploy a high level of cognitive and behavioural complexity. On the other hand, a context with low interpretive and inertial challenges may inhibit the development of cognitive and behavioural complexity of individuals in strategic leader roles.

It should be apparent that not all the relationships are equally robust; indeed it may be argued that some are tenuous. This merely reflects the state of current thinking in this study, and the available evidence does not permit the statement of more definitive propositions.

Despite this limitation, by bringing together different streams of thought in the strategic management, strategic leadership, organization theory, and cognitive and behavioural psychology domains, this research has offered a new perspective on individual strategic leader capability, an area that has been inadequately served by previous research, and has identified four key inter-related constructs.

"Face validity" of these dimensions was secured through two focus groups conducted by an independent facilitator. The focus groups were made up primarily from the management development and organizational consulting communities, but also included two practising managers – see details in Appendix 1(b). The findings were presented by the author to the participants in the focus groups. The facilitator then invited participants to discuss the dimensions, to consider if they fit with their own experiences and insights, and to highlight any omissions. While the groups considered the suggested relationships between the identified dimensions to be speculative, there was agreement that the dimensions themselves mirrored their own observations, and that they appeared to be comprehensive. The focus groups also suggested that it would be meaningful to explore capability development processes in a broad and open-minded manner, which should go beyond examining only formal development interventions. A decision was therefore made to proceed on this basis with the next phase of the research, with the objectives of informing and enriching the conceptual framework with empirical observations, and exploring the influential development processes experienced by individuals in strategic leader roles.

# 4
# Strategic Leader Capability: Field Notes

## Introduction to Phase II

Based on a review of the literature in Phase I, Chapters 2 and 3 offered a conceptual framework of individual strategic capability in the context of the realities of the strategic process. The four key elements of the framework identified in the research were:

*Engagement with strategic paradoxes*
The work of forming and executing strategy requires the exercise of strategic judgement, or the ability to synthesize or balance conflicting goals and processes.

*Cognitive and behavioural complexity*
High performance strategic leaders demonstrate high levels of cognitive and behavioural complexity i.e. they have a complex repertoire of ways of thinking and behaving.

*Ability to conduct a strategic conversation*
Strategy-making may be visualized as unfolding in the organization through a series of metaphorical conversations. These include a conversation with other people, a conversation with unfolding events, and a conversation in the mind of the strategic leader.

*Understanding and challenging context*
All strategy is contextual, and each context offers unique interpretive and inertial challenges. Individuals in strategic roles need to be able to understand the context and work within it, but at the same time be able to challenge it when necessary.

Individual strategic leader capability may therefore be viewed as a composite of the ability to engage with strategic paradoxes, the ability to think and behave in a complex way, the ability to conduct a strategic conversation, and the ability to both understand and challenge the unique context the leader is operating in.

Using these four dimensions of strategic capability as a starting point, the primary objectives of Phase II were:

1. to enrich the conceptual framework through an investigation into the experiences of individuals in strategic leadership roles, and their perspectives on the capabilities needed in their roles, and
2. to explore the processes by which individuals in strategic leadership roles acquired or developed their capabilities.

A subsidiary objective was to collect opinions of strategic leaders on formal management development interventions, to the extent that they had knowledge or personal experience of this.

Phase II findings were subsequently used in Phase III to develop recommendations for improving the effectiveness of strategic leader development processes (Chapters 5 to 7).

Following a review of the methodology used, this chapter presents Phase II findings under two sub-headings:

*Some voices: The dimensions of strategic leader capability* explores perceptions of the role of the strategic leader as narrated by the interviewees, as well as their observations on each of the four dimensions of strategic leader capability. Also included are some thoughts on how the conceptual framework derived in Phase I may be refined and adjusted in view of the empirical findings, in order to better reflect the managerial world and vernacular, and these are presented in *Summary of findings on dimensions of capability*.

*Some voices: The development of strategic leader capability* outlines the high level pattern in the range of influential development experiences narrated by interviewees. Within this theme, *Informal learning* explores the two broad types of informal learning processes – task-driven and people-driven – and their influence in the sample. *Formal learning* examines interviewee accounts of formal learning processes such as executive coaching, management development interventions, and formal education. The various strands of the influential development processes are then briefly pulled together in *Summary of findings on development of capability*.

## Methodology

Given the nature of the phenomena under study, and the need to see them through the eyes of the people being studied as opposed to imposing an *a priori* theoretical framework, a qualitative research methodology was adopted.

As a starting point, the target population of strategic leaders was defined as "individuals in strategic leader roles who have been in role for at least a year". Strategic leader roles were defined as the head of an organization or the head of an autonomous division or business unit within a larger corporation. The qualifying time period of one year was considered appropriate as a sufficient length of time that would enable interviewees to identify and articulate issues related to their role, and also to eliminate any individuals who may have failed early on in their roles.

A purposeful sampling scheme was followed. Although access was an important determinant, conscious efforts were made to achieve diversity of industry, organization size, nationality, and interviewee age and gender. As a result, the sample included interviewees from 16 different industries (including the not-for-profit sector), represented five nationalities (although the U.K. dominated) and had both men and women (although men dominated).

Individuals in the sample were identified through the author's professional contacts. As a result, one of the characteristics of the sample is that all interviewees had experience of, or interest in, the leader development process.

A profile of the interviewees is attached in Appendix 1(c). The identity of the interviewees and the names of their organizations have been disguised for reasons of confidentiality.

Individuals were formally asked to participate in the study via an invitation that explained the purpose and nature of the study. A "theoretical saturation" approach was followed, without a predetermined sample size. However, with the analysis of interviews 23, 24, and 25 not yielding any new insights, a decision was made to stop at 25 interviews.

A personal face-to-face interview was conducted with every interviewee. Interviews ranged from 30 minutes to 55 minutes in duration, and had an average duration of 40 minutes. This was considered satisfactory given the competing demands on the time of these senior executives. Each interview was tape recorded and was subsequently transcribed professionally.

The questionnaire used for the interviews is attached in Appendix 2(a). The questionnaire was piloted with two interviewees and then amended slightly before being rolled out further. Questions 1 to 3 were designed to be scene-setting in nature, and to elicit the interviewee's views on the business context, the role, and the strategic process in the organization. Questions 4 to 6 were intended to explore the capabilities required in that role. Questions 7 to 12 were aimed at exploring the development process the individual had experienced. Question 13 solicited the interviewee's views on the development of others in the organization.

The questionnaire was used as a conversational guide, rather than as a mechanical instrument. This flexibility was essential as it enabled sensitivity to emergent themes in the interview. Also, interviewee answers to a question sometimes made a downstream question redundant; for example a response to Question 3 frequently also elicited an answer to Question 4. Consequently the sequence in which the questions were asked varied from one interview to another.

However, for comparative purposes, each interviewee was asked a set of questions in five core areas, which concerned background and role, the strategic process in the organization, major challenges being faced, the capabilities required in the role, and the influential development processes experienced by the individual. With minor exceptions, every interviewee responded on each of these issues. Questions 6 (development of others) and 7 (additional comments) were not asked in every case due to exigencies of time.

Data analysis was conducted with the aid of NVivo, a computer based qualitative data analysis tool. This involved a study of all the text from all the transcripts, and a process of assigning text to different nodes. A node in NVivo is a way of bringing together similar ideas and concepts. Passages of text from one or more documents are connected to a node – through a process of coding – because they are examples of the idea or concept it represents. This enables the identification of patterns and recurrent themes while retaining an auditable trail of analysis.

For reasons of rigour, the text was initially coded "in-vivo" using words that were faithful to the voices of the interviewees. In the first stage of data analysis, this resulted in a process similar to the "grounded theory" approach (Glaser and Strauss, 1967).

Over 200 nodes were initially generated on this basis, and all text was coded. In the second stage, similar nodes were clustered, merged where appropriate, and then assigned to a hierarchy of ideas based on an emerging conceptual scheme. It should be noted that this was an iterative process. For reasons of clarity, a series of "trees" depicting the evolution and inter-connectedness of each set of ideas was generated and used to retain coherence. These are presented at the appropriate points in the ensuing narrative (Figures 4.1 to 4.6, and Figure 4.8) in order to maintain transparency of the thought process that resulted in a range of ideas being grouped into specific constructs.

Once the constructs had been assembled, text at each node was extracted to provide illustrations and examples. The discussion of findings that follows uses this text and the NVivo "trees" to develop the argument.

For the record, tables showing which interviewee raised or referred to which idea were also maintained. However, given the qualitative nature of this study, no attempt was made to conduct a statistical analysis.

It should also be emphasized that the data generated was based on "self-reporting" by interviewees and may therefore contain perceptual, memory, or current pressures based biases at the level of the individual. Collectively, however, numerous patterns were discernible.

## Some voices: The dimensions of strategic leader capability

### Scene setting: The strategic leader role

All interviews commenced with a brief scene-setting discussion on the individual's role. This served to establish at an early stage that the interviewees viewed themselves as principally accountable for strategy in their organization or unit. Responses did not result in any individual being disqualified from the sample, and some typical comments are given below:

> *Strategy formation and driving implementation is the job (Tom)*

> *Overall, as far as I'm concerned, strategy is the role of the CEO, full stop, that's what you get paid to do (John)*

> *I'm not solely responsible for strategy formation and implementation here but I would see it as my top priority (Thomas)*

Interestingly, in contrast with the distinction often made by academic thinkers, interviewees did not distinguish between the processes of strategy development and strategy implementation. A number of comments suggested that the two are inextricably linked together:

> *I see strategy as defining the vision in a practical way and then implementing it in stages (Heather)*

*Part of the strategy process has to be the strategy to execution matrix (Jed)*

It is also worth noting that despite their positions at or near the apex of their organizations, the strategic leadership role was often seen as a facilitative one:

*I'm a very good generalist, an orchestra leader. I don't play great music anywhere but I can bring it all together (Pat)*

*My job isn't necessarily to be the person who comes up with these big changes; it's to filter the ideas of the people that are pouring into this funnel (David)*

**The nature of the strategic conversation**

Consistent with literature previously cited in Phase I, interviewees tended to view strategy as an unfolding process, rather than as an artefact.

*I am thinking strategy every single day. I think about the business when I am in the shower in the morning, in the car on the way to work and in the car on the way home. Some bit of my brain is always thinking what can we do next, what do we need to do next, what should we do next (Judith)*

*I carry something around with me, it's from a guy named von Clausewitz and it says "Men could not reduce strategy to a formula. Detailed planning necessarily failed due to the inevitable frictions encountered, chance events, imperfections in execution and the independent will of the opposition. Instead the human elements were paramount: leadership, morale and the almost instinctive savvy of the best generals. Strategy was not a lengthy action plan; it was the evolution of a central idea to continually changing circumstances". So if you were to say to me what's my strategy, I'd say it's the continuous evolution of a central idea (Pat)*

*What I mean by strategy is the broad principles of the journey from here, to the business that you've decided you want to become (Jed)*

When interviewees were asked to characterize their strategic process, formal mechanisms were invariably cited in the first instance. Descriptions of the process were strikingly similar across interviewees with common features including small strategy teams, periodic strategic reviews that dovetailed with the budgeting calendar, and the identification of key issues and objectives:

> *We have a formal strategy formulation process which begins at the end of the first quarter, April. The management team, three or four of us, disappear for a few days to reflect upon the current market, current dynamics, our own group plan (Steve)*

> *The process of strategy formation and implementation is that I'm a member of the world-wide board with four colleagues, including the CEO of the world-wide group, and we meet on a quarterly basis to discuss all issues of global relevance, including strategy. We formulate a three-year plan every year in the second quarter, and we put annual business plans together on a rolling basis for the year to come in detail and the following two years in slightly less detail (Anthony)*

> *This is an extremely formal process in our company, it starts usually in September and leads to a business plan in October, and then the main budget issues are implemented at the beginning of the year and then mostly it's tracked. It's a three-year piece around which we budget the business and then once every two years there's a lot of new perspective (Reinoud)*

> *We operate strategy through a group executive committee who happen to be senior equity holders, so we are bound together by a common interest. It's driven across a three-year plan which is revised annually in a country house hotel and then it's told to the troops in a Novotel just off the A40 somewhere (Wilf)*

> *As far as strategy formation is concerned, I have a small central team, involved in strategic planning, then within each of our five main businesses there are business planning units, who do the detailed business planning. We have a conventional business planning cycle that kicks in around July, runs through till November/December, when we go to the board with our five-year view. If they endorse that then we take year one of that and it becomes the budget. Beyond that we also take a broader, wider view of strategy, given that we have a five-year regulatory cycle in electricity and water, we have a big price review, and our investment programmes are reset from 1st April. Every five years we can stand back to look at the general direction of the business (John)*

*The annual strategic review process is very thorough with loads of background data on your competitors, where do you want to be and how are you going to get there. There are usually two or three key issues which are identified for the business which you spend some time evaluating (James)*

However, descriptions of the formal process were frequently accompanied by comments about its limitations – scepticisms included the ritual, "box ticking nature" of the process; inadequate emphasis on creativity and innovation; and lack of engagement with people:

*It sometimes limits the breadth of our strategy work, because it already starts off in a box. Here's a well defined problem and a hypothesis. It says it's the best thing to do, you test it, and that ends up with putting you in a bit of a box with regard to what is possible (Ronnie)*

*We have a yearly strategy planning process but I would consider it more a mid-term budgeting process than a strategy process. We have submitted our strategy plan for 2004, but feel... it was box ticking (Pat)*

*The bit that's missing is the innovative bit, which we are just trying to address now, setting up a more creative group that's going to look at the next 3–5 years in terms of what are the big ideas that we can get into, which will genuinely give us some competitive edge (Wilf)*

*We were very rich in data but very poor in quality management information (Steve)*

*This process has been far too data intensive in the past and we need to put much more high quality thinking into the process (Anthony)*

The emergent and opportunistic dimension of strategy in reality was underscored by numerous interviewees:

*My favourite comment is the one about Harold Macmillan. When asked the question what keeps you awake at night, he replied events, dear boy, events. Most strategy is based on events, you're moving on, things happen and you have to respond and I guess it's engage and see, so strategy is the next big step, vision is the 10th or 12th big step (Tom)*

*A week after we'd done our strategy, one of our competitors decided that they wanted to get out of that particular sector, and we went from a desserts business with an average turnover at the plant of £35–40 million, to one of around £100 million. A fantastic and lucky break. At that point I went to talk to the board, and the board said, great strategy! (Jed)*

Consequently, it was suggested that the formal plan should be held lightly:

*Once you've dreamt up the new idea, you need some sort of a plan, but don't fall into the mistake of believing the plan; it's only an indication of a route. You take an engineer's plan and he would expect to stick to it with incredible rigidity. When plotting the future of a business all you know is that it plots a route and you will deviate left or right of it. You've got to build a deep sense of scepticism – be sceptical of everything you see (Rodney)*

Interviewees clearly aspired towards a hybrid of a planned and deliberate approach on the one hand, and a flexible and emergent approach to strategy on the other, as exemplified by one interviewee:

*The strategy process here is fairly formal in that we have financial management. Our basic idea is to have strategic flexibility but with financial rigour so at any given moment we have a very clear idea of what the financial expectations of the business are, but overriding that is a constant strategic flexibility (Tom)*

Nineteen interviewees offered comments about their strategic process. Of these, 13 characterized their strategic process as a combination of deliberate and emergent. Three interviewees described their process in exclusively deliberate terms, and another three in emergent terms only.

These findings substantiate an important element of the "strategic conversation" construct, namely that strategy is "a conversation with unfolding events".

When asked to comment on the abilities required to shape strategy effectively, interviewees highlighted a range of skills, some of which were directly linked to strategic thinking i.e. to the process of deducing or synthesizing a strategy, while others were linked to the need to engage people in the process and to articulate the strategy or vision.

Divergent views were expressed with regard to strategic thinking. The importance of analytical and abstraction abilities were emphasized by eight interviewees, and some typical comments in this regard were:

> *You should have a strong analytical focus. You must be a good analyser who comes straight to the point, reduces complex issues to a very essential point. You can describe complex issues on one piece of paper, and make simple models. The risk is that you go down into details as an analytical person and the challenge is to come up again, to make it condensed, compact (Udo)*

> *I believe you've got to have that analytical capability. There are certain businesses that you can run on an intuitive strategic model, but they are probably not in our position. It's difficult to see how a purely intuitive approach to strategy would work when you're not dealing with a clean sheet of paper, because our role is to take what we're given and make the best out of it. One is constantly trying to analyse and create compelling concepts as to what our strategy should be (Rupert)*

> *You must be able to see what's happening and you must have a level of abstraction, also you must be able to hover above the business to see what all the players are doing (Reinoud)*

> *I need the analytical skills to set out the road map for the business, to be able to formulate the strategy (John)*

However, even those who engaged in and made a case for analysis were mindful of the limitations of an over-dependence on analysis:

> *A lot of the work that's done analytically is frequently done to support a decision that somebody has already made, maybe as a nego-tiating tool or as a persuasion tool. People may have a gut feeling of what they want to do and then have a test at it (Ronnie)*

> *I still use Porter's five forces analysis for markets, and it's very valuable. But it's valuable because it's something, not because it's the right thing (Anthony)*

*You need to be able to articulate the strategy very clearly so those analytical skills are important, but I would say they are only one third of what it takes to make things happen (Thomas)*

Nine interviewees (interestingly, including three who had referred to the importance of analytical abilities) made a fervent case for alternative, "non-analytical" approaches such as creativity:

*Don't tell me you've done all the analysis and all the quantitative mathematics because all you're doing in my opinion is stifling creativity (Chris)*

*How do you get a giraffe in the fridge? The answer is you just open the door and put its head in the fridge. How do you get an elephant in the fridge? You open the door, take the giraffe out and put the elephant in. Over 60% of preschool kids get the answers right, and over 60% of CEOs get them wrong, because we train ourselves out of thinking outside these tram lines. You've got to get into giraffes in fridges as a CEO. You've got to be able to imagine outside the box; you got to get everybody to execute in the box, but you've got to be able to imagine (Jed)*

The ability to keep learning – from past experience or from others – was also cited. Learning was observed to require curiosity, open mindedness, flexibility, and a willingness to challenge assumptions:

*I am very curious, I ask a lot of questions, I don't have all the answers, I like to have a broad brush of people giving me thoughts, I'm looking for ideas, I'm looking for thinkers (Pat)*

*I see this as one of the most important things in strategic decision making, to be open minded. I've had this since I was small, I am naturally curious and open minded (Reinoud)*

*To be curious, you must be a scout, you must look in other sectors and what are they doing. You can then transfer and reflect this into your own operation. Scouting around is learning, picking up new ideas (Udo)*

*The ability to be flexible is crucial. When I look at the business I'm in now I think there has been a fundamental shift in some of the dynamics and therefore having the ability to adapt and the flexibility to change is required (Rupert)*

*Getting things wrong is a fact of life; getting it wrong twice, that's stupid (Chris)*

Figure 4.1 overleaf displays the various responses of interviewees on the subject of abilities required in the strategic process. Comments with regard to engaging others in the strategic process (for example, by getting input and buy-in, and communicating the strategic direction) are dealt with later in this chapter in the section titled *Behavioural complexity and mobilizing people.*

**The importance of contextual mastery**

Within the set of 25 interviewees, only five interviewees had prior work experience that cut across diverse sectors; the remaining 20 had been steeped in the same company or industry throughout their careers.

Given this profile, as well as previous observations in the literature regarding the importance of context, it was expected that interviewees would include in-depth understanding of context as one of the key capabilities required in the role. This expectation was met, as 20 interviewees (although not necessarily the same 20 who had spent their careers immersed in one company or industry) commented at length about the importance of understanding the unique context of their organizations.

Some framed the importance of context from a customer perspective:

*You need to understand the business. You don't need to understand exactly how the technology works. You need to know what goes in and what comes out and what happens to get it there. You don't need to have an engineering degree, or an IT background. But you do need to know what the customer wants, both our customer who is the betting shop, and their customer, in order to make the right decisions (David)*

*I have a wealth of in-built knowledge about my key customers, so I know people who are in those organizations and I talk to them, and I go and experience those organizations as a consumer of their service. I don't think that somebody could come in and do my job with no food experience (Jed)*

Others emphasized the need to understand the financials:

*The person in this role needs, like all other CEOs, to have strong capabilities, in respect of the financial anatomy of a business, the financial*

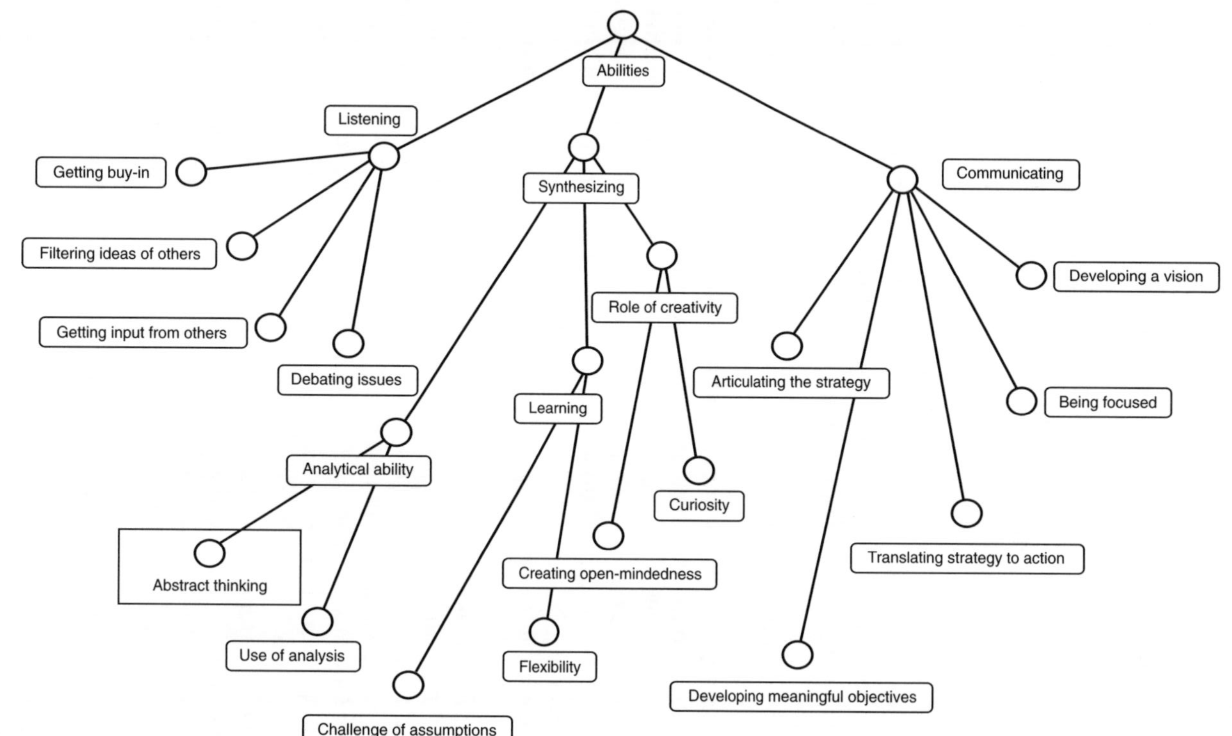


*Figure 4.1* Strategic Conversation Abilities

*dynamics of a business, the ability to understand in relatively financial terms, the levers you can pull to make the company perform (Anthony)*

Contextual understanding was also viewed as a key asset in the implementation of strategy:

*To understand what it takes to implement... having been in the market and having run a sales force and having experience in marketing; that's a really strong background in order to understand the difficulties in implementing your strategy (Steve)*

*The thing with media is that the concepts are really simple, so you go to the average social engagement and you engage them in a conversation about making a magazine or a radio station, and it's pretty simple. It's not the internal combustion engine. So the broad concepts are simple, but the detail is really hard, what makes page 4 a good page 4, what makes the 11 o'clock ad break a better break than the 12 o'clock break? (Tom)*

The need for credibility, effective communication, and the management of stakeholders were even more frequently cited as factors that made contextual understanding almost mandatory:

*From the external standpoint I think you could do this job regardless of your industry background. It's not the specific packaging knowledge that's required. When you start talking about the internal business area, that's where you have an advantage if you have the packaging knowledge and the company knowledge. It's important because of credibility, knowledge of how things work and culture, values, systems. It would take some time. If you put a Philips chap in my chair it would take at least 2–3 years for that person to get up to speed on these type of issues (Jan)*

*It is an asset, because of credibility. You can speak with knowledge; you can understand questions, particularly if you're talking to an aviation person. You know what they are talking about and you can ask intelligent questions. For a non-aviation person, that would be very difficult. The conversation would be much more superficial (Judith)*

*It helps understanding the dynamics of the market, it helps to understand some of the basic things of how it works, that gives you credibility otherwise you're having to work pretty hard and demonstrate to your troops that you are adding value (James)*

*Outsiders would actually find it very difficult. I have actually got one of my regional directors who came from Unilever and actually they find it quite difficult to achieve. He's a very smart guy, we did assessment centres on him, he comes out very good, and he has very good people skills, but the actual understanding of the medicines and the jargon, and he's been with us now four years, he still has difficulties. There is an aspect of this that is actually very difficult to actually put your hands around. It's not easy (Brian)*

*I do believe that when you're speaking to a team of fashion buyers it would be very different to speaking to a team of bio-chemists for example. So I think some kind of understanding of that actual business and the make up of the business is vital (Tim)*

*Knowing the way the mechanics of the industry work, particularly the regulated side of it, and how it links into the government machine, is crucial. I know that at the top level most businesses have to relate to government but we are very much in the public domain, our prices are a political issue, we have just said that we need to raise our prices by 39% over the next five years, that is a political issue and I will be talking to the Secretary of State about that. You need to understand all the subtleties of that (John)*

*The person also requires a high level of sensitivity and awareness, a set of antennae, for difficulties that can confront the business if it misreads or fails to spot non-financial issues and trends to do with those reputational points or to do with the personal relationship elements with key players in the other stakeholding groups of the business (Anthony)*

In discussions of context, the surprising pattern that did emerge was the large number of interviewees who also talked about the importance of not being constrained by context, and the importance of a willingness and ability to challenge the context. Twenty-two interviewees made a wealth of comments in this regard.

*There is the need to stand back from the detail. There is a danger that you understand the company and the industry so well that you understand too much what everybody is going to have to do and maybe it would be better for me sometimes to break out. In my 360 degree feedback a couple of my direct reports have said to me recently that you've started to ask us things that are unreasonable and I think that's good (Tim)*

Interviewees talked about the value of an "outsider perspective" and a "fresh pair of eyes", "new blood", and the need to challenge the mindset and overcome inertial tendencies within the organization:

*You must see it as a fun exercise to be able to step out of the business and look at it from an outside-in perspective (Reinoud)*

*The big challenges for me have been learning how to do that and to think more widely and to think outside the box and to be more strategically adventurous. Some people have quite successfully come from outside the industry into the industry and brought that freshness of perspective (John)*

*I do also see the significance of fresh ideas and there are many examples of people who come into other industries and do well. But I suppose we've all got our own idiosyncrasies and things that people couldn't possibly understand (Tim)*

*With any MD I think it's important that there's some kind of contact with the outside world because whilst you do need to understand your business, there's a serious danger that you do become indoctrinated and a bit closed (Tim)*

The NVivo model that displays the evolution of both constructs is displayed in Figure 4.2.

While the strong representation of both points of view may seem paradoxical at first glance, it may be ventured that understanding context is a necessary precursor to challenging it. This data is strongly supportive of the dimension of context as developed in Phase I.

### Behavioural complexity and mobilizing people

This was the dimension of strategic capability that clearly most pre-occupied interviewees. It was abundantly clear that the challenge of mobilizing people was by far the most significant one faced in the strategic leader role. Despite the positions of relative power and authority occupied by the interviewees, the need to listen, communicate, influence, network, lobby, inspire, persuade, and "sell", both internally and externally, was a constant refrain, and was articulated near universally.

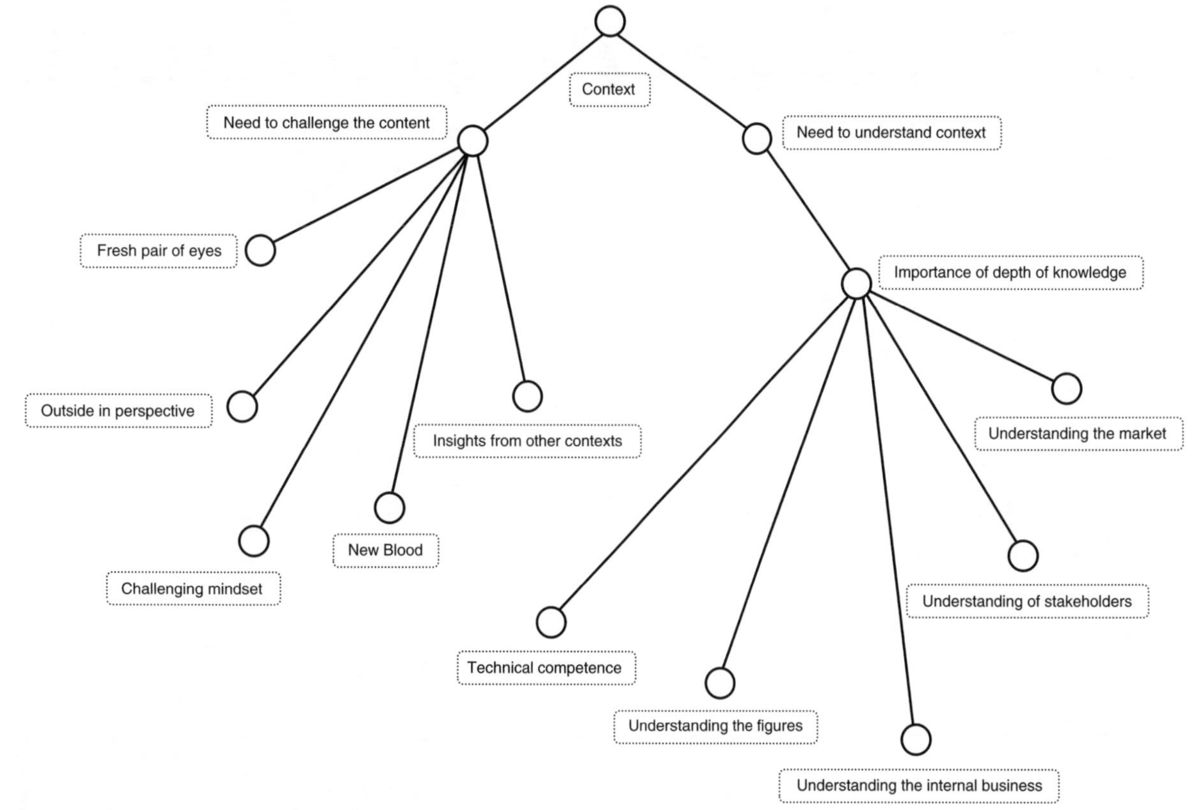


*Figure 4.2* Context

Eleven interviewees made observations about the need to engage with people, to listen to and filter their ideas, and get input while making strategy. An inability to do so was even considered dangerous by some:

> *I spend a lot of time just listening to people, hear what they've got to say and then decide (Rodney)*

> *Although I think the management team are important in strategic planning, everybody here and everybody in any business, is likely to have a good idea, which the management team may not see for one reason or another. I don't want to lose any ideas that anybody may have. Their idea may not be taken forward 100% but a seed of that idea can be allowed to grow and evolve into something useable (Judith)*

> *Sharing, talking, the whole process of strategic planning, it's in essence the most important thing I do in my work and that will shape the results that I'm aiming for in a very important way (Reinoud)*

Numerous interviewees highlighted the need to be able to articulate the vision or strategy in a compelling way once a strategic direction had emerged.

> *The biggest challenge is this: let's assume as the leader of the business you've got the skills to do the analysis and the interpretation, understand the issues and some of the solutions. Three thousand seven hundred and ninety-nine people in the organization have no idea what you're talking about or why you want them to go and do stuff, so the key challenge is about bringing everybody through... so that if people have a different point of view, I've got to get them to the same point (Jed)*

> *If you work in this business and you go to the pub tonight and you're chatting with someone and tell them you work for Company X and they ask you what's Company X's plan, I think if you as an employee can't articulate it for five minutes, the strategy is not good enough (Jonathan)*

> *The ability to formulate strategy is one part, but the other big part is the ability to communicate that strategy to the people in the business and to motivate them to go and achieve it (Jonathan)*

*If you don't take the time to talk to them about it, to explain, to see their concerns then your implementation will fail (Udo)*

*It's important to have this capability to create pictures, a vision. When I talk to my people after this strategic process, I try to have an easy picture for them, one that makes them hungry, to go for this self-fulfilling prophecy (Udo)*

*As a leader you do need to have a vision, to imagine yourself out of today and into tomorrow. That's the most important, everything else you can get somebody else to do for you. That bit is really tough. It's tough to lead a business and say what we're going to do is we're going to execute this vision (Jed)*

*I need to be able externally to relate to those people, to articulate what we want, to be able to network, influence, debate, and that needs communications skills and influencing skills (John)*

*You must have influencing capabilities, it's not what I say is law (Reinoud)*

*You need to be able to sell, not just to the customers but to other people in the industry, to their own company, to their boss, to their colleagues. I constantly find myself selling to everybody I speak to (Judith)*

*I have to be inspirational in some way, trustworthy, and I have to understand what this business is about that so I can talk about it in an interesting and inspiring way (Judith)*

*It's persuading people that the direction is right. Persuading individuals and groups as to what their role is, their ability to contribute to it, the difference they can make, how their performance is going to be measured against that, getting feedback, getting the buy-in of the shared objectives (Rupert)*

*Getting people to do things that you want them to do is vital. In many cases it's easy when the aims and ambitions coincide. If I want Joe to develop an IT system and he wants to do it, everybody's happy. Where I want him to do something that he doesn't want to do, then the skill comes in of managing him (David)*

Building teams and relationships, and nurturing them was another recurrent pattern:

> *I believe getting the right team in place is more important than the strategy. The right team will evolve strategy. If you've got the strategy but the wrong people, it's never going to work (John)*

> *Picking the right people to put on your bus is a really important skill and that's a combination of capability and fit (Jed)*

> *I have to build great relationships – I like to tell people that I move this organization through personal relationships, not reporting relationships (Pat)*

> *You need to be able to build trust. I need to be able to trust my team, they need to trust me. They need to know that if I say I will do something for him, then I will do it (David)*

> *Team building, getting the trust of people, getting them to realize that your intentions are to get the best for everybody, even if sometimes it means having to make an unpleasant decision… (Udo)*

> *It's more about having the right people at the heads of those teams, having the ability to motivate those people, to give them the right tools to do the job properly (Robert)*

When queried further about the demands made on the individual in a strategic leader role by the challenges of mobilizing people, 15 of the 25 interviewees made comments about the need to be elastic (including the need to flex style, tailor the message, treat people differentially, individualize, and to deploy different skills in different settings or times). Eight interviewees also talked about the need to have the social confidence to deal with different situations.

In other words, interviewees articulated the need for a complex repertoire of behaviours, to be employed in a discerning manner.

> *Trying to understand how to pitch a particular question or implementation plan to a German audience, versus an Italian audience or*

*Canadian audience is very difficult. You can go in with one plan but it won't be successful. You need to be elastic (Steve)*

*In a role like this the individual needs to be quite elastic depending on the situation. You are all things to all men (Rodney)*

*The way one deals with an American sales force, and the way one deals with a Japanese shareholder, and an R & D organization are all different and in a chameleon like way you need to change the way you deal with them (Brian)*

*It needs the ability to talk to Gordon Brown today and to talk to the shop steward at our Kendall Depot tomorrow and be equally credible in both roles. You've got to span quite a broad spectrum (John)*

*I need to be able to walk into a room, and either identify the character of the business I am talking to and adjust myself to fit that, or if it's an individual, to match my persona to the individual, perhaps to relax and have a chat when I meet a customer who has dressed in jeans and a T-shirt (Judith)*

*My theme is individualization. I treat everybody differently. I treat them fairly, but I discriminate not on race, colour, or gender, but I discriminate on capability and I treat my best people better than my worst people (Pat)*

*It's not a question so much of flexing your style as flexing the way in which you communicate that style to different audiences. Consistency is really important and therefore you need to have a particular style, it just needs to be a style that can be tailored to different sets of constituents (Anthony)*

*It is understanding your audience; understanding what issues are on their mind, what are the motivators for them, and then tailoring the essence of one's message in a way that they are going to respond to best (Rupert)*

*I think maybe I don't change my own personal style enough (Thomas)*

Figure 4.3 shows an overview of responses on the challenges of mobilizing people and the related skills. These findings are entirely consistent with, and serve to reinforce, the dimension of behavioural complexity discussed in Phase I.

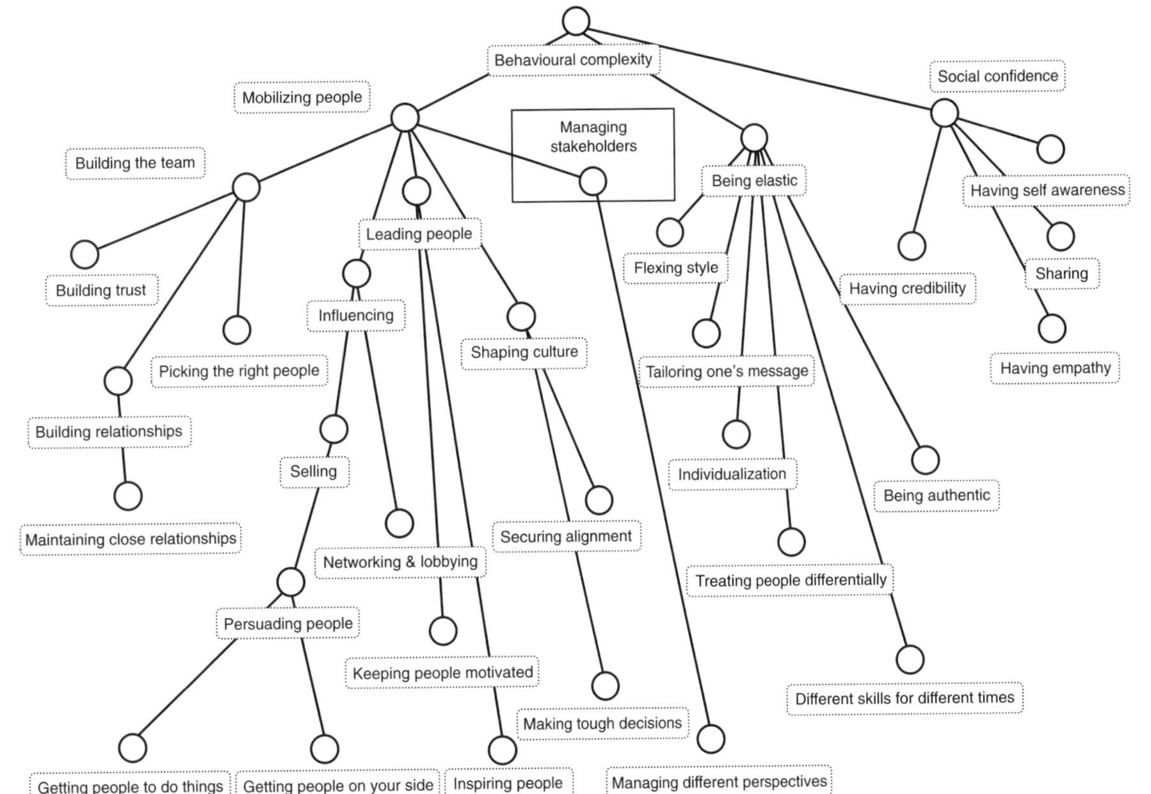


*Figure 4.3* Behavioural Complexity

## Strategic paradoxes and judgement

In response to questions about the major challenges they faced, 18 of the 25 interviewees indicated that balancing conflicting objectives was a key feature of their roles. These conflicts appeared to be essentially temporal in nature:

> *Trying to balance short and long-term: very often my organization is working on the plans for quarries which won't open for 15 years, and you can go through a 10 year planning process. So you're having to think about the replacement of strategic reserves, which is the lifeblood of the organization, versus the short-term demands of our customers. Our biggest customer is the government, it buys 48% of our products, either directly or indirectly, and political agendas can be quite short term (James)*

> *We need a convincing enough short-term plan, linked to a very exciting vision of what the group can become and we need to get them to buy-in to the changes in the strategy and the structure of the group to be able to deliver the long-term stuff at the same time as doing the sticking plaster exercise. That's an awful paradox (Thomas)*

> *I call it balancing today's results with tomorrow's expectations. There are a lot of decisions that, if today's results don't matter and only tomorrow's, I would make a lot of fast decisions today. But I also know that if I don't deliver today's results I don't get to deliver tomorrow's expectations. And I'm constantly balancing those (Pat)*

> *The biggest challenge I have is managing a balance between double-digit sales growth and a 2% margin enhancement every year. One doesn't normally come with the other– normally one comes at the expense of the other. Implementing that, and getting this balance between sales leverage and profit growth is probably the most difficult dynamic. We are trying to live with a paradox (Steve)*

> *In no order of importance, from a financial goal standpoint achieving improved growth, improved profitability, improved return on investment, improved cash generation are not mutually compatible (Anthony)*

> *We are seen by our investors as an income stock – they buy us for the dividend, so how do we protect that dividend in the regulated environment and how do we grow the business so we can produce additional returns. It can be a paradox (John)*

*If you say you have a business that you say you have to protect and sustain but you are also going to pursue opportunistic growth and development, it's a complicated place to be. What you do to protect and sustain a business is very radically different from what you would do in a business if you were going to look for new business and new places to grow and develop (Ronnie)*

On other occasions, interviewees expressed the need to inhabit different worlds simultaneously. Examples included the world of business and the world of art, of public service and commerce, or operations and strategy:

*I think that you cannot do strategy unless you're involved in operations, or strategy becomes better if you're also involved in operations, you need to link those together (Jan)*

*It's that schizophrenia that allows us to be at home in both the consumer and PR arena of our industry and at the same time at home in the financial arena of our industry. It is in my view absolutely fundamental to live in both worlds separately and fluently (Anthony)*

*At the end of the day the public purpose will always override the commercial considerations of its commercial subsidiaries. I often describe what I do as like running a brothel inside a church, and knowing that one has to run an effective brothel, but have a lot of sensibility to the nuns and the congregation on the other side of the wall (Rupert)*

*We are a charity, we are a company limited by guarantee, we have to operate as a commercial business.... I think the crucial thing for a manager is to understand the minutiae but also be able to take a long-term view (Sue)*

One interesting opinion was that these conflicting pressures were in fact beneficial:

*I don't think these contradictions are disturbing. I think they are rather value added. You have to be able to think both short and long-term (Jan)*

Nine interviewees attributed their ability to live with these conflicting pressures to judgement.

*Everything is judgement calls. There are very few black and white issues (David)*

*It boils down to making those judgement calls as quickly as possible (Wilf)*

*There are lots of judgement calls around that – wanting to encourage people to come up with ideas, but sometimes the idea will be impractical or just something we don't want to do, so the judgement call is about when to say yes and when to say no, but also how to say yes and how to say no (Judith)*

*I think judgement is one of my basic responsibilities, either alone or together with my team. You must have a certain way of judging. Judgement for me is proactive deciding (Udo)*

*We're making judgements every day. This is the plan, then an order comes in that is not part of the plan. Do you say, we ignore it, do we investigate it, or do we change the plan because we need to go for this (Nick)*

*You're left applying judgement as to where you're going to put your resources to pursue development growth and opportunities. How hard do you batten the hatches down on the rest of the business, because if you cut off all the fat from the business you can pursue the lowest cost position. But you won't have any capabilities left over when you do turn over some new opportunities. It's a fine balancing act (Ronnie)*

*It boils down to judgement calls in the end, and pragmatism. It would be great to always take the long-term view, but you see examples of the long-term view that never actually turn into profit and the shareholders won't give you that long (Rodney)*

Comments on the antecedents of judgement were offered by only seven interviewees, and included confidence in ambiguity, comfort with uncertainty, and courage:

*If you were to ask what's the cornerstone, to me it's to have confidence in ambiguity (Pat)*

*I also have a kind of paranoia, a healthy paranoia where I think am I missing something? Am I seeing things right? It's a continuous process*

> *and it can unsettle you, because I see it as a moving target and you have to be able to move with it, to keep it in your scope. It can be uncomfortable, and you must be able to work with uncertainty. The uncertainty also makes you sharp, because you have to keep looking (Reinoud)*

> *There are times when you just say, look we've got enough information on this, we've got enough conviction, how much more do we really need? I've seen people where they want more data because they didn't have the confidence to make the decision. And often that's a personal thing, a psychological thing, do you with your background have that confidence to pull the trigger? (Robert)*

> *I always encourage people to say things… because we might be able to distil something from it. So I widen the scope and collect more diverse ideas. If you judge very early on in the process you already go to a side, and in my view that's very dangerous. You have to be as open minded in the process as possible. And that helps the judgement call (Reinoud)*

Figure 4.4 overleaf shows an overview of interviewees' comments on different aspects of judgement.

The findings on the need to straddle conflicting goals and processes support a key element of the strategic paradoxes dimension developed in Phase I, with judgement now coming into sharp relief.

## Summary of findings on dimensions of capability

The Phase II interviews serve to enrich our understanding of the four dimensions of individual strategic capability previously presented in the conceptual framework in Phase I, viz:

- Engagement with strategic paradoxes
- Cognitive and behavioural complexity
- Ability to conduct a strategic conversation
- Understanding and challenging context

All four dimensions emerged clearly in the interviews. In particular,this study has helped to move from broad constructs to a sharper and more specific view of each dimension, and to populate the dimensions with notes from the field in the language used by strategic leaders.

A number of observations that emerged through the interviews have enabled the dimensions of strategic capability to be developed into specific abilities, without changing the areas that they cover. Taken together,

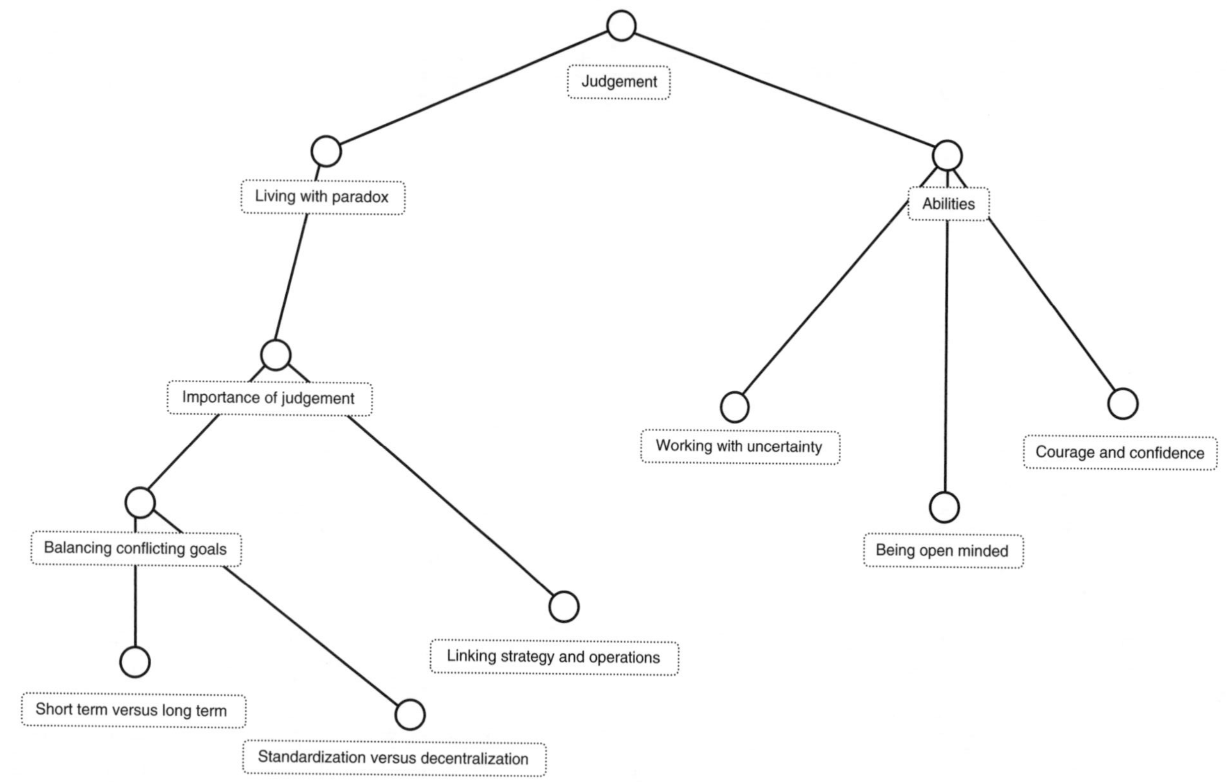


*Figure 4.4* Judgement

these yield an empirically adjusted framework of the dimensions of strategic leader capability, as described below:

Engagement with strategic paradoxes can be reframed as the exercise of Judgement, which has the act of balancing conflicting goals – most often, but not always, related to multiple time horizons – at its core. This goal or outcome focus was more evident in the interviews than in the literature.

Cognitive and behavioural complexity may now be expressed as "the ability to mobilise people based on a complex repertoire of behaviours", or behavioural complexity.

The ability to conduct a strategic conversation, hitherto largely metaphorical, has now come into sharper relief as being able to make strategy with both deliberate and emergent processes, and of synthesizing strategy in both analytical and non-analytical ways. In practice, the interviews also highlighted a lack of distinction between strategy formulation and implementation, and a mix of formality and informality in the strategic process.

The importance of both understanding and challenging the context has been supported, and may be reframed as contextual mastery, underpinned by "the ability to challenge context as well as to work within it", allowing for the context to be both accepted and challenged, rather than resolved.

During the study, not all the dimensions were articulated by interviewees in equal measure. This may be a result of the methodology deployed. Had a structured questionnaire been used, with clear definitions of each term, accompanied by ranking or measurement scales, then every interviewee would have had a common understanding and a common data collection experience would have resulted. As stated earlier, the interviews were not rigid in their structure, but conducted fluidly around the interview schedule. As such, some interviewees may have been constrained by their ability to conceptualize and/or articulate responses to certain questions. Hence the fact that a particular dimension of capability was not articulated in a particular interview does not necessarily mean that it is non-existent or not salient to that interviewee, but merely that it was not expressed in terms that the author recognized to code in line with this dimension. This complicates any attempt to evaluate the relative significance or strength of one dimension in relation to another, and this is a limitation of the chosen research methodology. Recognizing that a simple count of interviewees who did articulate a particular dimension is a surrogate and crude measure for what might otherwise be an ideal, it has nevertheless been adopted here as the best alternative available.

On this basis, this author suggests that the pattern in the dimensions of capability, ranked on the basis of the relative frequency with which they were observed, is:

1. *Behavioural complexity*, or the ability to mobilize people based on a complex repertoire of behaviours
2. *Contextual mastery*, or the ability to challenge context as well as to work within it
3. *Judgement*, or the ability to balance conflicting goals
4. *Strategic conversation*, or the ability to synthesize strategy using analytical and non-analytical approaches in deliberate and emergent processes

## Some voices: The development of strategic leader capability

We now turn our attention to the experiences and processes by which the interviewees acquired or developed the capability needed in their roles.

Although there was an aspiration early in the research design to develop causal maps and linkages between different development experiences and specific capabilities, it became apparent at the pilot interview stage that this was unrealistic. With a very few minor exceptions, the development processes of interviewees were unplanned, and "osmotic" i.e. characterized by unconscious absorption or assimilation. In addition, a wide variety of development experiences were reported. These factors rendered a deconstruction of development experiences and resulting capabilities impractical within the time available for each interview.

In broad terms, both formal learning and informal learning experiences were indicated by interviewees. Figure 4.5 displays an overview of formal and informal learning experiences as they emerged in the interviews.

Formal learning may be viewed as skills and knowledge acquired in a planned and purposeful manner. Formal learning is structured and may be institutionally sponsored. Formal learning on the job includes short-term work assignments designed with a development objective, executive coaching and feedback, and management and leadership development interventions. Formal learning off the job includes pre-work schooling and professional education.

Informal learning is predominantly non-institutional, often unintentional or a by-product of a different activity, frequently unconscious,

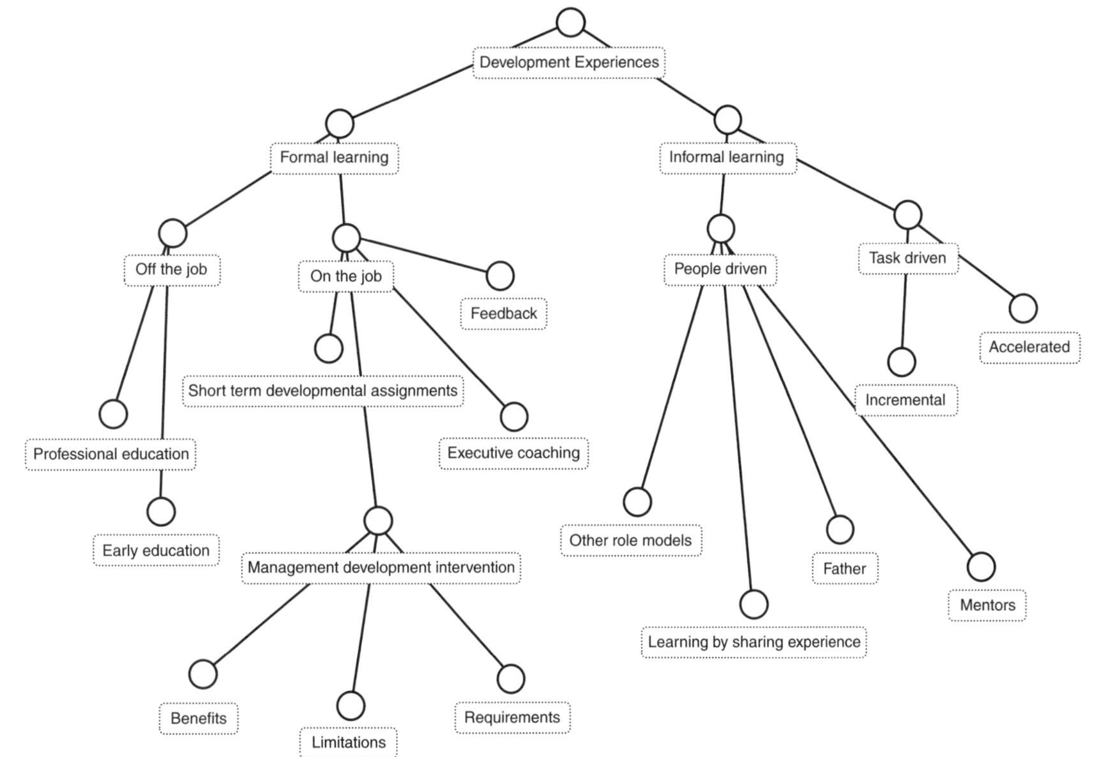


*Figure 4.5* Development Experiences

haphazard, and influenced by chance. Informal learning may be "people-driven" i.e. triggered off by encounters or relationships with other people, or "task-driven" i.e. induced by the task(s) at hand. At a subsidiary level, people-driven informal learning includes role models, parental influences, mentors, and learning by sharing experiences. Task-driven informal learning may in turn be "incremental" i.e. a slow accumulation of work related experiences over a long period of time, or "accelerated" i.e. an intense and challenging experience in a relatively short period of time.

On an overall basis, the interviews revealed a strong pattern of multiple development experiences.

When asked about their formative development experiences, interviewees tended to first narrate their informal learning experiences, and then supplement their narrative with instances of formal learning. It may be ventured that this could be suggestive of impact and value – or at the very least, memorability – and therefore it is in this order that interviewee experiences have been examined.

## Informal learning

All 25 interviewees reported task-driven informal learning, and 23 interviewees reported people-driven informal learning.

Scrutiny of the accounts of task based learning revealed that these could be further classified into incremental and accelerated.

Figure 4.6 displays an overview of the responses related to informal learning.

Informal learning that was task based was largely acquired by having undertaken a range of assignments over an extended period of time, primarily in the same industry or company.

Informal learning processes that were task based but of an accelerated nature were made up of stretch assignments and hardship situations such as being out of the comfort zone or in crisis mode.

People-driven informal learning was based on learning from mentors and role models, as well as parental influences.

Figure 4.7 shows the top three informal learning experiences viz. task-driven incremental learning, people-driven learning, and task-driven accelerated learning, and the ensuing narrative focuses on these, in order of impact.

### *Task-driven incremental learning*

A slow but steady accumulation and distillation of on the job experiences was universally acknowledged.

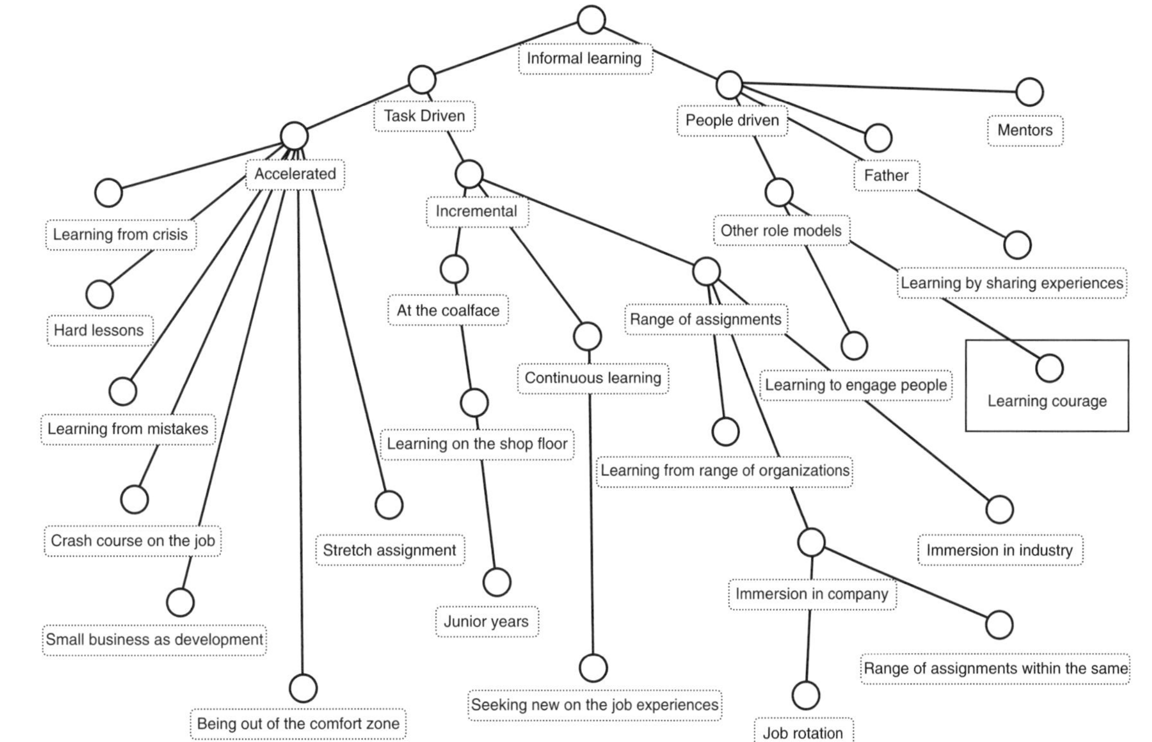


*Figure 4.6* Informal Learning

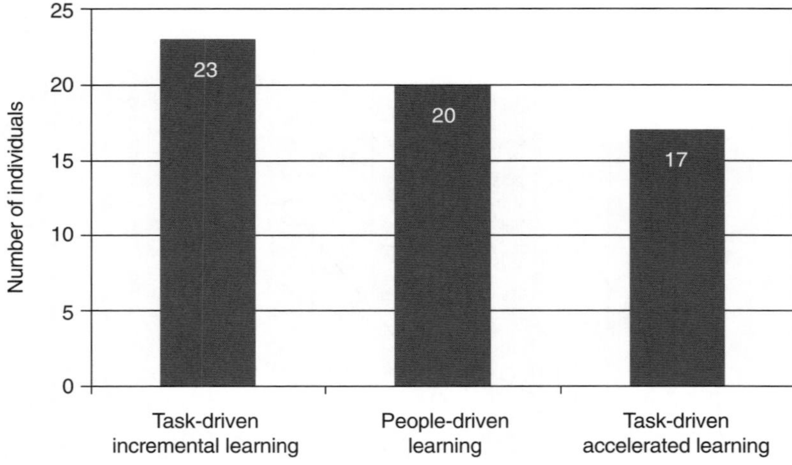


*Figure 4.7* Dominant Informal Learning Experiences

A typical trajectory, as described by one of the interviewees, was:

> *My career started at Bristol Airport, about 20 years ago, as a check-in person for Dan Air. I went on to ticketing and then on to the ramp to loading. I then got the opportunity to join a new regional airline in Bristol, as an Operations Assistant, from my early 20s. For the first ten years I hopped between airlines, I moved around and up the ladder. Then I was made redundant and fell into a business aviation job at Heathrow, as an Operations Controller, running Shell International's group fleet of business jets. That got me in to business aviation. I was there for 10 years and ended up as Operations Manager. We moved the business to Holland, and I moved with it for a couple of years, but then I decided to come back to the UK and joined Virgin Express as General Manager, UK. Spent a couple of years there at Heathrow, picking up some general management experience... I was then called by my current employer and offered this job (Judith)*

Similar observations were made by other interviewees:

> *I was working for a whole range of companies at a relatively senior level and at a young age. I consciously went through that career path because I didn't precisely know what I wanted to do but I wanted to see as much as I could see in terms of what businesses did, how they ran themselves, how they strategized. I spent 10–12 years doing that, in effect as a con-*

*sultant, their advertising adviser, being able to distil as much as I could and work with CEOs, senior board directors, picking up the tools of the trade (Robert)*

*I was really lucky joining Beechams when I did because over those seven years I got all the training in the world and when I left Beecham I was really quite rounded. At the time I didn't recognize it was doing anything for me, but when I look back I realize it was actually giving me a depth of understanding about why things happen the way they do (Brian)*

*I was moved around, I didn't have a job for longer than 11 months, I worked in two different countries. I think that was both chaos and development, or managed chaos. You had to move. But the mobility helped me personally. I learnt a lot about how people do business in different countries. For me the international and cultural exposure working for a genuine multi-national was a huge experience (Wilf)*

*I never had extensive development in terms of people development or strategic management. I've picked it up as I've gone along, I've learnt from others and I've learnt from my mistakes. I try to get myself out of the run of the business, whether it's just going on a conference for a couple of days to get exposure to new markets, new ideas, new technologies. I read extensively and I'm normally reading something to do with management or the business or the wider world. It is a continuous learning process, and I'll never get to the end of it (John)*

*I don't think in the first 20 years of my career that I received any component of training. It has always been through actual work experience that I have developed. It's always been informal, on the job (Robert)*

*I've seen every single role as a training role and that's why I've moved from industry to industry to build up my competencies in a whole range of different industries and when I'm about 65 I believe I might be employable (Rupert)*

While the dominance of incremental task-driven learning was inevitable given the track record and position of the interviewees, the contribution of mentors and role models, and accelerated learning on the job stood out as worthy of further scrutiny.

*People-driven informal learning*

By far the most significant informal learning experiences cited by interviewees came about as a result of mentors and other role models.

Six interviewees cited the influence of their father. For example:

> *I grew up in a family which had a family business. My father was the CEO of a company making leather goods and I was with him at work, and I spent every weekend in the factory speaking to the workers and had a good time. I learnt from him the way of relating to everyone in the company. I honestly think this is a great advantage, compared to many other people (Jan)*

> *I had learnt from my Dad about the maturity and discipline needed to focus on what I wanted to achieve (Robert)*

In all other cases, as well as for most of these six, the impact of mentors and other role models was very prominent. In all, 20 of the 25 interviewees talked at length about their mentors.

The value of mentors appeared to derive, among other factors, from the opportunity to learn by shadowing them, to learn new skills and perspectives, and to be able to use them as a sounding board. Mentors were also influential in setting standards for personal performance.

The effusive manner in which interviewees gave credit to their mentors for their development was particularly noteworthy:

> *I was very lucky during my time at BOC to have a number of mentor relationships. People who did have good leadership skills, were good leaders and who were good strategic thinkers. So I had some good role models without whom it would have been almost impossible to develop in the way I did (Ronnie)*

> *Everything that's stayed with me has been a product of people I've worked with or for. There are some shining examples. There are many people who have helped me to form my style of management. These were mentors who took a real interest in me (David)*

> *My job was to sit down with the CEO and ensure that the strategy made financial sense and we had the resources in the right place to deliver it and we knew when we were on track and off track... the mentality was that if he was out of the office I should have enough of a grounding to run the business. Great mentor, he's now CEO at BT (Chris)*

*I had a Group President in the US called Cy Johnson. He taught me more about organizational development than anyone. He's incredibly bright, he was able to bring a new perspective that I had not thought of, he was great thinker, if I needed 50 words to say something he could bring it together in three. He continues to help me. My first boss in Europe taught me more about the P&L and the numbers. This guy could look at a P&L and know exactly everything. I was nine years with him and learned a lot, watching, listening (Pat)*

*The 56-year-old on the board is like a mentor to me. He is my boss and also my mentor. The relationship includes very broad issues, about how you do things and how you implement things. He leaves the technical things up to me saying that's what I pay you for, that's your job (Reinoud)*

*The mentoring came initially from within NFC, it was my boss, I had a great deal of respect for him and the way he handled things. He was a superb communicator, and at that time I probably wanted to get to places fast and obstacles needed to be taken out of the way. He helped me enormously in saying how you take these obstacles out in a constructive fashion, because you'll actually get to your end goal much quicker than you think (James)*

*The chair of our board is fantastic, she has been a real mentor to me, and she's taught me an awful lot and I think I'm good at this job because of me, but also because of her. She has made such a difference to my ability to lead this company (Sue)*

*I worked for Mark for many years and he was an extraordinary motivator. That gave me one on one training in every form of leadership and motivational skills (Rupert)*

*He was a complete and utter bastard and I hated him. He was extremely demanding but very clear about what he wanted and expected, high standards, unyielding in dealing with failure and that set a pattern for me. He was a huge influence and we developed a good relationship. He was a good coach and he was going through a process of trying to toughen me up and was doing it his way (Jed)*

*I got from these mentors courage, confidence, recognition of what I was achieving when I didn't feel I was achieving anything. They'd make me go through what I'd done that day, to review what I'd done, they helped me to identify decisions I needed to take, to go through the process of decision-making in a senior role. I was suddenly responsible for budgets, whereas before I'd only had my little bit. So, confidence and a resource that I could tap into, so I could expose my complete fear and ignorance (Heather)*

*I think of this Canadian person as a mentor, also a friend, we do business together now outside the bank, I have a tremendous respect for him. I've learnt where you need to take risks, where you're dealing with your own money as opposed to shareholders' money. I think one of the great lessons is that you have to know your limitations in business, when to take risks, when to back your convictions, when to know if the chips are stacked in your favour (Robert)*

*I was lucky I worked with and for some good people. When you're green and you go into business and you actually believe what people are saying to you, you take them at face value. But you learn fairly rapidly to understand all the undercurrents that are going on in organizations, and what people actually mean and how you do influence people (Wilf)*

Not all mentors were positive role models – instances of "how not to do it" were cited as well.

*I was never formally mentored. I suppose I had some role models, people I did worked with from the earliest times. I also had a lot of role models about how not to do it (John)*

*I went to work for a quite extraordinary business leader, Stanley Kalms, and so I spent a lot of my early years probably picking up the wrong traits because he has a particularly bruising leadership style and I found that utterly fascinating (Rupert)*

*Task-driven accelerated learning*

Seventeen interviewees reported having undergone an accelerated learning experience on the job. The most common form was being stretched by being given a challenging assignment for which the interviewee did not feel well equipped at that time, for example, for reasons of youth as in the cases below:

*It was 20 years in Harvard compressed into three years. I had been in Europe for three years, I was 28 years old, and my boss said I want you to go run the UK. I said I don't know anything about P&L, I can't do that.*

*He said your FD will help you with that, what they're looking for is a leader (Pat)*

*I became a business leader quite young, I was 28. The organization was a good breeding ground for having to stand on your feet and having to convince 50 people that they need to do something, when politically they don't want to do it... what I learnt in having to change that organization, a monolithic, nationalized set up, with lots of trade union activity, was how you switch people on to the change. It was a hard road. That teaches you quickly that you've got to have your troops behind you (James)*

*What really accelerated my development was my working life, and the pure fact that I got the chance to do this job at a young age. Getting this business to run was in itself a formative experience. It's also learning by doing (Reinoud)*

However, stretch assignments were observed at later career stages as well:

*Being acting Chief Executive was a huge transition. That was a huge learning curve to me, both personally and how to deal with other people and how they perceived me (Heather)*

*I then became CEO of one of the smallest privatized regional electricity distribution companies. We were not given any hope of survival. That made me really determined that we were going to make it. It was a fascinating exercise in human relationships and organizational dynamics. I said to people we have two choices: we either get it right, quickly, or we go out of business. That had never been heard of before because you couldn't go out of business if you were owned by the government. That fear of failure completely transformed the business. In the next two years we became the best for customer service, and the most profitable. I learnt a lot going through that, taking people through the transformation, and the challenge of taking the organization through that transformation on to something else. All those experiences I think I have drawn on here in my current role (John)*

*The other challenge which formed me very strongly was the time in Germany when the wall broke down and I had the honour, mission, task, to go to East Germany and implement the new strategy. Learning by doing. To think, to analyse the situation, talk to people, and go forward. This was a big stretch because I had to completely throw away my Western set up. This was a completely different country, it had different rules and you had to forget what West Germany was. Suddenly you were dealing with socialism which had a completely different set up. And you had no connections. This was a very interesting learning experience. You certainly do learn if you're thrown in at the deep end (Udo)*

Some interviewees cited a different kind of stretch as an accelerated development vehicle – the opportunity to manage a relatively small business in its entirety:

*I had been picked out but I was not quite ready for the next move. When I moved to this role I became the head of a division and it did have the effect of allowing me to take a discrete business, which was relatively stable, to understand the dynamics of its P&L, balance sheet, cash flow statement in a way that was meaningful, where the various elements were joined up.... so it was a very good crash course, on the job about how to take the essence of a business and work it (Anthony)*

*There is something developmental about a small business, you can take on different roles, you can help people out, lots of opportunities to stray over into other people's areas, they tend to be more casual and not as structured as a larger business needs to be. The procedural element of the job tends to be a lot more relaxed. That helps if you're the sort of person who likes to wander about, learning what other people do, meddling a little in other people's part of the business. You get a flavour of the whole business (Judith)*

*I moved through a number of different roles designed to be steep learning curves and low impact in terms of value added to the business (Ronnie)*

Inevitably, when forced outside their comfort zone by stretch assignments, the interviewees recalled making mistakes – but that appeared to have enriched the learning and development process:

*I made quite a lot of mistakes. The most formative learning is making mistakes. The learning is huge, everybody says it, and it is a truism. You really feel the pain for a long time after, how I handled that difficult situation or the mistake I made when handling that, that particular event that had that effect on the business that basically was down to me, you don't forget (Thomas)*

> *Looking back on it I learnt more by my mistakes, in those first two years when I first went to the States (Nick)*

> *Most of your learning comes from things that you failed to do rather than things you achieved (Tom)*

Interestingly, those who had experienced stretch assignments were strong advocates of similar experiences for others.

> *I think that people gain a lot by being given responsibility quite early in life, as long as they are nurtured and not dumped totally. I can see the ones who are going to succeed; they are usually the ones who have had a bloody tough job at some early stage in their career. They assume nothing (James)*

> *To me the best developmental methodology is stretch positions. If I want to develop somebody, give them a big new job. That's how I was developed the best. Moving to Europe at 24, the European company had no marketing manager. Go to Europe, and live in Germany on your own. Not just the business skills, the social skills, the confidence skills; all these you learn in stretch positions (Pat)*

In conclusion, on the basis of this sample of executives, we may infer that in addition to on the job learning gained over an extended period of time, mentors and role models, followed by stretch assignments play the most significant roles in the development of strategic leaders.

### Formal learning

In the "on the job" category, 20 interviewees had experienced a formal management development intervention. Executive coaching, with 12 respondents, was also widespread. One instance of the use of a short-term developmental assignment was noted. "Off the job", 12 interviewees cited professional education as developmental, while five cited early education (e.g. schooling) as influential.

#### *Management development interventions*

Most interviewees had experienced management development interventions; usually business school-based customized programmes (for a particular organization) or open (publicly available) programmes. However, these experiences were either not front of mind, or were mentioned incidentally. It may be speculated that the benefits of formal management education are higher for those who are at more junior levels. In any event, given this author's specific professional interests in this regard, follow-up questions were asked.

Figure 4.8 overleaf displays the principal benefits of management development interventions, which were felt to be networking, and reflective time and space. Some interviewees also cited "new insights" as a benefit.

Networking was valued mainly as an opportunity to benchmark against peers from other organizations, and to learn from them and their businesses:

> *It gave me a lot of confidence that the peer group in the programme were not high flying, super managers. We were all of similar capabilities (Steve)*

> *I really enjoy going to business schools. Meeting other similarly placed people is really interesting and the only training or outside development I've done has been of that sort, the main benefit has been to meet other people (Anthony)*

> *The big advantage wasn't necessarily what I was taught there, because I don't think I was going in there with my radar on full, it was about meeting the other people, that was as much a learning experience as the pure content (Jonathan)*

> *I felt the need to break out for a week or two and see how other people were thinking, work with people at a similar level (Wilf)*

> *I went to Stanford, to the Senior Management Development Programme, summer 2002, a six week programme. It renewed my faith in my company. I realized that compared to the others we were no worse, but that we were significantly better. Lots of the things that other companies were really struggling with and people were talking about, we were streets ahead on. Our normal practice was their best practice, in terms of people and engagement and values (Tom)*

> *I think I was surrounded by some pretty good people at Harvard. There were 260 classmates, from around the world. I think the daily interaction was at a very high level (Pat)*

> *For me it's also spending time talking to and working with people from different backgrounds, industries; the financial services sector is notorious*

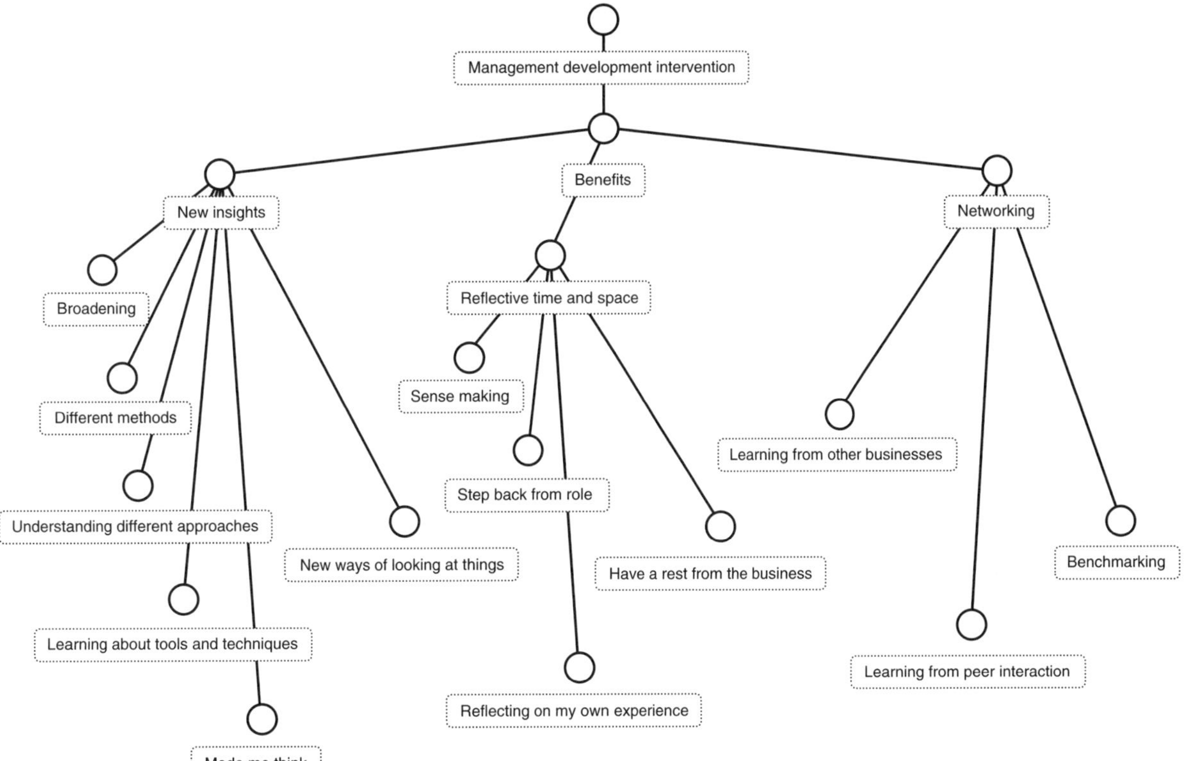


*Figure 4.8* Management Development Benefits

> *for tunnel vision and blinkered, it's the most overrated, overpaid, saturated sector, and I make my living in it, but I genuinely feel that way. Spending time with people from the public services and looking at their perspectives, not quite a humbling experience, but it's very enlightening (Rupert)*

The principal benefit of reflective time and space offered by a management development intervention appeared to be "sense-making" for the participant, described as acquiring a formal structure for previously unstructured learning on the job, and validating and re-framing prior knowledge and capabilities:

> *I think the formal classroom setting has a role in allowing us to take a step back and say hold on, have I got the priorities, have I looked at the fundamentals. That's a skill set where business schools can add value. It's the reflective time and space (Chris)*

> *I did have a chance last year to go back to Harvard for 10 weeks on their Advanced Management Programme. I learned a lot there. I was able to listen to what they were saying, reflect on my experience and think of what I'm doing that's wrong (Pat)*

> *Your own experience in life is a number of events which are often not correlated, you can often not deduce a theme – they are things that happen. What you then do is you put two fences around it and you say how can I structure it, how can I use it, how can I shape it in my everyday business (Reinoud)*

> *They give you time to reflect, they sometimes give you some tools to bring along, but I think it's the interaction, having the time to reflect, to pick out a few items that you would deal with differently and then you do that and you probably learn from that (Jan)*

> *The external training helps to put either certain skills or certain contexts of what you've doing into place, what you've seen and what you've done. The structure about what you've been doing and how you can do it even better (Brian)*

> *I came here also to hopefully gain confidence in what I am doing; I haven't got through six years as the organization's CEO without doing something right. But I don't know how to measure it or how to recognize it in myself (Heather)*

*Most of the formal training I've done has mainly confirmed or validated things that I have learnt on the job, with the exception of one or two little nuggets that you pick up on training courses that you hadn't thought of, or just gives you a different view because you're mixing with people from other businesses as well. On the whole, formal training has validated my own ideas (Judith)*

*It gives you a "standing outside work" ability to look in. It's useful; it reframes things (Sue)*

By contrast with networking and reflective time and space, a much smaller number of interviewees appeared to gain new insights from management development programmes. The value of new tools and techniques, new ways of looking at situations, exploring different approaches to problems, and broadening were all mentioned.

*From that course I got loads of phrases, loads of strategy models that we had been doing here in a much more haphazard way. It gives you the tools. One of the main benefits from the course is that it gives you the tools. You don't use them all but you might use 10% of them and that's a huge benefit (Judith)*

*For the last eight or nine years all I've seen is telecoms, but I'd also like to get the experience from other industries back into telecoms... a programme can give me some of the broader perspectives (Chris)*

Not all interviewees had positive perceptions of management development experiences. Some of the limitations of management development programmes that interviewees had experienced were a "one size fits all" approach by the provider, an overly broad scope of content resulting in superficial learning, elegant ideas that proved to be unexecutable in reality, an excessive focus on theoretical models, and an inappropriate peer group which undermined the potential learning. Indifference by the boss, and therefore an unsatisfactory transition back to the workplace was also cited.

Given these limitations, not surprisingly there was a plea for a greater focus on application, increased contextual relevance, and assistance with re-introduction to work. Since these conversations involved only a minority of interviewees, further discussion of this theme is not offered here.

*Executive coaching*

Although coaching is not always a formal learning process, 11 interviewees reported actual or planned use of a formal process of executive coaching and feedback. Those who had undergone coaching talked of their experiences in very positive terms. The benefits of coaching appeared to be gaining feedback, enforced introspection and reflection, being challenged, testing ideas, and enhancing self-confidence:

> *I'm trying to develop some executive coaching for myself now. I need this for me to understand how to do business at the very top of the organization. I need to understand the ways that a board works, the ways that a non-executive team works, what is expected of someone at that level, some of the politics as well as the external stakeholder pressures. Someone to say to me have you thought about doing this or that, what about this slight change of style. Someone to pose questions, questions I'm probably asking myself already. To bounce ideas off, and talk freely without any kind of pressure (Steve)*

> *I believe I need a one-to-one series of sessions with someone who will give me the confidence, who will give me the way of doing it (David)*

> *Executive coaching is important because it helps a person to prioritize in ways that are different from ways they prioritize in the workplace. There is a need to nourish the less grind orientated operational elements of my working life; it's the interface between my life and my working life (Anthony)*

> *What I need from the coaching is some help in making that fundamental shift towards being more effective in the allocation of my own effort and resource, working out ways of dealing with organizational complexity, day to day challenges and the need to be showing leadership and direction. What I've had from coaching before is challenging questions. I need a coach that I trust enough to bully me a bit and it'll be a bit hard to find that (Ronnie)*

> *I have a coach outside the company who I see every half year to talk about developments. I get a fresh mind from this and somebody who's able to challenge the way I am thinking, which is very important. But also someone who's able to put a mirror in front of me and say well you did this and that and it had this effect (Reinoud)*

*Formal education*

When recounting their development histories, interviewees frequently referred to their education, often as no more than biographical information. Some, however, did dwell on their formal education as formative. Interestingly, several comments were made with regard to early schooling as a driver of self-esteem, discipline, and inter-personal skills:

> *One of my life shaping experiences was boarding school, it teaches you to be extremely focused on the things you are doing and on yourself, it's not always the world people think of looking on from the outside. It can be quite unsettling, and you grow up quickly (Reinoud)*

> *I come from an educational background that's put a lot of emphasis on leadership skills. From having been to certain components of the public school system, I just happened to end up in a component that put a huge amount of emphasis at an early age on understanding what leadership and management was about. I went to a school that was run by the boys, you ran yourselves, and you appointed your leaders, your leadership group, and you relied on your peer group to lead the organization. That's fundamental if one goes through that experience when one is in one's teens. My training was my schooling (Rupert)*

Others focused on their adult educational experiences, and their role in developing analytical abilities:

> *I trained as an accountant, learned to be methodical, organized, to analyse, and to draw conclusions from the information. You could say that the Germans or the Japanese have the best engineers, but we've got the best accountants in the world if that's not being too arrogant. It's good business training (Rodney)*

> *I am by nature an analytical person, I have a scientific background and I did an engineering degree. I bring to everything that analytical approach. I went and did the engineering degree because I am an analytical individual. The choice of degree was more about my innate preference and ability (Jed)*

Overall, the formal educational patterns were weak, and did not appear to be as significant as the patterns in informal learning.

## Summary of findings on development of capability

At first glance, the development of strategic leaders interviewed seems to be characterized by a multiplicity of experiences.

However, closer scrutiny has suggested a remarkable pattern in the significance of informal learning processes in general, and mentors and other role models as well as accelerated learning experiences on the job in particular.

Evidence also suggests that formal learning and development interventions do have benefits, principally as a vehicle for reflection, structuring previously unstructured learning, being challenged, testing ideas, gaining feedback and validation, networking, and enhancing self-confidence.

These findings have implications for leader development practice, and these were explored further in Phase III.

# 5
# Developing Strategic Leaders: An Integrated View

## Introduction to Phase III

Phase I in this study examined the nature of individual strategic leader capability, and through an extensive and multi-disciplinary literature review, identified four key dimensions described as Engagement with Strategic Paradoxes, Cognitive and Behavioural Complexity, Ability to Conduct a Strategic Conversation, and Understanding and Challenging Context.

Phase II investigated patterns in the dimensions and development of strategic leader capability through in-depth interviews with 25 leaders in organizations. This empirical phase resulted in a re-framing of this capability as a composite of Judgement, Strategic Conversation, Contextual Mastery, and Behavioural Complexity. The related abilities which were observed most frequently in practice were:

1. The ability to mobilize people based on a complex repertoire of behaviours (Behavioural Complexity)
2. The ability to challenge context as well as to work within it (Contextual Mastery)
3. The ability to balance conflicting goals (Judgement)
4. The ability to synthesize strategy using analytical and non-analytical approaches in both deliberate and emergent ways (Strategic Conversation)

Phase II also highlighted the unplanned and informal nature of the formative development experiences of the strategic leaders who participated in the study. In particular, a remarkable pattern involving mentors and other role models as well as "accelerated learning experiences" on the job was observed. The benefits of formal interventions as opportunities to network and reflect were also noted.

Phase III continued the focus on the development of strategic leaders, with the following objectives:

1. to relate the empirical findings of Phase II to existing theory, and thereby improve understanding of the phenomena observed
2. to inform the design and delivery of two formal leader development interventions so as to investigate the possibility and consequences of simulating the influential development processes identified in Phase II, and
3. to develop a framework for leader development which could serve as a basis for further theory-building.

A key objective in Phase III was to develop a framework that would integrate the principal development processes identified in Phase II: mentors and other developmental relationships (such as role models and networks); "accelerated learning" experiences on the job (or "stretch assignments"); and reflective time and space. Phase III therefore commenced with an engagement with existing theory and knowledge in these domains. The key ideas that have emerged are presented here in a narrative structured on the following lines:

*Exploring informal learning* explores the power, and some of the limitations of informal learning.

This is followed by an examination of the significance, types, benefits, and limitations of *Mentors and developmental relationships*.

*Accelerated learning and mastery experiences* reviews the significance, types, benefits, and limitations of such experiences.

*Critical reflection* considers its role in leader development.

*Integrating the development processes* pulls the various strands of the discussion on development processes together.

## Exploring informal learning

Opportunities for learning are a natural feature of the manager's job. The evidence from Phase II suggests that most managers learn most of what they do learn from the work they undertake, and that experience often results in intense learning.

According to Cseh et al (1999), everyday life offers natural opportunities for learning, in which the person controls his or her own learning. Such informal learning is predominantly experiential, and often unintentional or a by-product of a different activity. Informal learning is unplanned, tacit, non-linear and serendipitous, and occurs while individuals are preoccupied with other tasks. Marsick and Volpe (1999) suggest that informal learning is not highly conscious, is often haphazard and influenced by chance, and occurs inductively through action and reflection. By contrast, formal learning may be defined as a structured, institutionally sponsored, and planned learning process, often supported by an instructor in a classroom (Merriam and Caffarella, 1991). The power of informal learning has been highlighted in numerous studies.

## Learning from experience

Davies and Easterby-Smith (1984) report that managers frequently describe their past careers in terms of slow maturity and growth through a gradual accretion of experience in each job, which in turn equips them for the next job. Studies by Akin (1987) and Kotter (1988) have shown that with the benefit of hindsight, managers see practical experience as the most influential development process in their preparation for leadership. Kotter (1988) also highlights managers' testimonies that their development as leaders was influenced to a significant degree by their early management experiences on the job. Cseh et al (1999) contend that formal learning accounts for only 20% of managerial learning. Others, such as Sorohan (1993) have estimated that nearly 90% of learning takes place through informal means.

Thomas and Cheese (2005) found that a wide array of leaders – entrepreneurs, corporate executives, social activists, and elected politicians – unanimously agreed that they had learned more about leading from real world experiences than from leadership development courses or MBA programmes. While formal programmes had helped them to gain technical competence, these had done little to help them learn the fundamental lessons of leadership.

Mumford (1992: 301) observes that most managers proclaim that they learn by experience, and that three types of incremental learning opportunities exist: "informal managerial" or accidental opportunities where the focus is on the task and there are no clear development opportunities; "integrated managerial" opportunities where the implicit intention is both task performance and development and there are clear learning objectives, and "formal management development" opportunities which are often away from normal managerial activities. Accidental opportunities are unplanned and are part of the day to day work, and are therefore unstructured in development terms; but the advantage is that they are owned by managers, and consequently the resulting learning is real and direct.

Informal learning is powerful because it is determined and directed by learners themselves; it is an active, relevant process, arising in the setting where the skills are used (Leslie et al, 1998). As a result, things are best learned by actually doing them.

For informal learning to be meaningful, the right conditions need to be in place. Davies and Easterby-Smith (1984) suggest that the factors that facilitate on the job learning are *opportunities* (the amount of change and turbulence experienced in the company's environment tends to be reflected inside the company in terms of opportunities for managers to learn from) and *culture* (whether managers are expected to adapt to changing circumstances and develop new principles for themselves, or to conform to norms of behaviour and performance that have been established beforehand). These two factors together produce higher or lower incidences of development experiences on the job.

### The limitations of informal learning

On the other hand, informal learning also presents significant challenges, as it occurs all too often in a "disorganized, inefficient, un-thoughtful and insufficient" way (Mumford, 1995: 9). The learning may remain intuitive and unrecognized, as though through some unconscious absorption process. Managers may even find it difficult and unnecessary to articulate what they have learned or how, and may fail to understand and make use of learning opportunities. Further, as Mumford (1996: 22) emphasizes, "not all managers have the same motivation to learn, they do not necessarily have a working environment which encourages learning, and they have preferred styles of learning which might not fit the kind of work environment in which they are engaged". Conlon (2004) emphasizes that a dependence on informal learning alone is risky, and that a "sink or swim" approach can result in an employee feeling frustrated, helpless, and directionless. A strong mentor or supportive colleague can mitigate such risks, and help the employee to learn.

Boud and Middleton (2003) observe that informal learning may remain unacknowledged as learning. It is typically viewed as a part of the job or a mechanism for doing the job properly, and thus rendered invisible as learning. Knowledge acquired through experience has an implicit character, and it is difficult to develop explicit knowledge through experience.

## Mentors and developmental relationships

The positive developmental impact of mentors was a key finding from Phase II. Mentoring relationships contain crucial elements of assessment, challenge, and support that are crucial for leader development.

There is considerable empirical and theoretical evidence that mentors make a significant contribution in the development of strategic leaders. Kram (1985) reports that mentoring greatly enhances the development of individuals in both early and middle career stages. Akin (1987) observes that some managers describe all of their learning experiences in terms of emulating a specific mentor. The mentor was recognized for having a well-developed, coherent, world-view; in effect, a system for "putting it all together". Kotter (1988) found that leaders in organizations reported they had learned a great deal about leadership from observing other managers, and that such observation of role models positively impacted emotional and social development. McCauley and Douglas (2004) report that in their narrative of significant learning experiences, managers often describe how they learnt from other people, with mentors being the most frequent influencers. Collins and Scott (1978) observe that "everyone who makes it has a mentor" and indeed, Clutterbuck (2004: 6) suggests that "everyone needs a mentor".

There is an intriguing relationship between mentoring and leadership. Appelbaum et al (1994: 64) explore the relationship of mentoring and leadership, and suggest that it is closely aligned. When mentors shape the values of others, act as an example, and define meanings, they are, in effect, acting as leaders, and hence mentors are perhaps just "leaders in disguise". This duality of mentoring and leadership is also considered by Westfall (1992: 11), who suggests that since "leaders prepare their people, develop them, challenge them, encourage them, and touch them with their vision and the passion for that vision"; mentors are leaders, and leaders are mentors. In other words, the act of mentoring someone is not just an act of leadership development; it is also an act of leadership. Mentors produce leaders, leaders become mentors, and so the cycle goes on.

### The impact of mentors

Zaleznik (1977) suggests that the mentoring relationship, if effective, offers a mini-course in leadership, and proposes that such one-on-one relationships are critical to the development of leaders; they are the recipients of intense tutorials on their organization by an individual with experience and knowledge.

Mentors contribute to the development of others by enacting a variety of roles. Clutterbuck (2004) describes mentoring as a multi-functional process that has four sub-roles of coach, offering job related knowledge and guidance; counsellor, providing emotional support; guardian, acting for the protégé's well being and interests; and networker or facilitator, providing access to networks and resources.

In a study of mentoring relationships as experienced by protégés, Burke (1984: 362) found that in terms of functions served by mentors, the most common role was "built self-confidence". Other highly valued functions were "provided a positive role model", served as "teacher, coach, and trainer", provided support or "went to bat for me", and "developed my talent through job assignments". Davis (2001) suggests that mentoring is an interpersonal engagement where an experienced manager acts as an advisor or coach to another, usually less experienced, manager. Mentoring is often both task based and psychosocial in nature – the protégé learns what to do and how to do it, through the skilled modelling of a more seasoned person. According to Kram (1983) and Colley et al (2003), mentors principally provide three functions:

1. psychological and social support, in which the mentor provides acceptance, affirmation, and friendship
2. role modelling, in which the protégé takes cues and learns from the attitudes, values, and behaviours displayed by the mentor
3. career development, in which the mentor coaches the protégé and insulates the protégé from adverse organizational pressures and forces, provides challenging assignments that stretch the capabilities of the protégé, sponsors career advancement of the protégé, and fosters positive organizational exposure and visibility for the protégé.

In general, mentoring offers a private and protected relationship that enables protégés to test out new ideas and examine issues with a fresh perspective in a safe and non-threatening environment.

Effective mentors foster nurturing environments in which protégés may develop faster and more completely than their peers, and are therefore better prepared as organizational leaders (Scandura et al, 1996). For the protégé, self-confidence may be enhanced by the knowledge that one has a significant ally, and given the protection often offered by the mentor, enables taking career enhancing risks. Equally, the mentor may also benefit from the mentoring process. The motives of the mentor may range from the selfish to the altruistic: an implicit *quid pro quo*; or organizational legitimization as a king-maker; or the very act of mentoring may be refreshing and rejuvenating to the mentor's interests and motivations, or the mentor-protégé relationship may create a professional or organizational legacy, and lastly, the act of giving time and effort to the protégé may be rewarding in itself. Mutual trust is a key element of the relationship, which can evolve towards one with familial undertones. Mentoring relationships are known to continue to flourish and evolve beyond specific organizational settings, even after either the protégé or the mentor has changed organizations or roles.

### Formal versus informal mentoring processes

It has been suggested that true mentoring is an inherently informal process in which mentors and protégés come together spontaneously. Successful relationships are therefore a combination of common goals, individual personalities, and a healthy dose of luck (Wasburn and Crispo, 2006). On the other hand, it may be argued that a reliance on informal mentoring alone, and therefore on chance events, is unsatisfactory.

As a result of the considerable evidence available in support of the developmental benefits of informal mentoring through inter-personal relationships that may play out either within a particular organizational setting or across organizations, there have been widespread attempts to replicate these through more formal and deliberate mentoring processes. However, these have frequently delivered mixed results. According to Sosik et al (2005), informal and formal mentoring relationships differ in terms of degree of organizational control, level of planning and intentionality, the specificity of the goals, the depth of the relationship, the degree to which participation is voluntary, the life-cycle of the relationship, and the nature of the setting in which the relationship unfolds.

Colley et al (2003) point out that informal mentoring involves a voluntary and natural learning relationship in which there is mutual self selection between mentor and protégé. Informal mentorships grow spontaneously and in an unplanned manner out of informal relationships and interactions, during which protégés may prove themselves worthy of the extra attention that a mentorship would demand. Such a relationship may be initiated by the protégé based on a perceived similarity in values, attitudes, demographics, or life experiences with the mentor. Similarly, mentors also frequently select protégés whom they can identify with, and who they are willing to devote attention to and develop. The relationships involve intense social interactions, joint decision-making, and sharing of perceptions about and feedback on the protégé's performance by the mentor. By contrast, formal mentoring involves an organizational matching process, in which the mentor and protégé are brought together with a deliberate goal of providing career development guidance to the protégé. Such an organizational arrangement may be undertaken by a programme coordinator based on perceived similarities between mentor and protégé, with the attendant risks that this may result in less identification between mentor and protégé, and therefore a poor fit and inadequate commitment to the relationship.

Friday et al (2004) argue that informal mentorships tend to evolve out of shared work or social interests that may result in mutual admiration and commitment between mentor and protégé, and this may add to the depth, personal commitment, and durability of the relationship. Informal mentorships are therefore more likely to move beyond the discussion of task and career issues into more personal arenas, and protégés in formal mentorships should not be expected to gain the same benefits as protégés in informal mentorships.

Sosik et al (2005) observe that informal relationships are enduring and typically last between three and six years, whereas formal relationships are significantly shorter as they are often contracted to last between six months and one year only. While the former focus on personal development, the latter focus on career development.

Chao et al (1992) observe that formal mentors may not view the protégé as worthy of special attention and support, and therefore a longer adjustment period may be required. Formal mentorships may also be accompanied by an organizational pressure to participate in the mentorship programme, and may therefore be less effective than informal mentoring relationships. Formal mentors are often less motivated and effective at communication and coaching skills, and more organizationally distanced from their protégés. Formal mentors provide may more superficial suggestions and ideas, and less career development, role modelling, and psychosocial support. By contrast, informal mentors enhance the ability of protégés to recognize the social and political dynamic within the organization, and acquire relevant career related knowledge and skills. As a result, report Ragins and Cotton (1999), protégés with formal mentors report less satisfaction with their mentor than protégés with informal mentors. It may also be the case that protégés who had some implicit freedom of choice in informal mentor selection, report a positive experience in order to validate and legitimize their choice.

### Making formal mentoring effective

If it is to be beneficial, formal mentoring must therefore occur within certain parameters.

Wilson and Elman (1990) emphasize that mentoring is a relationship that can and should be promoted by the organization, but should never be required. The mentoring relationship should be a voluntary one, so mentors and protégés cannot simply be paired off by some higher authority. The best mentoring relationships are relatively exclusive, intensive, and voluntary.

Chao et al (1992) suggest that if formal mentorships were more like informal mentorships, their outcomes would be more positive. Accordingly, management of the mentoring programme should instil a climate of mutual interest and participation, without obligating participation. Mentoring relationships should be carefully outlined and not promise specific benefits from participation, or disadvantages from non-participation, and matching should be based on compatibility of interpersonal factors.

Other considerations in maximizing the benefit from this relatively inexpensive and individually tailored process are offered by Arnold and Johnson (1997). The mentor–protégé relationship should be given time to mature, and there is likely to be a positive correlation between benefits and amount of contact. In addition, the mentor should not be in a role that could intrude on the day to day supervision of the protégé. While Clutterbuck (2004) suggests mentors should be two or more levels above in the hierarchy, there is an important balance to be struck: if the mentor is too senior, the mentor can consequently be too remote, geographically, interpersonally, and organizationally. Lastly, mentors must be perceived as having influence in the organization, but mentors who are too influential may also have constraints. Levinson (1979) highlights that good mentors have an interesting blend of work commitment coupled with being approachable and open, sensitive and empathic, supportive and helpful, and that mentors who are too old relative to the protégé are not as effective. There is also a suggestion that very high performing mentors may be less likely or able to provide psychosocial functions. It takes time and energy to mentor, and high performing mentors may simply not have the time or the inclination to engage in the more emotional and personally intense aspects of the mentoring relationship.

### Limitations of the mentoring process

It is also important to note that mentors are not a panacea, and there are some tensions inherent in the mentoring relationship – its emotional intensity encourages close bonding, but can create dependence on the mentor. The power of the mentor may be such that the protégé may feel obliged to comply. Additionally, the process makes heavy demands on mentor time, support, and resources.

Formal mentoring programmes, in particular, can also have significant organizational downsides. Hunt and Michael (1983) observed that mentoring could be complicated by suggestions of favouritism, and can be much less readily available and more problematic for female protégés. Wasburn and Crispo (2006) offer other caveats about formal mentoring, which may be based on the tacit assumption that the protégé is deficient in some way, and that the mentor is someone who should be emulated. Paternalistic overtones in the relationship can undermine self-confidence, some of the organizational values transmitted may be obsolete, and personality differences can doom a relationship from the outset. There may also be other dysfunctional outcomes such as mentors taking credit for or sabotaging a protégé's work, sexual harassment, and expectations of a submissive attitude from the protégé. In addition, only a small number of protégés can be selected, as it is unlikely that there will be a large enough number of effective mentors available within any one organization.

Within a development context, Clutterbuck (2004) asserts that offering mentoring as a sole activity would not be sufficient on its own to meet leadership development requirements, and mentoring would need to be part of a wider package of support and learning opportunities. Keele et al (1987) also argue that formal mentoring programmes are no panacea, and that if the assigned mentor-protégé programmes are to enhance protégé development, they must be but one element within a broader range of management development activity.

## Other developmental relationships

Although mentoring relationships have been studied and written about extensively, there is evidence that there are other people who also provide developmental assistance (Higgins and Kram, 2001). While mentoring has become a "catch all" term, and has been used to describe guide, adviser, sponsor, role model, teacher, protector, friend, coach, counsellor, patron, benefactor, and advocate, these numerous developmental roles can be played by different individuals (Friday et al, 2004). Individuals often rely on not just one but multiple individuals for developmental support in their careers, a phenomenon that Kram (1985) describes as "relationship constellations". In other words, individuals may receive mentoring assistance from many people at any one point of time.

The multiple developmental relationships and roles available to individuals have been summarized by McCauley and Douglas (2004) as follows:

1. *Assessment Role*: this includes providing ongoing feedback, assistance in integrating or making sense of feedback from others, allowing evaluation of strategies before they are implemented by acting as a sounding board, and offering a comparison point for evaluating own skill and performance
2. *Challenge Role*: this includes pushing the individual beyond the normal comfort zone, acting as a dialogue partner by offering different perspectives or points of view, enabling access to challenging assignments, providing pressure to fulfil commitment to development goals, and acting as a role model to provide examples of high or low competence in areas being developed
3. *Support Role*: this includes providing emotional support during the difficulties of the learning process, and acting as a counsellor who helps with examination of what is making learning and development difficult, as a cheerleader who boosts belief that success is possible, as a reinforcer who rewards progress toward goals, and as a companion who gives individuals the sense that they are not alone in their struggles, and that if others can achieve their goals so too can the learner.

Clearly, some relationships are more developmental than others, either because they fulfil more such roles; for example, over time, mentors are likely to play multiple roles, or a relationship can be especially developmental because it provides just the right role that the individual needs at that time.

Given the centrality of the boss-employee relationship, it is intriguing to note the mixed developmental impact of the boss. Bosses are in the unique position of working directly with the individual, having regular contact, feeling responsible for the individual's continued success, and having the power to access organizational relationships and resources for the individual. However, Boud and Middleton (2003) argue that bosses may be unable to foster learning due to the structural constraints of their roles. Individuals may have difficulty in trusting their boss to facilitate learning because of the boss's formal role in performance evaluation, and the need for individuals to portray themselves as competent. Levinson (1979) points out that not all managers can function effectively as mentors, and Mumford (1995) observes that bosses as coaches are "appallingly ineffective".

Within the context of other development influences, there has been an increasing interest in peer relationships and networks for their developmental value. Kram (1985) identifies a continuum of peer relationships, ranging from the "information peer" to the "collegial peer" to the "special peer". In an information peer relationship, individuals benefit most from information exchange about their work and the organization, and receive only occasional confirmation or emotional support. In the collegial peer relationship, there is a moderate level of trust and self disclosure, and an increased level of emotional support and job related feedback. The special peer relationship is relatively rare, and is characterized by a special sense of bonding, and provides valuable and candid personal feedback, friendship, and confirmation of self-worth. For individuals who do not have or want mentors, such peers seem essential – they can coach and counsel, provide critical information, provide support in handling personal problems and attaining professional growth. Indeed there may be times when it makes more sense to consult with a peer than a mentor; and Kram (1985) suggests that while conventional mentors are most important in early career stages, peers seem to be important at all stages.

Building on this theme of multiple relationships, Emmerik (2004) observes that a network of development relationships may be essential to achieving intrinsic career success, and the more developmental relationships there are in the network, the better. According to Higgins (2000), there is evidence that individuals do not rely on a single mentor or current boss, but rather on a network of relationships for developmental assistance and support. The effectiveness of an individual's developmental network is a function of the diversity and strength of the developmental relationships. Diversity is a function of range, or the number of different social systems the relationships stem from, as well as density, or the degree to which the developers know and are connected to each other. The greater the range and the lower the density, the lesser the redundancy of information, and therefore the better the network. Strength is a function of level of emotional affect, reciprocity, and frequency of communication. Based on these criteria, each relationship may be appropriate in different situations, and yield different outcomes.

Peer relationships assume a special significance in some settings and for some purposes. Peer networks result in an increased ability to access others for information and expertise, resources, and cooperative action. With the right networks, leaders save time because they know where to get information, and how to foster cooperation and collaboration (Spreitzer, 2006). Engestrom (2001) draws attention to horizontal or sideways learning and development in which problem solving occurs essentially through interactions with peers without resort to a conventional knowledge hierarchy. Holbeche (1996) observes that the need for peer mentoring may arise in some organizations where it can prove difficult to admit openly that one is in need of support, because it can be seen as an admission of weakness in an organization that may be entrenched in a command and control culture. In such an environment, individuals may also be mistrustful of support offered internally. Peer mentoring may also be a viable alternative to conventional mentoring in situations where there are simply not enough senior line managers who are able or willing to act as mentors. On the other hand there may be a history of hoarding information from peers and there may be a degree of suspicion and insecurity in developing the frank exchange of views needed. Snell (1992) suggests that close problem-solving relationships with peers can provide reciprocal counselling or a two-way version of low key mentoring in which joint problem-solving can take place.

In a development sense, experiences of colleagues can provide new insights on problems. Engaging with colleagues in critical conversations allows individuals to explore perspectives and ideas different from their own. Reflective learning alongside peers encourages individuals to surface and question their hypotheses about others and roles in organizations, allowing for changed leadership behaviour by the individual (Densten and Gray, 2001). Peers can also be a source of valuable feedback, and the act of securing feedback strengthens relationships that can be drawn upon during times of difficulty, and provide social support. These relationships are critical for leadership development because they build social capital, ensuring that leaders are better informed, more creative, more efficient, and better problem solvers (Spreitzer, 2006).

Peers also provide vicarious learning. Observing colleagues in leadership settings can provide positive and negative role models, and a largely cost-free resource for effective leadership development. Bandura (1994) observes that seeing people similar to oneself succeed often raises observers' beliefs that they too possess the capabilities required to succeed in comparable activities.

## Accelerated learning and mastery experiences

In Phase II, interviewees frequently characterized learning from certain types of intense experiences as formative development processes.

On the whole, experience appears to be a key to the development of managers and leaders, but some kinds of experience, such as stretch assignments, provide more effective development than others. It appears that individuals often develop primarily through confrontation with novel situations and problems where their existing repertoires of behaviours are inadequate, and where they have to develop new ways of dealing with these situations.

### Development through stretch

The concept of stretch appears to be intimately connected with the concept of development. Indeed it has been suggested that leadership development may be defined as the process of stretching capacity so that both leader and follower can perform more effectively (Davis, 2001).

McCauley et al (1995) suggest that some mismatch or stretching beyond current talents helps the manager continue to learn and grow, expanding his or her capacities and hence contributing more to the organization. Mahler and Drotter (1986) emphasize the importance of developing future high level managers by placing them in assignments for which they are not yet fully qualified. Similarly, McCall et al (1988) identify stretch assignments as a major source of the development of managerial skills and perspectives. Such assignments place the manager in dynamic settings full of problems to solve, and choices to make under conditions of risk and uncertainty, and these situations provide both the motivation and opportunity to learn rapidly. Such situations can surface shortcomings in current skills, frameworks, or competencies and stimulate a desire to overcome these deficiencies.

Smith and Morphey (1994) observe that managers frequently refer to learning from experience in work situations, and refer to difficulties, adversity, setbacks, failures, and mistakes, and that the majority of tough challenges are from significant job changes or changes in job content.

### Formative development experiences on the job

In their study of the formative development experiences of 60 managers, Davies and Easterby-Smith (1984) determined that none were associated with formal training, and all were linked to experience obtained in carrying out work duties. They suggest that development experiences can be categorized into proactive and reactive. Job moves are a common mechanism for proactive development and typically include a significant element that is completely new to the manager, for example, a shift from a specialist to a general management role. As a result it is no longer possible to use tactics and routines established in previous jobs, and it is necessary to work things out from scratch. In order to cope with such novelty it is necessary for managers to accept major changes in perspective from which they view the business, and the ability to shift perspectives is important in developing an awareness of the total context of the business. Davies and Easterby-Smith (1984) also found evidence of development for managers in static positions, or reactive development. Development within existing jobs happens in a changing business environment which requires adaptation, or in situations in which although roles and responsibilities are clearly defined, there is freedom as to how these goals are to be achieved. Other reactive development situations include temporary special projects and assignments which involve gaining a wider perspective on the business, meeting and keeping in touch with important and influential people, contributing to thinking and action on future policy, seeing existing jobs in a new light, and seeing new opportunities within existing jobs.

Similarly, McCauley (1986) identifies several studies showing that early job challenge, early broad responsibility, early leadership opportunities, and task force and staff assignments can have developmental significance.

In their study of the developmental influences of British CEOs, Cox and Cooper (1989) found that a major factor in the background of these successful individuals was the development of self-sufficiency and an ability to cope with the world, using their own resources, at a very early age. There were a number of reasons for this, but it was most often due to the loss of a parent or separation from parents in early childhood. Another common theme was that most interviewees had experienced considerable responsibility quite early in their careers. Often this involved "being thrown in at the deep end and left to sink or swim". Typical experiences were being sent off to manage an overseas subsidiary and left in a strange country to cope with local conditions, with virtually no support from the parent organization; or being given sole responsibility for turning around an ailing company or division – all associated with the acceptance of challenges involving risk. Cox and Jennings (1995) undertook a similar study and highlighted the extreme resilience of successful entrepreneurs and the ability to bounce back from catastrophic failure, sometimes more than once.

Snell (1989) observes that most successful managers have been through the "school of hard knocks" and offers a typology which includes: big mistakes; being over stretched or feeling deficient in the job; being under threat or facing unpalatable demands for a change in working approach; facing an impasse or a situation in which plans are abruptly and firmly obstructed; being unfairly or unjustly treated; becoming a victim of another's incompetence or lack of concern; losing out or experiencing disappointment of fair defeat; and being under personal attack or experiencing unjustified personal criticism.

Stumpf (1989) identifies six types of work experiences that aid thinking and acting strategically. Four of these involve a change in job assignment to one that differs from past assignments in several meaningful ways such as:

1. Starting a business or project from scratch, constituting a stretch due to the holistic nature of the assignment
2. Fixing or turning around a failing operation, a situation in which managers must learn to ask thought provoking questions, to diagnose what else could go wrong before it actually does, and to respond quickly and flexibly to many different situations every day
3. Special projects or temporary assignments that are viewed as central to the organization, and which challenge the manager's ability to understand a different work situation quickly and perform effectively with people they have not dealt with in the past
4. Moving from a line to staff position or vice versa, and learning how the business works from a different perspective, coping with uncertainty and ambiguity, and learning to think in more complex ways.

In addition, two additional stretch experiences relate to accommodating adversity, such as:

5. being demoted, missing a promotion, or getting an undesirable job, and

6. working through a personal crisis such as divorce, illness, or bereavement.

In a similar vein, McCauley et al (1995) have identified five broad categories of stretch related development experiences. These are:

1. Transitions, which involve unfamiliar responsibilities and a need for the individual to prove himself or herself, as well as novel situations that render previous frameworks, routines, and behaviours inadequate
2. Creating change and developing new directions, or dealing with inherited problems, both of which require numerous decisions and actions in a climate of uncertainty and ambiguity
3. Higher levels of responsibility involving high stakes, external pressure, a need to manage increased business diversity, job overload; all requiring greater breadth, complexity, and visibility under close scrutiny
4. Non-authority relationships or influencing without authority, and exposure to other perspectives that must be considered
5. Obstacles such as adverse business conditions, lack of top management support, lack of personal support, and a difficult boss; all requiring the individual to learn how to persevere.

Specific examples of assignments characterized by one or more of these developmental experiences are the first staff position, the first general management position, a fired predecessor, and an international assignment. McCauley et al (1995) suggest that some lessons such as self-confidence are learned from several types of challenging assignments.

### Assessing development potential of work experiences

McCall (1988) argues that the developmental potential of a work experience is driven by the challenges it presents, and identifies eight key job challenges:

1. By learning to adapt to a variety of bosses, both good and bad, executives develop the ability to deal effectively with a diverse array of people in authority
2. Incompetence and resistance from subordinates can lead to the realization that there is no one way of leading that will work all the time
3. Learning potential increases every time managers work with types of people they have not encountered before, and the stakes are further

raised when there is no formal authority over them and when there is no requirement to co-operate
4. Playing for high stakes, for example, being out on a limb on a project highly visible to top management, working against tough deadlines, taking a huge financial risk, or having to go against the preference or advice of bosses
5. Business adversity, creating a need to take action quickly, to cope with ambiguous problems, and make choices without sufficient information
6. Scope and scale changes, which can present demands to lead by remote control, and to find ways to run things when it's impossible to keep one's arms around them
7. "Missing trumps", which require the individual to work around a significant disadvantage, such as working in unfamiliar functions, businesses, and products, or being too young, or having the wrong background, or being in a foreign country and unable to speak the local language
8. High degrees of change in role can bring proportional challenges, as in being promoted multiple levels, moving from a line to a staff position, "fix it" managers sent to start something, free-wheeling managers given a "hands-on" boss: all these situations require executives to find ways of dealing with huge and usually unexpected change.

It is worth noting that none of these challenging assignments can be identified by reference to job title, salary, or hierarchical level.

### The role of hardships

Moxley and Pulley (2003) emphasize the extent to which hardships are important to the development of well-rounded leaders. Hardships differ from other developmental experiences because they are not intentional; people encounter them naturally. The challenges of hardships are also different from other developmental experiences, and they provide lessons in self-knowledge, sensitivity, control, and flexibility. Hardships often serve as wake-up calls; people decide what really matters, become clearer about their values and aspirations, develop greater self-awareness, and recognize their limits. Individuals also get an opportunity to learn how others really see them, and to see how their weaknesses matter. Moxley and Pulley (2003: 15) suggest that through hardship, people learn that they need multiple "involvements and images" to adapt to changing circumstances; they learn to be "both-and" for example, tough and soft, self confident and humble, a strong individual leader and team player. Research at the Center for Creative Leadership has identified six relevant types of hardships:

1. Mistakes and failures, in which learning happens when cause and effect are clear, the mistake is acknowledged, and there is no punitive outcome
2. Career setbacks, which can be unfreezing experiences that open people to new insights about their strengths and limitations, and what kinds of jobs they like and don't like, and what work is satisfying and meaningful to them
3. Personal trauma, which can teach valuable lessons in personal strength and resilience, ways and means of creating meaning from the experience, maintaining self-esteem and dignity, and foster a sense of belonging to a group and being useful to others
4. Problem employees, who can trigger learning about being firm, forceful, and confronting problems
5. Downsizing, which can result in reflection about loss, relationships, security, and community
6. Racial injustice, which forces learning about personal identity and values

Bennis and Thomas (2002) recount intense, often traumatic, always unplanned experiences that transform leaders and become the sources of their distinctive leadership abilities, and describe the transformative events that shape leaders as crucibles. Crucible experiences are a trial and a test, points of deep reflection that force managers and leaders to question who they were and what matters to them. Crucibles require leaders to examine their values, question their assumptions, and hone their judgement. Not all crucible experiences are traumatic, and can involve positive but challenging experiences such as having a demanding boss or mentor. Significant crucible experiences include adapting to a foreign territory, surviving disruption and loss, and enduring enforced reflection. Crucibles can play a key role in building self-confidence.

In summary, stretch may arise through work experiences on the job or through hardship events in the lives of individuals. Both processes embody a high degree of distress, risk, and novelty, and represent situations which demand skills and capabilities that exceed those currently possessed by the individual. After Bandura (1994), these processes may collectively be described as "mastery experiences".

Learning from mastery experiences requires learning about how not to repeat previous failures and mistakes, generalizing and making explicit the learning from a specific situation, and thereby avoiding or reducing such difficulties in future.

While there are some clear leader development implications, such as the notion that where there is a choice people must accept assignments that test and challenge them, and try out untested skills, organizations must also consider the developmental potential of assignments more explicitly. Davies and Easterby-Smith (1984) suggest that selection decisions in organizations should take greater note of the novelty that the manager is likely to encounter in the new job, and organizations must override risk-averse tendencies likely to dominate individual decisions.

### The limitations of stretch experiences

However, development through stretch is not without its costs and limitations, as outlined below.

*Variable Learning*: McCauley (1986) and McCall (2004) suggest that people do not automatically learn from experience; some people are more "learning agile" than others. Placing managers in challenging assignments offers developmental opportunities, but learning from these assignments is not guaranteed. Bunker and Webb (1992) found that managers who are most likely to learn are action oriented, self-confident, and willing to take the risk of moving beyond their realm of expertise to try something new. Dechant (1994) observes that it is left up to individuals to mine such experiences in whatever ways they have come to rely on over time, and this places the individual in the role of chief architect of his or her own development. It also engenders a sort of fatalism about learning from experience: one either learns or one does not.

*Organizational Costs*: developmental moves involve potential business losses due to errors, costs, and inefficiencies associated with the learning curve, and even possible loss of people if they do not succeed in meeting the performance objectives of the job. As a result, the organizational irony is that the person most likely to get a stretch assignment is the person who has already demonstrated the ability to do it. In addition, on the job development requires time (McCall, 2004). Stumpf (1989) observes that the size and scope of stretch events means that such learning on the job can be a costly and lengthy process. If stretch is to be used properly, the organization needs to wait for an appropriate situation to occur so that it can be assigned to someone for development reasons. Thereafter, the organization has no control over the learning that takes place, and when a skill is not learned effectively, the cost of failure is high. McCall (1988) argues that a portion of the organizational bottom line must be risked to put talented people in jobs for which they are not yet fully qualified.

*Problems of Over-stretch*: As Snell (1992) points out, repeated adversity is likely to yield diminishing returns in terms of learning. There is limited developmental value in repeatedly making big mistakes or being continually overloaded. Nor can one gain much from ongoing pressure, impasse, injustice, losing out, or being attacked. There is therefore a need to distinguish between stretch assignments and "dumb risks", and there must be some fit between an individual and the job otherwise the stretch is potentially overwhelming. A job should be challenging enough to stretch the manager, but not so tough that severe frustration and frequent failure is experienced.

As a result, on the job stretch needs to be accompanied with appropriate developmental support.

### Managing stretch: Organizational considerations

Moxley and Pulley (2003) observe that companies often encourage high potential managers to undertake stretch assignments for which they are not yet fully prepared; yet the company's response to mistakes may be punitive. Additionally, too much challenge accompanied by too little support is counter-productive. Seijts and Latham (2006: 1) argue that many organizations set stretch goals but fail to provide employees with the knowledge or skills needed to meet these goals, and suggest that it is "foolish and even immoral" for organizations to assign stretch goals without equipping employees with the resources they need to succeed, and still punish them when they fail. McCall (1988) suggests that managers must be encouraged to take risks and make mistakes, on the basis that mistakes are not fatal as long as they are not repeated, and they are a result of a real effort to do something useful.

Organizations must not only provide a supportive culture and resources, but also re-frame how goals for individuals in developmental roles are articulated. Seijts and Latham (2006) observe that goals framed only in terms of performance outcomes are limiting, and that goals framed in terms of skill acquisition are more powerful. An exclusive focus on performance goals encourages the individual to fall back on personal strategies or routines that have been known to be effective for the individual in the past. A learning goal draws attention away from the performance outcomes to the discovery of effective task processes. The increase in commitment resulting from a learning goal in turn results in higher performance. Learning goals stimulate the imagination, foster discovery, and thinking "outside the box".

Smith and Morphey (1994) observe that little attempt is made in most organizations to manage the difficulties key people are experiencing, and given the heavy task orientation of most managers, there is a lack of recognition of the learning opportunity while experiencing tough challenges on the job. Smith and Morphey (1994) also highlight the need for accompanying support systems and mechanisms. In particular, they identify an environment of supportive relationships which foster and encourage mutual trust. Securing a constructive development experience from the stretch requires the active involvement of others who can coach or mentor the individual who is experiencing the difficulties – for example, an experienced mentor who can help the individual make himself open to learning. In the same vein, Mahler and Drotter (1986) highlight the need for providing access to coaches to enable reflection and regular feedback on development progress. Easterby-Smith and Davies (1983) report a considerable benefit for managers through maintaining a long-term link with a manager who takes an interest in their development, such as a mentor. Typically, such a relationship is not time or role specific, but spans a number of experiences and situations, and mentors also help guard individuals against the shock of too much change. In other words, there could be a complementary relationship between mastery experiences, mentors, and critical reflection.

## Critical reflection

While we all learn from experience, experience is a very slippery teacher; most of the time we have experiences from which we never learn (Smith, 2001).

Reflection plays an important role in synthesizing the tacit learning from experience. By becoming "reflective practitioners" managers can generate new insights and develop new ways of working in practice (Schon, 1983). As Boud et al (1985) point out, the capacity to reflect is directly related to how effectively individuals can learn from their personal experiences. Reflection therefore provides a meaningful way for leaders to gain a deep understanding of their actions and environments. In other words, reflection helps to convert experience into "actionable knowledge" (Argyris, 1993). To paraphrase Smith's work on action learning, reflection seeks to cast a net around slippery experiences and capture them as learning (Smith, 2001). Conversely, the absence of reflection results in poor decisions, bad judgements, and repetitions of previous mistakes (Brookfield, 1995). Without the re-consideration of events that reflection entails, leaders may be mistakenly persuaded of their invincibility by past successes, and fail to consider alternative viewpoints and scenarios with possibly disastrous outcomes (Densten and Gray, 2001).

The requirement for conscious and frequent reflection is a key feature of all learning models (Honey and Mumford, 2000). Additionally, reflection as a critical component of informal learning is less of an outcome than an ongoing process (Kolb, 1984). We learn by doing, thinking over and reflecting on what has happened, making sense of it, and arriving at some tentative conclusions on how to use the learning and what to do differently next time around.

However, reflection does not come naturally or easily to most managers and executives. This may be because of their task orientation, or as Conger (1990) suggests, leaders may avoid reflecting because such reflection might be discomforting and challenge their favourable perceptions of themselves.

Reflection is not by definition critical, and "simple" reflection, as in muse, think, or consider, is not adequate. Smith (2001) observes that simply thinking back over what worked and what did not is not enough. Critical reflection involves becoming conscious of previously implicit assumptions, beliefs, templates, and criteria, and critiquing them vigorously.

Reflection should not simply be an "improved understanding of experience" but should involve serious internal criticisms of it. According to Mezirow (1990: 14), through critical reflection an individual becomes more open to the perspectives of others, less defensive, and more able to accept new ideas, and all these elements contribute to "transformative learning". Through critical reflection, a manager can examine feelings, beliefs, and actions, as well as the assumptions that underpin them. Transformation occurs through a challenge to underlying assumptions, and the identification of new possibilities for thinking, feeling and acting.

Brookfield (1995) suggests that critical reflection can be characterized by a deeper, more intense, more probing form of reflection, and can create discomfort and dissonance. Densten and Gray (2001) argue that deep reflective learning requires questioning basic assumptions and practices. Yost et al (2000) observe that learning through critical reflection happens when there is a desire to learn, an open mind, a willingness to question even the firmest of beliefs, and an ambition to make meaningful change.

Schon (1987) argues that effective reflection entails diagnosis, testing, and belief in personal causation. It needs a safe environment in which reflective conversations can take place. Raelin (2000) contends that through talk and reflection people can learn to recognize their taken for granted values, appreciate the connections between their own practices and the organizational contexts in which they are embedded, and participate in a learning process that may transform their world by their very participation in it.

Schon (1987) also makes interesting connections between mentoring and reflection, and describes three modes of learning: follow me, joint investigation, and hall of mirrors. "Follow me" is the simplest learning mode, at the core of which is imitation of the actions and behaviours of an expert, and is appropriate for problem situations that are highly focused and specific, and in which the correct actions and behaviours can be practised and replicated precisely. "Joint investigation" is a relatively more sophisticated learning mode in which the learner and the instructor together explore the problem at hand, and the experiences of the learner, in order to arrive at a solution and derive meaningful principles, concepts and actionable knowledge. This is a form of coaching conducted by means of reflection on experiences. "Hall of mirrors" is a metaphor used by Schon (1987) to describe the idea of reflection from all possible sides, particularly from perspectives that may not be easily available or evident to the learner. At an operational level, for example, a 360-degree feedback system is an example of a "hall of mirrors" approach, and is therefore a positive aid to reflection.

## Sense-making

Critical reflection is closely linked to, and possibly an enabler of, sense-making.

Sense-making involves "turning circumstances into a situation that is comprehended explicitly… it is about the interplay of action and interpretation, and about stabilizing the streaming of experience" (Weick et al, 2005: 409). Against a raw flow of activities and events confronting the individual, sense-making is the attempt to understand "what's going on here", and to answer the question "what should I do next". Explicit efforts at sense-making occur whenever ongoing action becomes disorganized, and whenever events disrupt normal expectations and established patterns of meaning.

Sense-making begins when there is a lack of fit between what is expected and what is encountered. Uncertainty and ambiguity increase when existing patterns or structures are interrupted, thus creating a need for new efforts to make sense of one's world (Seiling and Hinrichs, 2005). Hence, sense-making is a process of dealing with uncertainty. Sense-making is more than mere problem-solving, and happens before and after it. Sense-making provides input to successful problem-solving, and in turn is informed by the decisions and outcomes that are a result of problem-solving. It is the process through which information, insight, and ideas coalesce into something useful, or stick together in a meaningful way: "managers must literally wade into the ocean of events, and actively try to make sense of them" (Daft and Weick, 1984: 266). Alternatively, sense-making may be defined as an interpretive process in which people assign meaning to ongoing occurrences, and as such it is a necessary precursor to all purposive activities: planning actions, forming judgements, and reaching decisions (Wagner and Gooding, 1997).

Toit (2003) argues that sense-making requires overcoming the barriers of previously held thought patterns, a process which is a key feature of critical reflection. Additionally, the creation of knowledge is not a solitary process, but is a result of interaction with others, and therefore sense-making requires interaction with others. It is fundamentally a social process: people interpret their environment in and through interactions with others, constructing accounts that allow them to comprehend the world and act collectively.

## Integrating the development processes

The previous empirical study documented in Phase II identified mentors and accelerated learning on the job as dominant formative development experiences, with reflection and networking playing a supporting role. Although these have hitherto been expressed as independent or parallel processes, the preceding review of other studies and prior theory suggests that these processes are, in fact, inter-related. Such an integrated perspective is depicted in Figure 5.1.

Implicit in this perspective are the suggestions that:

1. *Accelerated and mastery experiences* are often provided by influential mentors, and mentors support protégés as they cope with stretch and hardship
2. Mentors, peers, and other *developmental relationships* facilitate not only a "cathartic discharge" (Snell, 1992) but also critical reflection

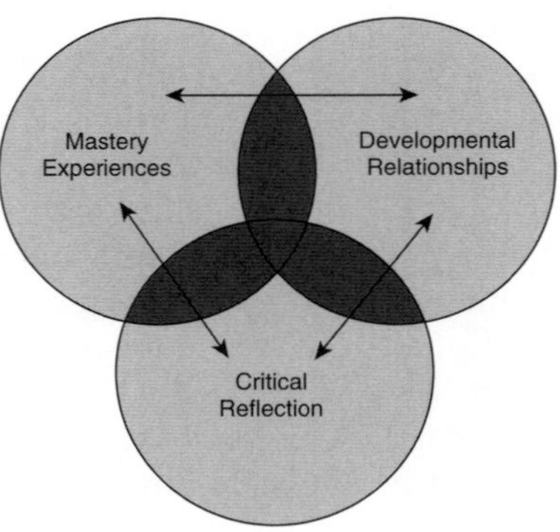


*Figure 5.1* Integrating the Development Processes

and sense-making, and critical reflection in turn enables individuals to better leverage mentors and other developmental relationships such as peer networks

3. *Critical reflection* and consequent sense-making help convert the tacit learning or stretch and hardship on the job into "actionable knowledge", enabling the individual to engage deliberately with more mastery experiences such as stretch assignments.

# 6 Leader Development Interventions: Action Research

## Overview of the interventions

Phase II findings suggested that formative development experiences occur, in the main, in informal learning environments. However, as suggested in Chapter 5, an exclusive reliance on informal learning processes presents problems of inefficiency, cost, and lack of control, and may be of limited value to organizations and individuals interested in pursuing development in a planned and proactive manner.

For these reasons, an important element of this Phase was to undertake action research in which two formal leader development interventions were designed and delivered in order to explore the feasibility and consequences of simulating the dominant informal development processes identified in Phase II.

The first intervention was customized for a leading media company in the UK, and the second was an open enrolment executive development programme launched at Ashridge Business School in the UK.

Both interventions were aimed at improving the strategic leader capability of participants, and both included similar components of workshops intended to stimulate learning about strategy and leadership capabilities, a real or simulated "stretch assignment" designed to facilitate accelerated learning, mentoring or peer mentoring of varying degrees of formality, and networking. Both interventions had a longitudinal dimension as opposed to a traditional development offering that is cynically but perhaps accurately described as a "sheep dip".

## Methodology

An action research methodology was adopted for this element of Phase III. The term action research in this context is being used as "an approach to applied social research in which the researcher and a client collaborate in the development of a diagnosis and solution for a problem, wherein the findings will contribute to the stock of knowledge in a particular domain" (Hult and Lennung, 1980: 183). The interventions were employed as a "voyage of discovery", that is to say, in an exploratory manner, with the objective of "illuminating the effects of implementation" (Patton, 1987: 172).

The leadership development interventions described here were deliberately designed using the emerging findings from this research, with the objective of simulating the influential development processes, and evaluating the outcomes of doing so. Both interventions were longitudinal, and spanned four to eight months.

The first intervention, The Leadership Circle (described hereafter as the Circle) involved this author's engagement within a major media company in the UK for a customized strategic leader development initiative. Nine senior (but not top) managers participated in a development experience that was specifically designed to provide:

- a workshop, led by the author, that offered participants both formal and experiential learning about strategy and leadership, alongside opportunities to reflect and network
- in-company mentoring, managed by the client
- four simulated "accelerated learning" or "stretch" experiences.

The second intervention, the Top Leader Journey (described hereafter as the Journey) was a senior leader open-enrolment development experience with 12 participants, designed and delivered by two leadership development specialists at Ashridge Business School using the author's previous findings in Phases I and II as a basis for the design of the intervention. The author was actively engaged in this process. The Journey offered participants learning opportunities through debate and discussion on the nature of strategy and leadership, as well as through mentoring, stretch, and structured reflection aided by an executive coach.

In both cases, although the development processes deployed were explicit, the dimensions of strategic leader capability identified in Phases I and II were implicit elements of the design of the interventions.

As "real" interventions, each development experience operated under certain constraints which restricted freedom of design. For example, in the Circle, the client had specific needs which took priority. In the Journey, it was not possible to arrange a formal mentoring process, and hence a co-mentoring solution (in which participants mentored each other) was adopted. In both cases, the time available to work with the participants was limited by the work pressures the participants were under, as well as by client budgets.

Nevertheless, the interventions provided useful and thought-provoking outcomes for this study. These were captured by interviewing all participants after the intervention in the case of the Circle, and both before and after the intervention in the Journey. In addition, feedback from the Circle client, as well as the Journey facilitators was also sought. All interviews were semi-structured, at the least; in the case of the Journey the interviews also included a structured element. *Inter alia*, participants' specific learning goals and the extent to which these were achieved, the differential impact of various development processes, and overall development outcomes were investigated. Interviews lasted between 30 and 45 minutes. All interviews were recorded, and professionally transcribed. All responses were clustered by question, and the data carefully scrutinized for emergent patterns. Since the clusters could be anticipated, it was not considered necessary to use software based analytical tools such as NVivo in this instance. The findings from the interviews were used to enrich understanding of key leader development processes, and also triggered a further scrutiny of the construct of self-efficacy, and its role in leader development and performance.

The details of the development interventions and their outcomes are reviewed in the sections *Intervention #1: The leadership circle* and *Intervention #2: The Top Leader Journey.*

The section titled *Self-confidence and self-efficacy* explores self-efficacy as a variable in leader development and performance.

*Towards a new framework* concludes the account of Phase III with a brief summary which sets the scene for further theoretical development.

## Intervention #1: The leadership circle

The Circle commenced with nine participants, but one participant withdrew due to pressures of business midway through the intervention.

Participant profiles for the Circle are summarized in Appendix 1(d). In general, Circle participants were mid-level managers who had been identified as high-potential within the company. The objectives of the Circle were to broaden the business and strategic exposure of participants, and to make them "mobile" across business areas within the company as part of a longer-term career development plan.

In the words of the client:

> *The specific development issue is around strategic capability in that our people come from a very narrow world, and the toolkit and experience range they have is relatively bounded. We want to give them some just-in-time strategic input, and also the opportunity to play with that on a bigger canvass, and learn to be less tactical in the way they think and operate. A lot of these people have grown up being passionately attached to the business they are in, and we want to give them an experience where they don't necessarily have that passion, but where they will have to be more disciplined and objective in the strategy they are recommending and taking. Lastly, we also want them to learn to work with and lead diverse groups, not just people who are like them, and we want to give them a really challenging experience of having to form a team and work with it around some specific business challenges.*

The Circle commenced with a two-day workshop that explored the strategic process and strategy formation from both analytical and creative perspectives. Additionally, participants were also offered self-insight through a 360-degree feedback instrument, and a learning styles inventory. A team-work exercise designed to help participants form effective teams was also included. The workshop was facilitated by the author working alongside an in-company facilitator.

The workshop was followed by a formal mentoring process, supported by senior managers, including the chairman and chief executive of the company, which ran for the duration of the intervention i.e. eight months. Participants were assigned to mentors – typically senior managers within the organization – by the client, but the mentoring process was left deliberately loose and unstructured thereafter. On average, participants met their mentors four or five times.

Another key component of the intervention was the "stretch assignment", which was an attempt to stimulate accelerated learning through a "live" case study. This required participants to work in two teams as in-house strategy consultants and deliver to a brief developed by a business unit within the company. Typically, this required engaging with a high stakes "live" strategic dilemma or issue being experienced by a "client", assimilating a large amount of data of different types from various sources, working under time pressure, in an environment of market uncertainty and information ambiguity, and making recommendations to the top management of the business. In acknowledgement of the cautionary notes presented in the Chapter 5 discussion on *Managing stretch: organizational considerations*, the top management team was briefed to evaluate the recommendations primarily in a development context, and secondarily in a business context. This gave the participants a degree of freedom to make mistakes, and learn from them. In other words, the challenge posed by the stretch assignment was matched by a supportive setting. The objectives of the stretch assignment were to expose participants to strategic issues across different business areas within the organization. In addition to pre-work, the stretch assignment typically involved two days of "live" work. Each stretch assignment was followed by all participants joining a virtual review meeting using a web conferencing platform.

The overall structure of the Circle is displayed in Figure 6.1.

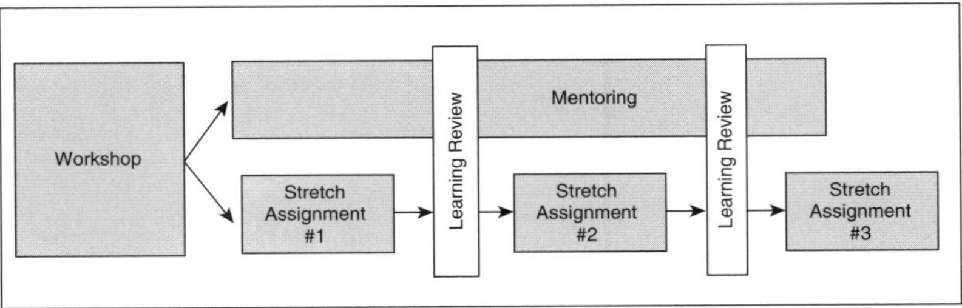


*Figure 6.1* The Leadership Circle

Participant work schedules and the timing of the Circle did not allow "pre-intervention" interviews with participants. However, eight months into the Circle all participants were individually interviewed, primarily to ascertain their account of their original learning goals, how they thought they had developed as a result of the Circle, as well as to test if it was possible to establish any co-relations between the dimensions of strategic leader capability of Phase I and the formative development processes of Phase II. The questionnaire used in these interviews is attached in Appendix 2(b).

### *Learning goals*

Perhaps reflecting the nature of the process within the client company by which participants were nominated onto the Circle, different participants came with different learning goals and expectations. When asked to recall what they were hoping to learn at the time they were nominated onto the Circle, participant responses were distributed across the acquisition of a better skill set, gaining broader business exposure, and networking and learning from peers. For example:

Better Skill Set:

> *I think it was getting a better skill set and tool set to enable me to make decisions, and take some of the risk out of my decision-making and to be more confident about the decisions we make around the business (Louise)*
>
> *Learning strategically how to run a business, what tools I could use to measure if what we were doing now was effective, and more importantly what tools I could use to measure the thinking we were having and would that be effective (Tracey)*
>
> *I've always found these things fantastic for networking and learning different things about different bits of the business, also that it always gives you better strategic insight and tools because day to day running around operationally, you don't have much opportunity to use these kinds of things (Dan)*
>
> *The one thing I was hoping to get out of it and still hope to get out of it, is about being able to synthesize information and develop a response to that rapidly. I guess the people that impress me most are those consultants that we often come across in working life who are able to grasp concepts very quickly and reach conclusions, more often than not relatively correct conclusions. My view about myself is that I tend to reflect too long, and tend to be a little bit ponderous (Fraser)*

Broader Business Exposure:

> *For me, it was to get a greater insight into other businesses, and the way that they operated. Having been in radio for 12 years, and the way the media industry is moving, it's unlikely that progression for me means sticking just inside radio. So the attraction was to learn other areas, almost to stretch myself by looking at an internet business or a publishing business, and seeing if I could adapt the skills that I have developed, and apply them to other areas within a wider industry (Adrian)*
>
> *One of the big draws for being on the Circle for me was the ability to interface with different areas of the company. I was very much in a place of always being in radio as a business, and it started to feel smaller and*

*smaller to me. I was really welcoming getting involved in other areas of the business (Tracey)*

*I mainly wanted to explore possibilities, what it's like to be on the other side of the business. And trying to figure out, do I have the ability to go and run a product as opposed to selling someone else's product and could I shape a product? I wanted to understand business strategy, in different types of markets (Darren)*

Networking and Learning from Peers:

*It's a real motivation for me to work with more inspiring people and to learn from them. I'm always very interested to know how successful people have become successful and how I can learn from their behaviour, their knowledge, their skills (Adrian)*

*I thought being exposed to a group of people who are not necessarily involved in magazines, is something that would fascinate me because that's where my career has been focused on for some time, it's been about learning about lots of different platforms and how they work and then bringing them together at some point (Mark)*

When asked if any part of the Circle had made a particular impact on them, the stretch assignments featured most prominently in the responses. Six of the eight participants confirmed they had felt stretched, and that they had benefited from the process. The workshop at the start of the Circle was also considered beneficial, as it helped prepare participants for the stretch. Mentoring received mixed reviews. Despite the previously stated learning goals of networking and learning from peers, in this instance, networking seemed to be of marginal value. These themes are elaborated below, in the voices of the participants:

**Stretch assignment**

For participants, the stretch assignments seemed to be characterized by a requirement to operate outside their "comfort zone", under time pressure, and in a high stakes environment. While this induced a degree of anxiety, support was also available, and the overall effects seemed to be positive:

*You go in to a real live situation and work through it over two days, with the knowledge that some of your ideas may really be used, that's has been the biggest thing for me. It made me feel uncomfortable. It's made me more able to take on things that I don't 100% understand but that I can definitely add to, and thinking in a slightly different way as a result of being on this course, that I can adapt to more easily (Darren)*

*I had to lead the group when we did the first live case study, and I found it spectacularly hard because I was trying to lead a group of people I didn't know, I was dealing with a subject matter that I didn't know and I had a toolkit that I didn't know. I found it an incredibly difficult two days. There was no area of comfort for me to revert to. That was extremely challenging. And also trying to lead the group whilst simultaneously trying to collate the information in my head and come to some sense was very hard in such a pressured environment. In the work environment there's an implicit hierarchy, whereas in this situation we are all equal, but I am the leader trying to exert authority without knowing the people (David)*

*I felt under pressure in terms of time, mentally, trying to keep everyone engaged, trying to focus, I found it mentally exhausting. It's made me think more before I react, people around me would agree that I'm very action orientated and it's good for me to learn from other people, for example David is someone who thinks things through before deciding on a course of action and it's good to try to emulate some of those skills (Louise)*

*It was an extraordinary two days. We had half a day to take on the information and try to formulate a plan. I found myself very frustrated at the end of the first day as I felt we hadn't made much progress… I felt inside me a great deal of panic at that point. I was really concerned that we weren't going to reach that end goal in time. The next real epiphany came the following morning when we talked to you as a group… that was really telling. It was extraordinary. It suddenly just cleared a lot of fog that had immersed both me and the people in that group. I was quite pleased with our conclusions; I thought we did at least a half decent job in the time given. Our conclusions were relatively brave and certainly ambitious. We genuinely felt it was one that as a business we could go out and do. It was a pretty petrifying experience (Fraser)*

Two of the participants framed the outcomes of the stretch in terms of enhanced self-confidence and self-belief, and a sense of self-discovery:

*Every night we were doing something like this and having to turn it around quickly for the board to review, and that is a fantastic stimulus for the brain and confidence in your own ability to do stuff at speed. Looking back, it's reminded me that you can do it (Dan)*

*One of the biggest learning outcomes for me was I was quite nervous about going into a business with a limited amount of information, being asked to look at its issues, and work to a brief within an arena where the information was what I had been given. I was nervous on two planes, one because I am quite reflective and analytical and I do like lots of information to base decisions on. I also like consideration time and I had limited information and two days with that business and then an audience. The biggest thing for me was that I enjoyed it so much and realized that I enjoyed having strategic conversations and building ideas and a strategy for a business with limited amounts of information. So what I expected to happen, the opposite happened. I realized that, with the right tools, even with limited understanding, having the important information not just lots of information, I enjoyed working on that level and building strategy from there (Tracey)*

**Workshop**

Participants viewed the workshop as a lead-in to the stretch case studies. In other words, participants viewed the workshop as providing base skills and support for the stretch that was to follow.

In particular, the "analytical toolkit" elements of the workshop, which served to clarify thinking, and offered the security of discipline and method, were considered helpful. Little or no comment was made with reference to the self-insight and team-work components of the workshop.

*I think the models we were talking about were practical and surprisingly through my mentoring session with Tom, they came up a number of times. I've also used some of them to illustrate certain things with my team here and I felt that the two days we had were over too quickly (Adrian)*

*Just having all the toolkits that you can keep is very helpful (Dan)*

*Getting a refresher on the consulting tools was good, in my day to day I don't have much use to reflect on those skills and processes. It's good to go back and test the things I'm doing on a day by day basis. We all just slip into getting the daily grind done and forget about drawing the questions up to a higher plane (Mark)*

*It was very good to learn about the models, I refer to my notes an awful lot. With hindsight I would have loved to spend more time on those models and to test them more, it felt like a real rush through them. They give you a certain feeling of security, putting these things into matrixes, using the tools like Porter's 5 Forces, just having systems to work to really helps to clarify my thinking and acts as a safety net as in have I missed anything. In terms of being able to interpret what is important I found the models really valuable (Tracey)*

*Instinctively the first thing I go back to is the 5 forces model, I always think what value can we create over our competitors that is unique to us, and that helps my thinking (Louise)*

The workshop also helped in converting an approach based on instinct and experience into a more formalized and explicit approach. In the words of one participant:

*For me the workshop was really valuable, I'm the kind of guy who tends to work from instinct and experience, the approach to the workshop gave us a toolkit and this is something I've realized I need to apply. It's clear that I cannot survive without using it more, a truth that I must face, and I have begun to do so. There are occasions when I've had a problem that I didn't know how to resolve, and I've gone and had a look at the toolkit (David)*

**Mentoring**

The mentoring process received decidedly mixed reviews, with the group of eight participants being evenly split on the value of the process. It is worth noting that this was an organizationally sponsored and formally managed mentoring process, whereas the descriptions of the value of mentors offered by interviewees in Phase II were based in informal learning settings.

In the Circle, those who had found the mentoring beneficial highlighted ease of access to the mentor, a learner-driven agenda, a sense of identification with the mentor, and trust and openness as key characteristics of the process. The mentoring provided these individuals with psycho-social support in addition to career and task support, as well as critical reflection. For example:

Ease of access and learner-driven agenda:

*David and I meet every four to five weeks, face to face, we have two or three hours together. In between those meetings we always have an open line policy, I can always get hold of him and he can get hold of me by telephone. When we have our one-to-one meetings, David lets me set the agenda at the outset, but then throughout the session he will often link back to a thread that was created in our last session (Tracey)*

*We meet once every six weeks, and we have e-mails whenever. He sees what I'm doing from afar, and he might make a comment on what I'm doing, offer encouragement, ask me questions. The structure is for me to talk and for him to advise (Darren)*

*We meet roughly every five weeks, we have a couple of hours, it's fairly casual (Adrian)*

*We are talking more frequently as time goes by, we talk every two or three weeks, about six or eight times in total so far, some of it is about our work, some is more personal stuff about the work environment (Mark)*

Sense of identification with mentor:

*What was really nice with my mentor, Travis, is that we have some common ground of experience because we're from the same background. He's working in radio but wants to branch out into other platforms, I've worked in radio in the past, I'm trying to get into other platforms as well, so there's a common ground that we can exploit the synergies. Also we've both been in the company the same short amount of time; he has that outsider feel as well. He's a great ally and he's a brilliant guy, it's very inspiring, I always walk away from a conversation with him buzzing with thoughts and ideas... I think in the case of Travis there's been a personal connection (Mark)*

Trust and openness:

*We started off by doing a SWOT analysis on me which was quite a challenge; it took a while for both of us to become totally open, just because of the nature of who we both are. We're past that point now and it's a much more fruitful relationship (Adrian)*

*I'm getting advice on some of my worries; he relates it to when he was going through the business. He's made me realize it's not just me, and he's quite confidential with some other people way above me who have gone through the same situation. I would say that I am not the most articulate, and he's reassured me not to worry saying that lots of people use big words and they've no idea what they mean. That was good to hear, it's very honest and open and we talk about a lot of confidential stuff, both personal and work related (Darren)*

Psycho-social support:

> *It's been fantastic for me, I do feel a bit of an outsider in the company, the way I behave, my accent, and my background is very different from other people. I can be made to feel a bit of a foreigner, an alien at times (Mark)*

> *One of the biggest benefits to me is that I refer to David as my stupid question person, I am sometimes quite insecure and worry that things that I don't know I should know, and that creates quite a lot of pressure for me. I always feel like having someone you can call on and ask what appears to you to be an incredibly stupid question is so valuable. The further up you get in the leadership chain, the more painful it feels when you think there is something you should know but don't. On that level I've found it really valuable (Tracey)*

Career and task support:

> *The way it works is that we may use radio as a fallback for discussion around strategic thinking; it may be used as a case study for us to talk around how I might develop my own strategic thinking, which has been really useful. Within that, if I have frustrations about the way the company does something, Tom would use that element as something he could help to develop my leadership or personal skills. One of my issues is around not having a big enough voice around the corporate table, he has helped me as to how I could influence this situation, not necessarily having the presence at the table but influencing other people so that my ideas and thoughts get heard (Adrian)*

> *Both of our bosses went off to Stanford Business School this summer and both of us were left in charge of their divisions. We had a lot in common, with suddenly this big chunk of extra stress thrown on us at a really tough time in media. Both of us not getting a huge amount of support from above, trying to figure out how to do things. Are we a safe pair of hands or are we meant to move the game on. It was weird that both of us would go through this process together over the summer and it was great to have each other to run things off each other (Mark)*

Critical reflection:

> *David really makes me stretch my thinking, when we start to talk about the subject David will say, why do you think it's that way, could it be*

*anything else, if you looked at it from a different angle what would it look like. He's very good at making me walk around a subject (Tracey)*

*We make notes on every meeting. Prior to the meeting we'll both read up on the notes and I will prepare for our next meeting. We don't set an agenda beforehand, but I'll prepare on how have I progressed on things that we last talked about and as a result of that progression what are the new things that have come up that I want to talk about and what self awareness has happened over the last four to five weeks that creates change... he creates the notes as a result of our meeting. When the notes come through they are very insightful, when I read them it crystallizes things that I already know about myself but don't necessarily act on. When you see them in writing and in context it makes it easy for me to think carefully about if I do that for those reasons when the next opportunity presents itself, it might create a different outcome (Tracey)*

*He will bullet point a few thoughts under each heading so that we can reflect on them next time we meet. This helps me to think how I am progressing in those areas of development. We both enable each other to see things in a different way. The key thing is that he makes me see things in a different way (Adrian)*

Interestingly, one protégé also described the relationship with his mentor as mutually beneficial:

*I now say things to Tom that other people might not say to him, and that might be different to what he hears from his board or from the people he communicates with on a daily basis. I hope he's also getting something out of this. I want him to go away thinking that he's also had to think about some things. I try to make sure that I give him something to stimulate him and make him think (Adrian)*

Those who did not find the mentoring process beneficial attributed it to a loss of trust, lack of clear objectives and process, time pressures, and an overly remote mentor.

Loss of trust:

*I don't think it's brilliant, we've met three times and during that period I nearly swapped jobs and nearly worked for him. I applied to run the business in Australia. I thought I was going to get the job. I talked to my mentor quite enthusiastically about going to Australia and he talked about how to tackle that challenge and I found that constructive. But when it became clear that it wasn't what the company wanted me to do, and he said to me oh I didn't really see what was in it for you in Australia, I was a bit confused. I was a bit disappointed because I thought if you were my mentor why didn't you tell me that when I was enthusiastic about it, there's no point telling me now. So I lost a lot of trust there. It wasn't honest enough (David)*

Lack of clear objectives and process:

*I was unclear about how the process was supposed to work and I think my mentor was unclear also. If I had the opportunity to reshape it, I would be looking at an open agenda driven by things you want to discuss, in an open and honest manner and to be challenged about them (David)*

*I'd say on balance that it's not working very well. There's not much of a process, we agreed to meet before the live case and we did that. We haven't met before this next one, so it's fallen down. I'm not sure why it's not working. It's not because he's not interested, he is, he's been really good. Neither of us is used to it, there doesn't seem to be the bond, maybe the objectives have just not been laid out clearly. I think it needs clarity of responsibility to make it happen (Fraser)*

Time pressures:

*I haven't really used the mentoring opportunity to best effect, purely because I am currently working on a launch project and I am really struggling with time, it's one of those vicious circle situations. Chris has been chasing me to meet up with me and I have had to postpone meetings. I need to spend more time with Chris. I'd prefer to have my direct boss as my mentor, I know that's not the situation with most people as they would like a different view, but I think I'd find it more useful in terms of my own development, you're able to go to someone who actually knows and understands what you're working on and the challenges (Louise)*

Overly remote mentor:

*I did feel sorry for the guys when I saw who their mentors were, I was thinking they're never going to see them. These are guys way up the food chain (Mark)*

*It didn't work very well for me. My mentor is Alan, the new chairman. He's slightly older than the other mentors would be, slightly more old fashioned. He tries to talk open and candidly, but I think in his 17 years as chief executive and as chair of three boards, he's not an individual who is about bringing on people, he expects a certain level of ability, he's almost avuncular. He exists in a different world. He's interested in the way an uncle would be, but I don't think he's ever worked on the personal development side. I do realize that other people will be getting more personal development stuff out of it than I'm getting (Dan)*

These observations on the limitations of a formal mentoring process are fully consistent with the points of view in the Chapter 5 section *Formal versus informal mentoring processes*, and are also suggestive of the need to develop mentors into their mentoring roles.

**Networking**

Lastly, despite the professed learning goal of working with and learning from peers cited earlier, networking in reality appeared to offer a modest "task benefit", but no developmental benefit for Circle participants.

*I feel that if I had a particular issue within my business right now, I could go and discuss it with pretty much anyone on that course. I've used it from a business point of view, I've been thinking about acquisitions within my business, I've been able to go and talk to Lucy so there are some doors that have been opened (Adrian)*

*In such a pressured environment the opportunity to work that network on a day to day basis isn't there, but over time when I work with those people, having had this experience first will make that work better then (David)*

*I don't think anything has happened yet, so I haven't had any specific outcome in terms of the business I'm in. Working with another part of the business, that would be a fantastic outcome to achieve (Louise)*

*On the Circle group itself I feel at a slight disadvantage in being able to network with those people because everyone but me is in London, I'm in Manchester (Tracey)*

It may be speculated that Circle participants did not value networking with peers from within the same organization. This could be because the peers represented a similar set of organizational backgrounds and experiences, and therefore engaging with them lacked novelty and developmental value.

### Mapping learning processes with abilities

One of the explicit research goals in the Circle was to attempt to link previously observed learning processes with previously defined strategic leader abilities. In order to do this, participants were given a brief description of the four abilities during the interview, and were asked if any of the four learning processes they had experienced during the Circle had contributed to the development of any ability. Participants were allowed to make more than one co-relation for an ability.

Table 6.1 summarizes the frequency of responses in which a positive co-relation was made:

**Table 6.1** A Map of Learning Processes and Abilities

| | Workshop | Stretch Assignment | Mentoring | Networking | Total |
|---|---|---|---|---|---|
| **Strategic conversation** | 8 | 6 | 2 | 0 | 16 |
| **Contextual mastery** | 2 | 4 | 5 | 5 | 18 |
| **Behavioural complexity** | 2 | 0 | 2 | 1 | 5 |
| **Judgement** | 3 | 8 | 3 | 1 | 15 |
| **Total** | 15 | 18 | 12 | 7 | |

This data may be interpreted as follows:

The workshop at the commencement of the intervention, which was a formal learning process that offered participants tools and techniques for strategy development and execution, was reportedly most effective at developing their ability to conduct a strategic conversation. The stretch assignment, which offered participants an opportunity to practice this ability, was the second most useful development process for the strategic conversation.

Mentoring and networking with peers were the primary sources of improving understanding of the industry and organizational context. Given that the stretch assignments offered in-depth exposure to a range of business units within the organization, these also contributed to contextual mastery.

Behavioural complexity was the ability that benefited least from the development processes offered by the Circle. This may be explained by the fact that this intervention was "content and task" rich with a limited requirement to lead, influence, or mobilize people. Additionally, given that all participants were from the same organization, albeit from different parts of it, the available set of individuals had limited diversity and a high degree of similarity in their world view.

The stretch case study, which by design simulated an environment of incomplete and conflicting information, was cited as most useful for the development and practice of judgement.

On the basis of the total number of positive co-relations made, the ability to conduct a strategic conversation and contextual understanding, based as they are on largely cognitive processes, appear to be the most amenable to development through conventional learning processes.

With two exceptions, all the learning processes contributed – even if only modestly – to all the abilities.

In terms of impact, the dominant learning processes in the Circle were the stretch assignment, the workshop, and mentoring. It may be noted that the "managed" mentoring process, although beneficial, delivered mixed results. Networking did not make an impact, except with regard to contextual understanding.

Given the small number of interviewees, all these co-relations should be viewed as tentative.

### Developmental outcomes

When asked how they had changed as a result of the Circle, a range of comments were offered by the participants. Some re-emphasized their previous observations made within the context of the different learning processes. In addition, three participants offered increased self-confidence as an "overall outcome", and some of these comments merit repetition:

> *It's made me more able to take on things that I don't 100% understand but that I can definitely add to (Darren)*

> *Every night we were doing something like this and having to turn it around quickly for the board to review and that is a fantastic stimulus for the brain and confidence in your own ability to do stuff at speed. Looking back it's reminded me that you can do it (Dan)*

> *It's done a lot for my development. It's allowed me to believe that you can do a lot in a very short period. Prior to the exercise, I'm not sure I would*

*have been sufficiently confident in my ability to sit down with those guys and work with them on how that investment could be improved (Fraser)*

## Intervention #2: The Top Leader Journey

The Top Leader Journey is an open enrolment senior executive development programme at Ashridge Business School. The programme targets recently appointed or potential chief executives, division directors, and heads of business units, who are therefore more senior than participants on the Circle. The programme is restricted to a maximum of 12 participants. The primary objective of the programme is to help participants develop their "capability for leadership at the highest level".

The Journey is run twice a year by two leadership development specialists based at the business school who have an extensive track record in this area. The design of the Journey at its launch in late 2005 was informed by this author's previous research on strategic leader capability and formative development processes, as well as some of the outcomes of the Circle intervention. Inevitably, however, a degree of interpretation by the Journey delivery team was involved. A brief over-view of how the various concepts were operationalized into the design of the intervention is provided in Table 6.2:

**Table 6.2** Operationalization of Concepts in Top Leader Journey Design

| Concept | Descriptor | Operationalization |
|---|---|---|
| **Judgement** | Synthesize conflicting goals and processes | Scenario development, courage, improvisation, working with ambiguity |
| **Context** | Manage challenges of interpretation and inertia | Systems thinking, challenging industry and organizational recipes, understanding current reality and desired state of the organization, and related actions |
| **Strategic conversation** | Make strategy in analytical and non-analytical ways using deliberate and emergent processes | Scenario development, co-creating a vision, frameworks for industry and market analysis, managing emergence and organizational learning |
| **Cognitive and behavioural complexity** | Complex and elastic repertoire of behaviours | Self-awareness, credibility, authenticity, resilience, communicating effectively |

The structure of the Journey is summarized in Figure 6.2:

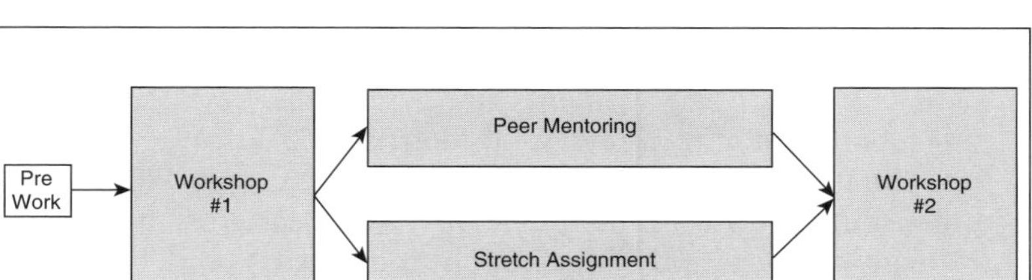


*Figure 6.2* The Top Leader Journey

The first rollout of the programme was used as the subject of this study. Twelve participants commenced the programme, but one subsequently withdrew due to reasons of ill-health. A profile of the participants is presented in Appendix 1(e).

All participants were required to complete a 360-degree feedback instrument in advance of the programme. In addition, all participants were interviewed before the commencement of the programme in order to gauge their learning expectations, to help the facilitators to understand the context each participant was coming from, to ensure that participants were of the appropriate level and that collectively they made up a good mix, and to put participants in a reflective frame of mind. In addition, they were asked to respond to a questionnaire designed to elicit the relevance of previously identified dimensions of strategic leader capability in their roles, as well as their self-perception of their effectiveness on each dimension. This questionnaire is displayed in Appendix 2(c).

Workshop #1 was a three-day residential event, and offered a mix of cognitive and behavioural learning, including:

1. A research presentation on strategic leader capability and the dominant patterns in development processes as reported by strategic leaders
2. An appreciation of different learning styles (Honey and Mumford, 2000), aimed at making individual learning preferences explicit, and identifying potential bottlenecks in the learning process, thereby improving the capacity of participants to learn
3. A discussion on ways and means of understanding and challenging industry and organization context, so as to begin the process of developing a strategically driven developmental and/or change agenda

4. Self-awareness through Executive Profilor, a 360-degree feedback instrument, followed up by a 1:1 session with an executive coach, resulting in enhanced self-insight. It may be noted that this instrument evaluates many elements relevant to this research, such as judgement, shaping strategy, leadership versatility, and cross functional and industry knowledge (which approximate the dimensions previously identified in this research as judgement, strategic conversation, behavioural complexity, and contextual mastery)
5. A discussion on the "mythology of leadership" and what authentic leaders "really do". In particular, this session focused on the contextual nature of leadership, the need to operate while facing high levels of ambiguity and uncertainty, and to learn how to manage your own anxieties and deploy yourself
6. An experiential learning session, working with actors, designed to take participants out of their comfort zone and to explore issues of their presence and impact, as well as their ability to improvise
7. Several opportunities for peer group networking, as well as structured critical reflection.

The first workshop was designed to disseminate and debate, as well as experience, ideas related to the constructs of context, behavioural complexity, and judgement, and their significance in the work of leaders.

Since mentoring could not be managed or orchestrated by the facilitators on an open enrolment programme, a "co-mentoring" or "peer mentoring" process was adopted at the end of the first workshop. Each participant was encouraged to support a fellow participant on the programme in achieving an outcome which the other person believed to be an improvement on where they were when they started the programme. Individuals were assigned into peer mentoring pairs by the facilitators, based on a subjective assessment of "fit", informed by data from available psychometrics.

Similarly, participants were encouraged to undertake a "self-selected" stretch assignment during the intervening two months between the workshops.

Participants also had the option of additional executive coaching sessions. Some exercised this option between modules; others did so during or after the second workshop.

The second workshop was also a residential event, but of two days duration. In addition to further reflection and networking, the second workshop focused on:

1. the construct of the strategic conversation, and in particular the development of scenarios to stretch participants' cognitive capabilities, and the construction and communication of a strategic vision
2. a discussion on ways and means of influencing, inspiring, empowering, and mobilizing others
3. participants' personal leadership agendas, and how they might lead in the future

In both workshops, an attempt was made to explore every issue from multiple perspectives. The facilitators followed a dialectical rather than an expert approach, and the workshops were immersive and intensive experiences that offered both challenge and support. The modular approach was intended to allow for internalization of the learning through its interaction with work experiences, and for a "working through" of competing interpretations and ideas.

Approximately two months after the conclusion of the programme i.e. four to five months after the first workshop, each participant was interviewed once again to explore their development outcomes as a result of the Journey. The time gap was deliberate as first impressions were not of interest, but considered and thoughtful observations were. The questionnaire that was used for this purpose is displayed in Appendix 2(d). In addition, Part 3 of the pre-programme questionnaire was administered once again to enable "before and after" comparisons.

*Learning goals*

Unlike the Circle, Journey participants did not have a task orientation, and did not aim to develop specific skill sets or broader business exposure. Rather, their learning goals were couched in terms of curiosity about other leaders, self-discovery, and a desire to seek reassurance and comfort. For example:

> *I was keen to learn what life was like for leaders in other sectors. I was also keen to learn about how other people saw me (Will)*

*I was really intrigued to meet people of similar age, background, and position. They were either new CEOs or hoped to be CEOs and they were going along that route and meet and find out what their concerns, their challenges were. To pick up any advice, tricks from peers (Gary)*

*I guess I was looking for some sort of benchmark for myself against other leaders, feeling more capable about dealing with the challenges in my career that were looming; to make new friends, a new network of people… not having had an academic background and leaving education quite early, I wanted to understand why some of the things which I naturally do, in terms of my judgement, the way my mind works, why that has been to date successful (John)*

*I was quite open minded… what I said at the time was that I wanted to learn what the difference was to go from just under the top level to the top level. At the time I suppose I was fairly open minded about what it might mean (Jon)*

*I was hoping to learn how to improve my leadership style – how to improve my leadership effectiveness (Ian)*

*To assess my leadership style, to learn what the different sorts of leadership style are, and what was most relevant. And to get some reference point as to the best way for me going forward for the company, how can I best lead the company (Robin)*

*I was hoping to learn characteristics of leadership roles that I would aspire to deliver, that I could mimic, and how I could keep myself motivated to keep learning and to develop (Mik)*

*I wanted to learn about the intellectual and practical characteristics of effective leaders (Edgar)*

*To get this leadership issue resolved, getting an understanding of how to live with it, and also to get an understanding as to whether I was the only one feeling like that, or whether it was a general feeling from everybody else in a leadership position (Stefan)*

*I wanted to know whether or not I wanted to progress any further in management and running a business, as opposed to being on the creative side of things (Martin)*

Despite these learning objectives, all participants scored themselves very highly on their self-assessment of strategic leader capability before the

Journey. These high self-attributed scores may be a function of "defensive routines" (Argyris and Schon, 1996) that is to say, they may reflect a tendency of people to present themselves in a positive light that improves their image. Wagner and Gooding (1997) observe that a self-serving bias can be explained by both motivational and informational origins. From a motivational perspective, self-serving attributions grow out of desires to create, in oneself and others, positive perceptions of one's actions and personal worth. From an informational perspective, self-serving bias originates in cognitive structures or mental maps that develop as repeatedly successful individuals grow accustomed to taking personal responsibility for occurrences of success.

As a result, the absolute scores participants awarded themselves are of little interest. However, it is interesting to note that when asked to repeat the exercise after the Journey, and without reference to their previous scores, there was evidence of a further improvement in the capability of participants as perceived by them. As a result, a tentative inference of a perception of a positive developmental experience was made.

Unlike the Circle, and due to the absence of a shared organizational context for the Journey, key learning processes such as the stretch assignment and peer mentoring were led by participants themselves, rather than by the facilitators. On the other hand, the executive coaching sessions injected a degree of structure into the reflective process. Collectively, this resulted in variations in commitment and outcomes, and different individuals appeared to benefit in different ways, with no clear pattern in the differential impact of the stretch, peer mentoring, and structured reflective processes.

Some typical comments in each case are given below:

**Stretch**

> *The in-between assignment that I took on was to structure my team and deal with some personnel issues that I had been sweeping under the carpet. I really just had to grab the nettle and with discussions with other people on the first module in October, very much coming out of that was to deal with the big business strategy and crisis management stuff, and get stuck into the people bits and that has paid dividends. It was a stretch because from my perspective it's not something that I would consider as my strength. I tend to be more strategic and analytical, rather than inter-personal. Some of the people things I tend to put off. But I'm pleased to say that I think I've learnt the lesson now and put it behind me, not just at that time but since then as well. I'm certainly prioritizing my day differently now (Mik)*

*I really wanted to do the thing for real. In the end I decided I was just making things up for the sake of it, I realized that where I am I'm doing things that are stretching all the time. My own job is quite stretching for me and I push myself quite hard in it and I do things out of my comfort zone, so I've certainly done things at work that are stretching, and quite courageous and difficult in conflict management situations with individuals. I do that on a regular basis, I try to front up to those things. I don't find them very comfortable. So I thought I'm doing that stuff, out of my comfort zone so I haven't done anything in particular that I wasn't going to do anyway (Will)*

**Peer mentoring**

*I did run past him some of my thoughts on some of the problems I had and there were a couple of staff issues that I'd been ducking, probably because I was a bit tired and I was thinking that they would resolve themselves. He looked me in the eye and said you know you really have to deal with these because it will just get worse. He was entirely right. Those aspects of saying you know what you have to do, why aren't you doing it, and challenging me, was very useful. That was very valuable in itself (Gary)*

*The advantage Gary has is that he's worked in a lot more companies than I have, he's been through a lot more situations. He was able to give me his views and recommendations, he challenged me and questioned my logic – not saying I would do it this way but questioning why are you doing this, what are you trying to achieve, do you think this is the best way, lots of open questions. But also drawing on his own experience and reflecting some of the good and bad things that he'd experienced (Paul)*

*You don't really have anyone in the organization that you can use as a sounding board. I see him as an independent sounding board, with no axe to grind, no agenda, no politics, just someone who was going to tell you straight as it was. It's hard to find someone in the organization that's going to be independent with the advice they're giving, because there's always so many objectives they've got (Ian)*

**Structured reflection**

*I've created time and space for myself. I was probably the sort of person who never had a plan to my life, no real structure, I now have a better understanding of exactly who I am and what I want to do, and that my whole life is not about work, and I think it makes you a much more rounded person with a better character if you do have stuff away from work (Ian)*

*We all charge around at 100 mph in this industry and never sit down to reflect, if you're reflecting you're reflecting by yourself, you're certainly not going to reflect with your work colleagues, that doesn't tend to happen unless you've got a very trusting relationship. Being able to reflect with similar minded people who are not a threat in terms of what they know about you, because they don't work in your company was very useful. The one thing it made me realize is that we had drawn similar conclusions, having taken time to reflect and discuss our similar situations with like minded people (Paul)*

*I have definitely benefited from it. I had my last coaching session yesterday. For me it's opened up a number of doors. I went into it with typical CEO arrogance, I know what's going on, I don't need anybody to train me. But for me it's turned out to be a great way of helping me to provide some of the answers to some of the questions I have, or frustrations I have in my leadership role. One big element is that you take time out of your schedule to reflect, you book that time, and you can't get around it. The coach facilitates the full process and brings it into shape (Stefan)*

*We talked about the 360 feedback, and that was a useful session for me. My coach, Michael made a good assessment of me and was able to ask me some interesting questions and pose questions of a type or in a way that I wouldn't, had he not done it. There was a degree of challenge in those questions. Also an element of support, almost more support than challenge, but equally valuable (Jon)*

### Networking

The one learning process that appeared to have had the most impact on participants was networking, from which participants appeared to take much comfort and reassurance, particularly from the idea that there were others like them, facing similar challenges, and that they "were not alone". These findings are consistent with the observations in Phase II regarding the developmental value of networking.

*I learnt a lot about other people's jobs in other sectors and that most of those jobs are very similar in some regards, irrespective of which sector you're in, in terms of the managerial and leadership challenges that you face (Will)*

*I learnt basically that others have similar problems, and this helped a lot in understanding better how I should do it. This was valuable because in my position you are not able to speak about these things and it showed me that people are in similar situations. It has shown to me how important it is to network with other people you can speak about it with, not just to rely on others to recognize how good you are (Edgar)*

*I found that I wasn't unique in the things that I had going on. That was good to know. Also that these were common things and it wasn't just yours truly that had these concerns. I found it quite liberating to realize that there were a lot of people in the same position. There aren't many peers that I have here that I can have that discussion with and be honest, so that was absolutely brilliant. I couldn't wait to come back for the second session – I was really looking forward to it (Gary)*

*A thing that I learnt which I enjoyed about the course enormously, is that if you want to develop as a leader it's not something you read in a book, but there's an enormous amount to be gained from just being able to talk to people who are on much the same sort of level. The world café was actually quite good, and I probably learned more about how to develop as a leader by observing others and having the chance to talk to them than I would have by trying to learn it in a purely academic context (Ian)*

*I came out feeling not only refreshed but emboldened as well. I realized that there are so many different sizes of organizations that being the leader of a small or medium sized organization is no different from being the leader of a big chunk of a larger organization. Meeting the other people there, most of whom were leaders of their organizations in a way that I'm not, I'm the leader of a chunk of an organization, but I felt there wasn't any difference. That was a nice thing to learn. All the attributes you need, all the things you need to learn, all the tools you need to master are the same (Jon)*

*I was concerned that I didn't want to go into the strictly managerial end of things. But I was pleasantly surprised, and I think why I didn't want to go into it was because I thought that I probably couldn't do it. I was pleasantly surprised to see that I probably could do it after all, and everybody on the whole course was in the same boat as me. Some were your more regular, orthodox kind of management people, and others were a bit more maverick like me. But we were all together and we were all going towards the same journey. Rubbing shoulders, and gleaning information from my fellow classmates was very useful and I made some good friends and listened to the way they ran their businesses and the problems they have and you realize that you're not alone (Martin)*

*Talking to other people on the course enabled me to understand that there isn't somebody out there of a calibre significantly different to me doing a similar job role (Paul)*

The theme of learning from each other was so strong that one could almost have concluded that the rest of Journey was of marginal value compared to these "chance encounters". However, as one of the participants acknowledged:

*As individuals we gelled, due to the climate and environment that you established, which I appreciate is part of the programme as well. One of the chaps, Martin, I think, said couldn't you just charge us fees and put us in a room like Big Brother and put us on an island and wouldn't we all have got the same value out of the course? I don't think we would have done (Gary)*

**Developmental outcomes**

It was when participants were asked to reflect on how they had changed as a result of the Journey (question 7 in Appendix 2(d)) that another significant pattern emerged.

Ten out of 11 participants reported feelings of increased self-confidence or self-belief on an unprompted basis:

*I've grown in confidence. I think, having used the opportunity to reflect, I am more decisive as a result of the course. It comes with being confident. I'm quicker to take decisions. When I look back to when I took on this job, I was unsure about it, and also I was working my way up from my peers, so I lacked a particularly decisive style, because I think it's quite difficult and discordant to suddenly start bashing out decisions when you've gone from being an essential part of the team. Some of the feedback I got from the 360 was that people wanted me to be a bit better on that, in knowing when to take a decision and when to say look we've had enough discussion, now this is what we're going to do. I think that now I am more confident about doing that (Will)*

*I'm so much more decisive in myself and firmer in where I'm coming from, and my grasp of the issues (Will)*

*I'm probably more strategic now, or I'm more comfortable in trying to articulate strategy and communicating it. I think I am more confident and in the past I thought there was a formula as to here's how you strategize. I think I came away realizing that this is something you learn from the heart, you have to have that passion inside you, you have to believe in it, it's not something that anyone else can do for you. The only answer you guys gave me was to really trust in my inner self and what I believed in and that passion burning inside me, and to ensure that I communicated this to the people who work for me (Ian)*

*Much more self-belief. I feel that the course put me in a room with 11 other guys in senior positions, worldwide, some of them running much larger businesses. I didn't feel out of my depth, I didn't feel my concerns and anxieties were unique, they were shared by everybody. It made me feel you've got what you've got and you can use that and still achieve the things you want to. It also made me realize that the things that aren't my strengths aren't necessarily going to be obstacles in achieving. The message from the course was you play to your strengths, be aware of your weaknesses; where you have weaknesses you can always utilize other people to reinforce those areas. You haven't got to be the perfect leader, you can't cover every aspect to the highest standard, and there's a team ethic here that you can utilize. It's made me think about my weaknesses and raise my view of my strengths (John)*

*I've realized that in principle I could be a topper leader than I am, whereas before hand I didn't know that. I might not have thought I could be. It made me think, I can do this, and I could do perhaps even more than I'm doing. I've got more confidence that the style I have anyway isn't a bad style, which before the course I wouldn't have necessarily known (Jon)*

*It's given me confidence outside my own business when I am with other business people. I learnt that I can make a difference, albeit a small difference. And if I can tell one or two different people here how to do things differently, come along with me we're all in this together, I could change the way this company progresses. It gave me confidence to go to board level and say we should be doing this or why aren't we doing that. It gave me confidence to question just where the company as a whole stood, what its values are and where it plans to go (Martin)*

*It's proved to me that I can do that stuff and it's not such a pain anyway. It's given me the confidence to do it again (Mik)*

*It's given me more confidence in myself. When I entered into it I was really delighted that I'd been offered this job, but I was acutely aware that I was lacking the formal qualifications, and wondered whether there were gaps in my abilities that I wasn't aware of and that people around me assumed I had. The course helped me realize that the amount of experience and good base of strategic knowledge which I have in the industry and the organization was sufficient to compensate for that lack of formal qualifications (Paul)*

*One of the big things in the Journey experience, it gave me the confidence to think "I can do this". It's a bit scary but the others are doing it too. Paul is now CEO, he's running it (Gary)*

*It made me think I had some courage, I'm not a wimp. That I actually do lead and my team do see me as a leader. It confirmed that, and I'm much more comfortable in the role of the leader. If we now go somewhere as a team the automatic propensity after the meeting of my team is that I'm the leader. I was before but now I'm comfortable with it, that's the difference. Being more comfortable with the constant nature of leadership is not draining any more (Robin)*

*I have become much more resilient. I realize that if something goes not exactly as I want it, then it's not necessarily because of my doing or not doing. As a leader, I realize I can't be superman, I need support from others, particularly outside my own remit. I've known that already, but it's just got clearer to me. It has resulted in resilience, self-confidence, and it's given me the additional learning and tools to move on in my career (Stefan)*

These findings echo those of Vicere (1988), who observes that formal development interventions enable cognitive learning, contribute to self-insight, broaden perspective, and increase confidence.

However, the findings also appear to be anomalous when viewed alongside the high scores participants awarded themselves on the self-assessment of their strategic leadership capability before the Journey. Possible explanations offered by the Journey facilitators are as follows:

*In the heroic leadership model, the heroes have to have all the answers. By the second workshop, we and they had legitimized "non-heroic" leadership. By unhooking themselves from the need to have all the answers, they were more able to deal with the ambiguities life has to offer, and this gave them more confidence (Albert)*

*I would say that participants had limited depth and perception of the complexity of the world they operated in, and they lacked the insight to understand some of the risks they faced or dangers they were in, nor did they have the language or the conceptual models with which to describe the reality they faced. Consequently, they judged their competence to be high against a set of limited scales. Many of them had evolved personal strategies, sometimes inappropriate ones, for coping with the toughness of the situations they were in. The Journey had the effect of deepening and broadening their perceptions. It meant they learned to see inside these coping mechanisms, and by the end of the first workshop, in the short-term, the self-assessment of their competence went down. However, as they began to question their behaviour patterns, and reviewed the way they applied their judgement, and became more thoughtful over the longer-term of the full programme, their reported competence and confidence increased (Phil)*

Based on the facilitators' insights, it may be conjectured that during the Journey, participants' perceptions of their competence in relation to the competence needed followed a trajectory displayed in Figure 6.3.

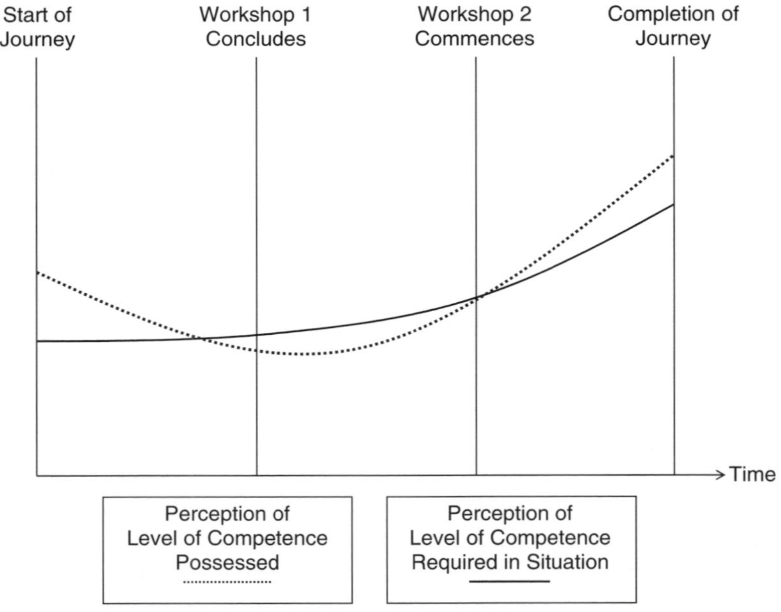


*Figure 6.3* Trajectory of Participants' Perceptions of Competence

It may be noted that this account of the participant experience is very similar to the "stages of competence" model popular within the training and management development community, in which learning is described as a transition from unconscious incompetence, through conscious incompetence and conscious competence, to the desired state of unconscious competence.

The large proportion of Circle and Journey participants (13 out of 19) who cited enhanced self-confidence as a primary developmental outcome in this study makes the significance of this phenomenon in leader development and effectiveness worthy of further scrutiny, and this task is undertaken in the next section.

## Self-confidence and self-efficacy

Although the power of self-confidence has long been a staple of sports psychology, Hollenbeck and Hall (2004) observe that self-confidence has been a neglected area in leadership because it is such a common sense concept that it has not been deemed to be worthy of study, and has been pursued in the self-help rather than academic literature. Self-confidence in leaders has been taken as a given, and it has been assumed that self-confident leaders are born not made.

The literature in this area is inconsistent and confusing. Although Hollenbeck and Hall (2004) use the term self-confidence interchangeably with self-efficacy, others make a distinction. Peterson and Arnn (2005) suggest that while self-confidence refers to an overall or general feeling of competence, self-efficacy is a more meaningful construct as it refers to perceived capabilities to act in a specific domain.

For the purpose of this study, and in an attempt to bridge the language of the practitioner with that of the academic, a decision has been made to take references to self-confidence in the narratives of the interviewees to mean "task specific self-confidence", and therefore synonymous with self-efficacy.

Self-efficacy may be defined as people's beliefs about their capacity to produce designated levels of performance that exercise influence over events that affect their lives (Bandura, 1994) or belief in one's capabilities to organize and execute the courses of action required to produce given attainments. Stajkovic and Luthans (1998) describe self-efficacy as an individual's convictions to mobilize the motivations, cognitive resources, and courses of action to successfully execute a specific task within a given context.

Self-efficacy beliefs determine how people feel, think, motivate themselves, and behave (Bandura, 1994) and the construct is therefore closely related to the dimensions of strategic leader capability identified in previous research in this study.

According to Bandura's seminal work (1997), people with high self-efficacy approach difficult tasks as challenges to be mastered, rather than as threats to be avoided. They set themselves challenging goals and remain committed to them in the face of adversity. They persist, and heighten or sustain their efforts in the face of failure. They recover their sense of efficacy after setbacks, which they attribute to a lack of adequate effort or deficient skills that need to be developed. Such a world-view supports personal accomplishments, and reduces stress. By contrast, people with low self-efficacy have low aspirations, and are reluctant to take on difficult tasks. They demonstrate weak commitment to goals, and are likely to abandon them if achievement proves difficult. They attribute unsatisfactory performance to deficiencies in their own aptitude. As a result, it does not require much failure for them to lose faith in their capabilities, and they may suffer from stress and depression.

### The role of self-efficacy

Bandura (1997) suggests that self-efficacy affects the thoughts, feelings, and actions of individuals in four ways:

1. *Selection Processes*: self-efficacy can shape the course of people's lives by influencing the types of activities and environments they choose. Through their choices, people cultivate different competencies, interests, and social networks. People avoid tasks where their self-efficacy is low, but engage in tasks where their self-efficacy is high. People with a self-efficacy significantly beyond their abilities overestimate their ability to complete tasks, and this can be very damaging. On the other hand, people with a self-efficacy significantly lower than their ability are unlikely to grow and expand their skills. The optimum level of self-efficacy is therefore a little above ability, and this encourages people to tackle challenging tasks and gain valuable experience.
2. *Motivational Processes*: self-efficacy plays a crucial role in the self-regulation of motivation. People with high self-efficacy in a task are likely to invest more effort, and persist longer than those with low self-efficacy. Self-efficacy also influences causal attributions, that is to say, high self-efficacy results in attribution of failures to insufficient effort, and low self-efficacy results in attribution of failures to low ability.

3. *Cognitive Processes:* low self-efficacy can lead people to believe that tasks are harder than they actually are. Since most action is initially organized in thought, this can result in poor task planning. People's beliefs in their efficacy influence the types of scenarios they construct and rehearse. Individuals with high self-efficacy anticipate and visualize success scenarios that provide a positive impetus for performance.
4. *Emotional Processes*: people's beliefs in their coping capabilities affect how much stress and depression they experience in threatening or difficult situations. People who believe they can exercise control over threats do not conjure up disturbing images and scenarios. By contrast, those who believe they cannot manage threats experience a high level of anxiety that is self-induced. They magnify the likelihood and severity of possible threats and worry about unlikely events and outcomes – this in turn distresses them and further impairs their level of functioning.

Not surprisingly, given the significant impact of self-efficacy on performance, a number of interesting connections between self-efficacy and leadership have been made.

### Self-efficacy and leader performance

Several studies have emphasized the parallels between leadership and self-efficacy. Podsakoff et al (1990) contend that leaders influence followers by role modelling appropriate behaviours. Followers identify with role models who are seen in a positive light, and this empowers them to achieve the leader's vision through the development of self-efficacy and self-confidence. Eden (1992) argues that leadership is a process primarily concerned with enhancing self-efficacy, in order to increase performance. In a similar vein, House and Shamir (1993) suggest that the primary motivational mechanism through which leaders influence their followers is by enhancing followers' self-efficacy and sense of self-worth. A study by Redmond et al (1993) observes that leader behaviour aimed at increasing follower self-efficacy results in higher levels of subordinate creativity in problem-solving situations.

Paglis and Green (2002) suggest that perceptions of leadership self-efficacy are an important source of a leader's motivation for taking on the difficult task of attempting change initiatives at work. Leadership self-efficacy is a person's judgement that he or she can successfully exert leadership by setting a direction and goals for the work group, building relationships with followers in order to gain their commitment, and working with them to overcome obstacles in the achievement of the agreed goals. Managers with high leadership self-efficacy therefore take on more leadership roles.

There are many reasons why a leader needs self-efficacy, assert Kirkpatrick and Locke (1991). A person riddled with self-doubt would never be able to take the necessary actions that leadership requires, or command the respect of others. Self-efficacy plays an important role in decision-making and gaining the trust of others. Not only is a leader's self-efficacy important, so too is others' perceptions of it. Leaders with high self-efficacy are more likely to be assertive and decisive, which gains others' confidence in the decision. Even if the decision is poor, such a leader admits the mistake and uses it as a learning opportunity, often building trust in the process.

Popper (2005) and Smith and Foti (1998) argue that one of the principal psychological components relevant to a leader's influence on people is self-confidence, or in more empirical terms, self-efficacy in influencing people. Research on followers' perceptions of their leaders has determined that the self-confidence attributed to the leader is a key variable in the positive evaluation of the leader. Popper (2005) concludes that self-efficacy in leadership, that is to say, a belief in one's ability to lead, is a major condition for the behaviours of a transformational leader.

## Self-efficacy and leader development

Task specific self-confidence and self-efficacy are individual perceptions, and therefore, judgements. Like any other judgement it can be accurate or inaccurate, influenced by how well the individual makes judgements, the accuracy of the data on which the judgements are based, the data that is selected for consideration, and how it is processed (Hollenbeck and Hall, 2004). As a result, self-confidence and self-efficacy can be changed by changing the perceptions of either the individual's capabilities, or of the task at hand.

Based on the work of Bandura (1994, 1997) and Hollenbeck and Hall (2004), it may be concluded that there are four primary sources of self-efficacy. These are:

1. *Experience:* having done it before, and succeeded, is the most powerful way to build self-efficacy. Successes build a robust belief in one's personal efficacy. A resilient sense of efficacy requires experience in overcoming obstacles through sustained effort. Setbacks and difficulties serve a useful purpose in teaching that success usually requires per-

severance. The experiences that are most valuable for this purpose are mastery experiences that are challenging, that stretch the individual's capability, while still providing a reasonable chance of success. Equally, through the slow aggregation of experiences, leaders may have done more of it than they realize, and critical reflection and sense-making can help to re-evaluate capability, or recall capability that may have been applied in a different setting or task. It may thus be possible to cobble together "successful experiences" from the diverse background that leaders bring to a task.

2. *Modelling*: it is simply not practicable for leaders to have experience in everything they do. Modelling, or vicarious learning based on the successes and failures of others, can show leaders what works and what doesn't. Formal educational settings lend themselves well to such social comparison, and such environments also enhance individual abilities in the form of new knowledge and skills gained. Models are especially important in learning interpersonal skills, and they may also provide inspiration. Seeing others like themselves succeed, leaders can come to believe that they too can succeed. The greater the perceived similarities between the model and the individual, the more persuasive the model's successes and failures. Models provide a social standard against which to judge or benchmark one's own capabilities. People seek out proficient models who possess the competencies to which they aspire. Through their behaviour and ways of thinking, competent models transmit knowledge and teach observers effective skills and strategies for leading and managing. It may be noted that mentors provide many of these developmental functions.
3. *Social Persuasion*: the encouragements or discouragements we receive from others have an important impact on our self-efficacy. Many leaders report accounts of a boss or colleague or mentor who believed in them, when they themselves were feeling unsure and uncertain. People who are persuaded verbally that they have what it takes to succeed are likely to mobilize greater effort and sustain it than if they harbour self-doubt and dwell on personal deficiencies. It may be noted that it is more difficult to instil self-efficacy through social persuasion than it is to undermine it. Malone (2001) makes links between the development of self-efficacy and coaching and suggests that many aspects of coaching facilitate the development of self-efficacy. Successful efficacy builders – such as effective mentors – do more than convey positive feedback and appraisals. They proactively construct situations in ways that increase the likelihood of success and avoid placing

people in situations for which they are significantly under-prepared, and in which they are likely to fail.

4. *Emotional Conditions*: how people feel about events around them, and their mood, affects their judgement of their personal efficacy. A positive mood strengthens self-efficacy; a despondent mood weakens it. Once again, critical reflection plays an important role in enabling the individual to make correct causal attributions between abilities and events, and therefore the evaluation of their self-efficacy. As Gundlach et al (2003) point out, causal attributions can have a significant impact on efficacy assessments, and how individuals identify the causes of their successes and failures affects the development of their self-efficacy beliefs and their mood. Excessive self-confidence can impede learning, and reflection may foster some of the humility that is required to stay in learning mode (Spreitzer, 2006). There are also other circumstances e.g. escalation situations (Chakravarthy and White, 2002) in which high self-efficacy may be dysfunctional if it is not tempered by adequate and appropriate reflection.

It may be noted that there is a close alignment between the drivers of self-efficacy development and the integrated model of development processes presented earlier. Clearly, positive self-efficacy assessments are, by themselves, inadequate. Individuals also need to continue to develop their capability. What is interesting, however, is the link between self-efficacy and the development of capability.

While managers may learn from experience, Densten and Gray (2001) argue that experience is more than just a stream of events, and involves the perceptions of events. By selectively attending to particular situations, leaders actively shape and construct their experiences. These selections and choices are influenced by individual expectations, prior experience, feelings, needs, and self-efficacy beliefs.

Hollenbeck and Hall (2004) suggest that self-confidence develops in self-reinforcing positive cycles. As people succeed in achieving a goal, they become more confident in their abilities, and set higher goals, and with success gain more self-confidence leading to a higher level of aspiration. Akin (1987) suggests that when managers have had a significant learning experience, in general, they sense "I can do it". The increased self-confidence also results in seeing oneself as a skilled learner who knows how to gain new knowledge and competencies, and this in turn paves the way for further learning. Davies and Easterby-Smith (1984) observe that an important result of development is far more confidence in dealing with new challenges, and that self-confidence is both a cause and effect of development. In other words, success in mastery experiences results in increased self-efficacy, and this in turn results in a willingness to engage with greater mastery experiences: a virtuous circle of leader development, as shown in Figure 6.4:

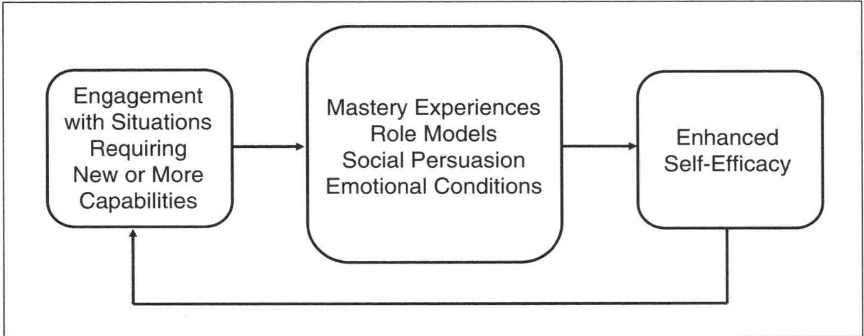


*Figure 6.4* Self-Efficacy as a Variable in Leader Development

Based on this discussion, it may be asserted that self-efficacy is an important mediating variable in both leader performance and leader development. In summary, the significance of self-efficacy is that it influences how capabilities are deployed, thereby impacting leader performance. Performance successes give rise to increased self-efficacy; which also feeds back into the challenges and experiences leaders engage with, thereby building more capability. This "multiplier effect" suggests that an explicit focus on the development of self-efficacy should be an integral part of leader development interventions.

# 7 Making Strategic Leaders: Some Reflections

## Towards a new synthesis

It is generally recognized that superior managerial skills that are rare and difficult to imitate are a valuable potential source of sustainable competitive advantage (Castanias and Helfat, 1991; Hart and Banbury, 1994). In particular, it has long been argued that strategic leaders – who by virtue of their roles make an organization-wide impact, and shape, orchestrate, or facilitate both the short-term and long-term future of the organization – make a vital contribution to organizational success or failure (Ireland and Hitt, 1999). Within a business context, it has been suggested that being able to exercise strategic leadership in a competitively superior manner facilitates the firm's efforts to earn superior returns on its investment (Rowe, 2001).

Strategic leader roles, which are characterized by a broad perspective as well as power and influence, are most commonly found at the apex of the organization or business. The ability to improve strategic leadership requires an understanding of the nature of strategic leader capability, and how it might be developed and deployed most effectively.

This study was motivated by a developmental perspective, and in particular, by the mounting concern about the doubtful returns from increasing investment in formal development interventions in the areas of strategy and leadership. In this debate, which continues to be contemporary, the abilities that such interventions focus on, as well as the learning designs that underpin them, have both been subject to critical scrutiny, with adverse conclusions often being drawn.

Within this context, this research has focused on three key questions:

- What are the dimensions of strategic leader capability?
- How is strategic leader capability acquired or developed?
- Can the influential development processes observed be deliberately managed, and if so with what effects?

Phase I identified key dimensions of the strategic capability of individuals. Phase II enriched our understanding of these dimensions, and surfaced several seemingly disparate learning processes influential in the development of strategic leaders.

Engagement with theory in Phase III has resulted in a synthesis of these processes into an integrated framework, which suggests that mastery experiences, supportive developmental relationships, and critical reflection should be at the core of leader development efforts.

The Circle and Journey interventions suggest that while some of these processes, for example, stretch assignments (one form of mastery experience), can be partially simulated to good effect, others, such as mentoring, are more challenging to replicate effectively as a managed process in a formal development intervention, and need careful attention to potential limitations.

Although it would be rash to suggest that formal interventions can be made to substitute for the profound and enduring development that is forged by experience, it may be argued that at the very least, formal development interventions that model reality can play a valuable contributory role. In addition formal interventions are also clearly beneficial for cognitive learning; for example around the process of strategy-making, or understanding an industry or organizational context. Formal interventions can also offer valuable opportunities for critical reflection and for learning from peers.

As far as developmental outcomes are concerned, whether from informal or formal processes, this research has suggested that these can manifest themselves in terms of enhanced task specific self-confidence or self-efficacy.

This study has also served to highlight the significant effect of self-efficacy in leader development and performance.

The leader development industry is currently burgeoning because of the perceived inefficiencies of learning on the job. Ironically, this study suggests that what is needed, in fact, is a willingness and ability to embrace the natural and informal learning that are a feature of the lives of all managers, and re-define the role and contribution of the leader development industry towards supporting the development processes that really work, and developmental outcomes that really matter. These issues, and the implications for the leader development industry, are a useful basis for the development of a new framework.

A discussion of the key findings from this study in relation to the *Dimensions of strategic leader capability*, the *Development of strategic leader capability*, and the *Deployment of strategic leader capability* are presented here in the next three sections. In the process, an attempt has been made to weave different strands of the narrative so far into a coherent whole, by taking an imaginative and creative look at the findings. *A theoretical overview* then offers a new and integrative framework, with a following section which explores the *Implications for practice*. Finally, an overview of this study's contribution to theory and practice, as well as some of its limitations and possibilities for further inquiry are presented in the concluding section titled *Further research: A springboard.*

## Findings: The dimensions of strategic leader capability

With the objective of developing a comprehensive and coherent understanding of the nature of strategic leader capability, a critical review of multi-disciplinary streams of literature such as strategic management, strategic leadership, organization theory, and cognitive and behavioural psychology was undertaken in Phase I. This resulted in the premise that strategic thinking, and acting strategically, is at the heart of strategic leader capability, which is a "gestalt" and is fundamentally concerned with both establishing organizational direction and leading change. Four dimensions of strategic leader capability identified at this stage were further enriched and refined through empirical work in the first phase of Phase II. The principal ideas that underpin these dimensions are:

- Much of the work of leaders is characterized by paradoxical demands, and apparently contradictory goals and processes. Making sensible decisions in the face of these requires the exercise of judgement.
- The process of shaping the organization's direction may be visualized as both a literal conversation with people and a metaphorical conversation with events. The ability to conduct a strategic conversation requires fluency with deliberate and emergent processes as well as the ability to synthesize analysis, creativity, and learning.
- All strategy and leadership is contextual. Context influences what is considered strategic, the nature of the strategic conversation, and the appropriate strategic leader style and behaviour. Each context offers an interpretive challenge, which is to do with which issues are recognized as strategic, and how they are framed and responded to; as well as an inertial challenge, which is to do with ways and means of moving forward effectively, when necessary, from the status quo. Leaders must not only understand the context and know how to get things done within it, but they must also challenge existing frames of reference and challenge the context when appropriate – in other words, they must possess contextual mastery.

- Given the complexity of organizations and markets, and the fact that strategies and behaviours effective in one situation may not work in another, or that methods that served their purpose yesterday may not be effective today, effective leaders must be able to think and act in an elastic and multi-dimensional manner. In order to mobilize people and orchestrate action, strategic leaders must have behavioural complexity, that is to say they must have a wide repertoire of behaviours, be able to discern what is appropriate and when, and engage with people and situations accordingly.

These ideas are summarized in Table 7.1.

**Table 7.1** Overview of Strategic Leader Capability

| Dimension | Underlying Rationale | Ability |
|---|---|---|
| Judgement | Paradoxes are endemic in the world of the leader<br><br>Paradoxes need to be tackled on a "both/and" basis, rather than an "either/or" basis | The ability to exercise judgement in order to balance conflicting goals and processes |
| Strategic Conversation | Strategic conversations are the process of sensing change, generating options, provoking ideas and innovation, shaping strategy, inspiring action, learning from what happens, and sharing that experience<br><br>Strategic conversations are the real or metaphorical interactions through which choices are made, tested, and the rationales underpinning them developed | The ability to synthesize strategy using analytical and non-analytical approaches in deliberate and emergent modes |
| Contextual Mastery | As a result of distinct configurations of internal and environmental factors, every organization represents a unique context<br><br>Each context offers both interpretive and inertial challenges | The ability to sense and interpret a unique context, as well as to challenge it when appropriate |
| Behavioural Complexity | Effective leaders are able to think and act in a cognitively and behaviourallycomplex manner by playing out multiple or even competing roles inan integrated and complementary manner | The ability to mobilize people based on a complex repertoire of behaviours |

These dimensions are inter-linked, and taken together (and adjusted in light of the empirical findings of Phase II), they yield the adjusted conceptual framework displayed in Figure 7.1:

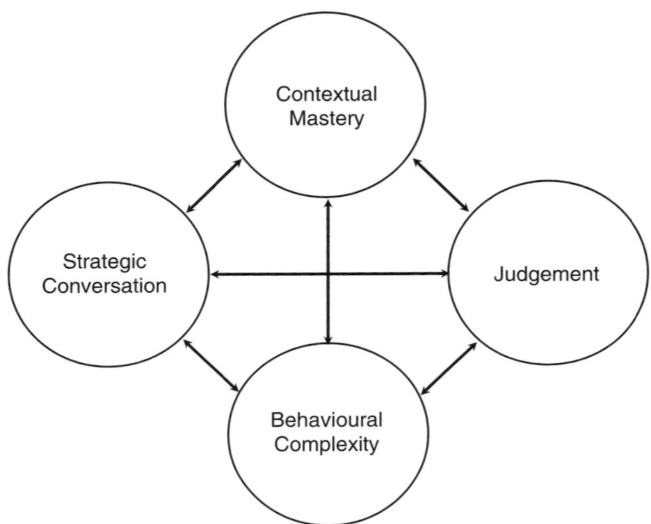


*Figure 7.1* Strategic Leader Capability: Empirically Adjusted Framework

Although this research did not purposefully seek out to establish such a pattern, it may be noted that this framework combines what are commonly described as the "hard" aspects of strategic leadership (strategy, context) and the "soft" aspects (judgement, behaviour).

This framework represents a theoretical contribution to the domain of strategic leadership in a number of ways.

Firstly, it offers a perspective on the implications of the realities of the strategic process for the individual in a strategic leader role. The framework acknowledges the diversity of strategic process archetypes – typically studied at an organizational level – offered by scholars such as Mintzberg (1978), Hart (1992), Mintzberg and Lampel (1999), Moncrieff (1999), Liedtka and Rosenblum (1996), and Cummings and Wilson (2003), and distils these into the individual's ability to conduct a strategic conversation.

Secondly, by focusing on the interpretive and inertial challenges, the framework builds on the work of Bower (1970), Mintzberg (1981),

Burgelman (1983b), Johnson (1988), and Daft and Weick (1984), and highlights the implications of context for the actions and behaviours of the individual, and the need for contextual mastery.

Thirdly, the framework assimilates the competing pulls and pressures that leaders face, as identified by Quinn (1988), Quinn et al (1996), and Pascale (1990, 1999), and crystallizes these into the need for judgement as an individual capability.

Fourthly, the framework incorporates the construct of behavioural complexity offered by Goleman (2000), Hooijberg and Quinn (1992), and Vilkinas and Cartan (2001) as an integrator of the wide range of ways of thinking and acting that strategic leaders need.

Finally, by integrating dimensions of strategy and leadership, which are all too frequently examined in isolation from each other, the framework offers a degree of comprehensiveness higher than that previously available. The framework offers new relationships between these dimensions, and also has a potential diagnostic value. Indeed, it can be suggested that the dimensions displayed in the framework influence and reinforce each other, resulting in six possible linkages:

- Effective strategic conversations facilitate the exercise of judgement, and the outcomes of judgement represent strategic learning that will influence the strategic conversation
- High behavioural complexity will result in a more meaningful strategic conversation, and the cumulative experience of diverse and numerous strategic conversations will enhance the behavioural complexity of the individual
- High behavioural complexity will result in a greater ability to exercise judgement, and the practice of judgement will in turn enhance behavioural complexity
- Contextual mastery helps clarify and determine the nature of the judgement to be made, and the outcome of the judgement will reinforce or reshape the individual's contextual mastery
- The nature of the strategic conversation is greatly influenced by the contextual mastery of the individual, in that this will determine what issues are considered strategic, and the process by which they are dealt with. Equally, a robust strategic conversation that challenges widely held mental models in the organization may result in a re-framing of context, and therefore enhanced contextual mastery
- Lastly, behavioural complexity enables working through the inertial and interpretive challenges embedded in a unique context, and therefore enhances contextual mastery. At the same time, contextual

mastery aids discernment of what is appropriate within that context, and therefore facilitates effective deployment of behavioural complexity.

It may also be apparent that the configuration or "mix" of the dimensions of capability is contextually bounded. The empirical findings from Phase II indicate that not all dimensions have the same salience for strategic leaders across various contexts, but this research has not established the degree to which each dimension must be present. Instead, a working assumption has been adopted in this research that strategic leader capability requires mastery on all four dimensions. Given that capability varies across individuals, and that capability may evolve over time, it is likely that gaps in capability will exist. Such gaps in capability have implications for practice, as well as interesting possibilities for further research, and these issues will be re-visited later in this chapter.

## Findings: The development of strategic leader capability

Having suggested what might be regarded as the dimensions of strategic leader capability, Phase II turned to the influential development processes recounted by individuals in strategic leader roles. A dominant pattern around informal learning – defined as unconscious, unplanned, and often unintended development that unfolded mostly on the job or in workplace settings – was identified.

Most of the informants in this research had also experienced formal learning i.e. learning that was planned, purposeful, and structured. The action research in Phase III provided further insights into formal learning.

Phase II revealed that both informal and formal learning modes have distinctive characteristics, and strengths and weaknesses. Informal learning is real, "sticky", immediately relevant to the individual's context, and has low direct costs. On the other hand it is haphazard, and the learning may remain tacit and variable across a group of individuals. By contrast, formal learning offers a more consistent experience across individuals, and is amenable to customization to the situation and to the individual. It is particularly suitable for cognitive learning. The principal disadvantages of formal learning lie in the direct and indirect costs involved and the potential for low relevance to the workplace context, as well as in the fact that some abilities and skills, while "learnable", may simply not be "teachable". Both informal and formal learning may be impeded or enhanced by the individual's preferred learning style.

These issues are summarized in Table 7.2.

**Table 7.2** Comparing Informal and Formal Learning Modes

| Mode | Characteristics | Strengths | Weaknesses |
|---|---|---|---|
| Informal Learning | • Results from natural opportunities in everyday life<br>• Often unintended or a by-product of a different activity<br>• May be an unconscious process | • Real and direct learning, owned by the individual<br>• "Sticky" learning; lessons often learned the hard way<br>• May have high relevance to context, and likely to be better integrated with work<br>• Can be low cost, or even free | • Often haphazard and influenced by chance; process may be disorganized and inefficient<br>• Learning may remain tacit, and may not be recognized as learning<br>• Learning may be variable<br>• Learning may be slow and unpredictable<br>• Process may not fit preferred learning style of individual |
| Formal Learning | • Structured, often institutionally sponsored<br>• Deliberate attention to planning, delivery, and review of learning | • Particularly suitable for cognitive learning<br>• Curriculum can be customized<br>• Offers a shared or consistent learning experience across individuals | • May have limited relevance to workplace context<br>• Can be high cost<br>• Process may not fit preferred learning style of individual<br>• Some abilities and skills not "teachable" |

Within informal learning, all the informants in this research narrated accounts of maturity and growth through a slow but steady accumulation and distillation of on-the-job experiences. In addition, when asked to reflect on formative development experiences, two processes stood out as especially significant: mentors and other role models (or "people driven" learning) and stretch assignments (or "accelerated learning on the job" induced by the nature of the tasks at hand). Mentors provided psycho-social support, role modelling, and career development, whereas stretch assignments offered lessons in judgement, resilience, flexibility, and self-knowledge; all acquired through the "school of hard knocks".

Formal learning processes such as management development workshops were valued principally for the opportunity to reflect in a structured manner, and the chance to network with peers. In the action research phase of this study, in the Circle intervention which involved mid-level rather than senior executives, such a workshop was also found to be valuable for developing or enhancing technical competence. In the Journey intervention, executive coaching was also found to be beneficial in terms of encouraging reflection and enhancing self-knowledge.

Table 7.3 compares the benefits and limitations of each of the influential development processes under consideration.

Phase II offered an integrated view of the informal development processes, and this included some tentative but high-level relationships between some of the processes. The formal interventions undertaken in Phase III suggested that informal and formal learning can usefully complement each other. In addition, self-efficacy, or an individual's belief in his or her capability to act effectively in a given context (Bandura, 1994) may be another important outcome of development.

A synthesis of the development processes and their relationships that emerged from Phases II and III is presented in Figure 7.2.

This framework represents a theoretical contribution to the domain of strategic leader development.

Development processes have traditionally been studied on a standalone basis e.g. mentoring by Kram (1985), McCauley and Douglas (2004), Clutterbuck (2004), Burke (1984); and mastery experiences by Colley et al (2003), Chao et al (1992), McCall (1988), Davies and Easterby-Smith (1984), Snell (1989, 1992), Stumpf (1989), and Bennis and Thomas (2002). This framework brings these seemingly disparate processes together and offers increased clarity regarding the relationships between them.

The framework also highlights the complementary nature of formal and informal learning modes, and the role of formal learning in promoting developmental relationships and critical reflection, linkages hitherto not prominent in the literature.

In addition, the framework builds on the work on critical reflection by Argyris (1993), Densten and Gray (2001), Smith (2001), Schon (1987), and Weick et al (2005), and positions this construct as an important mediator of the influential learning processes.

**Table 7.3** Comparing the Influential Development Processes

| Process | Description | Benefits | Limitations |
|---|---|---|---|
| Stretch | Confrontation with a high-stakes novel situation and hardship, for which current capabilities are inadequate | • Accelerated learning in areas of self-knowledge, flexibility, resilience<br>• Promotes deep reflection and questioning of assumptions<br>• Hones judgement | • Potential high cost of failure<br>• Variable learning<br>• Over-stretch can be damaging<br>• Requires time and appropriate opportunity |
| Mentoring | Inter-personal engagement in which an experienced individual acts as advisor to another | • Psycho-social support, role modelling, and career development<br>• Safe environment to test ideas and issues<br>• Personal, long-term bonds<br>• Can benefit mentor as well | • Requires mentor time and access<br>• Can be paternalistic, may result in dependence, or envy<br>• Benefits hard to replicate in an "organizationally controlled" setting |
| Peer Networks | Sharing experiences and insights with peers | • Personal "benchmarking" and reassurance<br>• Learning about and from different contexts, and vicarious learning | • Ad hoc and unstructured |
| Critical Reflection | Ongoing process of critiquing experiences, assumptions, and ways of thinking and acting | • "Sense-making" of experience<br>• Identification of new possibilities | • Requires open-mindedness, and frequently, support and feedback e.g. executive coach |
| Formal Training | Usually classroom or workshop based, often serves as "shell" for range of pedagogic practices | • Efficient for knowledge transfer and aiding understanding<br>• Can stimulate and energize<br>• Can provide structured networking and facilitate critical reflection<br>• Provides a safe environment for learning | • "Release" from "day job" required<br>• Learning transfer may be problematic |

Lastly, although most scholars have focused on the relationship between development and capability, the framework explicitly incorporates the idea that development also has an impact on self-efficacy (Bandura, 1994).

The framework in Figure 7.2 may be interpreted as follows:

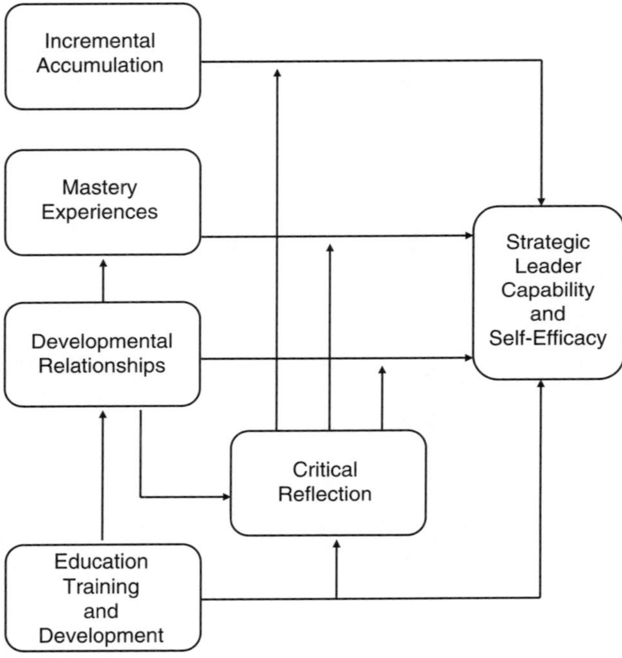


*Figure 7.2* The Development of Capability and Self-Efficacy: An Integrated View

Development may be seen as occurring through informal learning and formal learning, and aspects of strategic leader capability and self-efficacy may be acquired through either or both modes.

Informal learning as a category includes a slow and incremental accumulation of experience, with intense stretch or mastery experiences, and developmental relationships with mentors, other role models, and peers. Mentors often provide protégés with mastery experiences, as well as providing support when protégés try to cope with challenge and hardship. Mentoring may also be deliberately managed as part of a formal development intervention.

Formal learning – such as education and training and development – is valuable for the acquisition of teachable skills and cognitive aspects of strategic leader capability such as strategic analysis, resulting in an enhanced contextual understanding of the industry, market, or organization. In addition, formal learning can deepen self-awareness and knowledge of one's impact on others, through feedback and critical reflection. Formal learning also provides an opportunity to network with and learn vicariously from peers, and to build developmental relationships with them.

Critical reflection enhances the impact of developmental relationships, mastery experiences, and incremental accumulation of learning by making the implicit learning explicit, converting it into "actionable knowledge", and enabling the individual to leverage it. Facilitating critical reflection is a commonly observed facet of the mentoring process. Critical reflection can also be provided by formal learning experiences (aided, for instance, by an executive coach).

In general, the learning processes appear to be "osmotic" in their effect. In other words, they are characterized by unconscious absorption and assimilation, and it is difficult to co-relate a specific learning process with the acquisition of a specific ability with certainty.

However, by taking advantage of the tentative linkages between learning processes and abilities identified in Phase III, it may be conjectured that the following relationships are plausible:

1. Stretch assignments, which require individuals to cope with incomplete, ambiguous, and conflicting information in a high-stakes setting, appear to be particularly potent in terms of developing judgement.
2. Given that mentors are usually senior and more experienced figures within an organization, mentoring has a positive impact on the development of contextual mastery of the individual. Networking with peers from within the same organization improves understanding of the context, whereas relationships with peers from other organizations offer a window into other contexts, which may further assist in the appraisal of the focal organization. As a result, both types of networks can contribute to contextual mastery. Formal learning can also contribute to contextual mastery by equipping individuals with sense-making frameworks.

3. The ability to conduct a strategic conversation may benefit, in particular, from stretch assignments and the experience of being in unfamiliar situations in which pre-conceived structures and plans may break down, as well as from formal learning about tools and techniques.
4. Positive and negative role models in an individual's set of developmental relationships may enhance behavioural complexity. Stretch and mastery experiences that require the individual to act flexibly and adaptively in order to get things done in settings where previously successful coping strategies are unlikely to work, are also likely to contribute to behavioural complexity. Lastly, accurate feedback aimed at increasing the individual's self-knowledge (often provided by mentors or formal learning), and a safe environment in which to discover and practise new behaviours (a potential advantage of formal learning) is also likely to contribute to the development of behavioural complexity.

Although informal learning processes appear to be particularly effective in capability development, an exclusive reliance on these presents organizational problems of inefficiency, lack of control, and an indirect but high cost of failure in the development process. Informal learning is also of limited value to organizations and individuals interested in pursuing development in a proactive manner, and it could be argued that a development strategy that requires individuals to "sink or swim" in the workplace represents an abdication to the vagaries of circumstances.

The action research phase of this inquiry in Phase III has demonstrated, albeit on a small scale, that influential informal learning processes such as stretch assignments and mentoring relationships can be simulated in planned and managed development interventions, with caution and attention to the potential risks. In addition, critical reflection can be encouraged in a structured and supportive manner, to good effect.

Phase III also indicated that the overall outcomes of development are frequently articulated by individuals, in their vernacular, in terms of increased self-confidence. Further scrutiny suggests that self-efficacy, a specific form of self-confidence, is an important variable in the deployment of strategic leader capability, and that there is a "virtuous circle" of self-efficacy development. Thus this study would appear to confirm Bandura's view (1994) of the critical importance of self-efficacy, which is examined in the next section.

## Findings: The deployment of strategic leader capability

Although self-confidence has long been recognized as a staple of coaching in the sports arena, in which it is often viewed as a driver of positive performance outcomes, the construct has lacked a similar prominence in leadership theory. For the purposes of this research, the related but more specific construct of self-efficacy is considered more meaningful. While self-confidence may be used to describe a general feeling of competence, self-efficacy refers to an individual's perception of his or her capabilities to act in a specific domain. In other words, self-efficacy may be viewed as task-specific self-confidence.

Self-efficacy is perceptual, and contextual. It may be defined as an individual's belief in his or her capability to organize and execute the courses of action required to attain desired performance levels. Alternatively, self-efficacy may be described as an individual's conviction to mobilize the capability and resources required to successfully execute a specific task within a given context.

It may be argued that self-efficacy is an important variable that affects leader performance. People with high self-efficacy approach difficult tasks as challenges to be mastered, set themselves challenging goals, and heighten or sustain their efforts in the face of failure (Bandura 1994, 1997). By contrast, people with low self-efficacy lose faith in their capabilities, shy away from difficult tasks, set low aspirations, give up quickly in the face of difficulty, and attribute inadequate performance to deficiencies in aptitude. The implication is that having the right capability is a necessary but not sufficient condition to be an effective leader; individuals also need self-efficacy if the capability is to be deployed effectively.

Additionally, leader performance is also affected by perceptions of followers. Research suggests that followers' perceptions of leaders are positively influenced by the self-efficacy they attribute to the leader, and this in turn improves the leader's ability to mobilize people towards a certain goal or desired state (Popper, 2005).

The interaction between capability and self-efficacy is therefore an important determinant of performance. Figure 7.3 outlines four possible outcomes in this interaction.

This framework represents a contribution to the theory of strategic leader performance, and by making explicit the link between capability and self-efficacy, and offering a typology of outcomes in this interaction, it adds to the work of Bandura (1994, 1997), Hollenbeck and Hall (2004), Kirkpatrick and Locke (1991), Popper (2005), Akin (1987), and Davies and Easterby-Smith (1984).

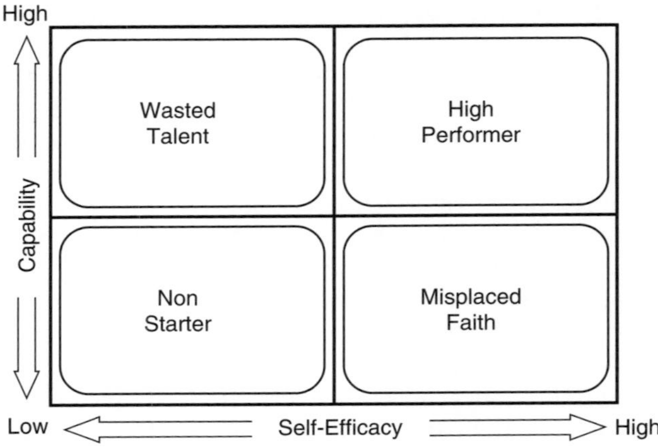


*Figure 7.3* The Interaction of Capability and Self-Efficacy

The framework suggests that High Performers are those individuals who possess both a high capability and high self-efficacy. At the other extreme, a lack of both capability and self-efficacy may relegate an individual into a Non-Starter category. An individual who possesses the appropriate capability but lacks or has lost the belief in his or her ability – perhaps by wrongly attributing a temporary setback to inadequate ability – may be described as Wasted Talent. Lastly, an individual with high self-efficacy beliefs, but lacking commensurate capability, may be nursing a Misplaced Faith, and this may result in undertaking rash acts destined to fail.

Self-efficacy is a perception, and therefore can be changed by changing the perceptions of either the capability or the task at hand. The development of self-efficacy may be visualized as a self-reinforcing cycle. Self-efficacy is increased by experiencing success in challenging situations (e.g. through stretch assignments), learning from role models (such as mentors, who provide social standards and many development functions), social persuasion (i.e. the encouragement we receive from others, such as mentors, peers, or coaches) and emotional conditions (which are influenced by the ability to reflect critically and make the correct causal attributions between abilities and events). On the other hand, self-efficacy beliefs influence the nature and manner in which individuals engage with available development processes. Individuals with high self-efficacy are more likely to expose themselves to situations which will stretch their capability, and this gap between capability possessed and capability required may stimulate further development. There is, therefore, a potentially virtuous circle of self-efficacy development.

**Table 7.4** The Impact of Self-Efficacy

| Area of Impact | Relationship with Performance | Relationship with Development |
|---|---|---|
| • Selection: which tasks are taken on, and which competencies, interests, and networks are developed<br>• Motivation: the degree of effort invested in a task, and the degree of persistence<br>• Cognition: perceptions of the degree of difficulty of the task being faced<br>• Emotion: the degree of anxiety and distress experienced | • Individuals with high leadership self-efficacy will take on more leadership roles, and will persevere longer in these<br>• Individuals with high self-efficacy are more likely to cope better with stress and hardship<br>• Leaders with high self-efficacy are more likely to be assertive and decisive, thereby inspiring the confidence of others<br>• Followers' perceptions of leaders are likely to be positively influenced by high self-efficacy in the leader<br>• Excessive self-efficacy may be dysfunctional if not tempered by critical reflection | • Self-efficacy is both a cause and effect of development, with self-reinforcing cycles. For example, individuals with high self-efficacy are more likely to take on stretch assignments, and success in these is likely to enhance self-efficacy<br>• Self-efficacy in learning paves the way for further learning (although excessive self-efficacy impedes learning)<br>• Individuals with high self-efficacy are more likely to admit mistakes and use them as learning opportunities<br>• Self-efficacy can be built by mastery experiences (e.g. stretch assignments) and role modelling and social persuasion (e.g. by mentors and networks)<br>• Causal attributions of perceived performance success and failures affect the development of self-efficacy beliefs, hence critical reflection is important |

Table 7.4 summarizes the impact of self-efficacy on individual selection, motivation, cognition, and emotional processes, and the relationship of self-efficacy with leader performance and development.

## A theoretical overview

This study has inquired into and corroborated the dimensions of strategic leader capability, identified influential development processes and the relationships between them, simulated these in planned leader development interventions, and evaluated the outcomes.

It is interesting to reflect upon the possible interactions between the dimensions, development, and deployment of strategic leader capability that have been identified in the process. A new framework that integrates these constructs and attempts to offer such a theoretical overview is depicted in Figure 7.4:

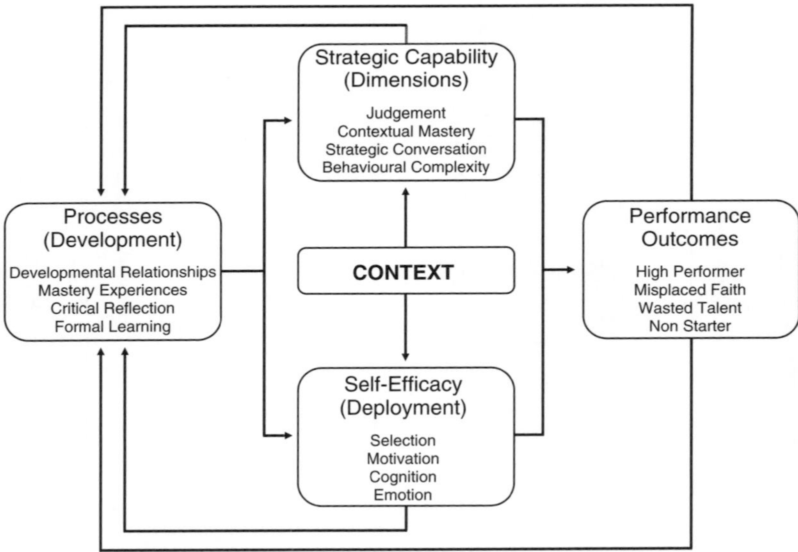


*Figure 7.4* Strategic Leader Capability: Dimensions, Development and Deployment

The framework may be viewed as a way of making sense of the conceptual and empirical findings from this study. This synthesis is based on a set of exploratory interactions between the various constructs, explained as follows:

1. It may be conjectured that performance outcomes, as perceived by the individual, are determined by the individual's capability and self-efficacy, and the "fit" of these with a given context. As suggested previously, High Performers may be said to have high capability and high self-efficacy, whereas Non-Starters are perhaps low on both. High self-efficacy accompanied by low capability may result in Misplaced Faith, and high capability without a commensurate self-efficacy may be characterized as Wasted Talent.
2. Both capability and self-efficacy are contextually bounded. In other words, an individual with high capability in a given context may have low capability in a different context, and vice versa.
3. Both capability and self-efficacy are shaped by development processes, although it may be possible to develop one without the other. For example, if the development of capability remains tacit, the individual may continue to have low self-efficacy. Equally, the social persuasion aspect of developmental relationships may result in high self-efficacy beliefs, but the actual capability, not having been tested or honed in mastery experiences, may continue to be low.
4. Perceived performance outcomes, through a developmental process of critical reflection, are likely to impact the individual's assessment of capability. If capability is perceived to be inadequate, the individual may seek a developmental experience to build capability further. If the capability is assessed as adequate, the individual may seek to deploy it more deliberately in future.
5. Perceived performance outcomes, through a developmental process of critical reflection, also impact the individual's assessment of self-efficacy. Critical reflection is likely to help individuals with low self-efficacy to avoid falling into the trap of attributing unsatisfactory outcomes to deficiencies in capability. Equally, critical reflection may discourage individuals with high self-efficacy from getting carried away by their accomplishments and developing an exaggerated belief about their capability.
6. The individual's assessment of capability and self-efficacy is likely to impact the nature of, and manner in which, the individual engages with development processes. In other words, the individual may form a specific development agenda based on one or more of the

dimensions of strategic leader capability. Additionally, the degree of self-efficacy of the individual may influence the preferred development process – for example, the degree of challenge and risk the individual may find acceptable.

This framework meets the tests of theory development suggested by Hjelle and Ziegler (1981). The constructs presented have been defined and related to one another to the extent that current knowledge allows, and all are amenable to verification by other researchers investigating the domains in question. The framework should stimulate further research, as outlined towards the end of this chapter. The constructs are internally consistent within the perspectives adopted. The framework is parsimonious in that it comprises only five constructs, but at the same time it assists in exploring a comprehensive range of phenomena. Lastly, the framework is functionally useful in understanding the nature, antecedents, and deployment of strategic leader capability.

## Implications for practice

The dimensions, development, and deployment of strategic leader capability, as identified in this research, have significant implications for practice in a range of processes such as the preparation, selection, diagnosis, development, and performance management of strategic leaders. Some of these implications are discussed here on a tentative basis, and would need to be explored further beyond this study. It may be useful to consider such implications in terms of three principal stakeholders: the Individual, currently in a strategic leader role or about to move into one, the Organization (including those responsible for leader development inside the organization) seeking to create, attract, and retain strategic leaders, and the leader development industry or the Developers.

### The individual

At the level of the individual, a simple but direct implication of this research is that the articulation of the dimensions of strategic leader capability may be valuable in itself. These dimensions can help an individual in moving from an intuitive understanding towards an explicit awareness and a holistic sense of the strategic leader role. This can help prepare the individual for the role by giving purpose, and clarifying what might be expected from the individual. Knowledge of the dimensions of capability may also help the individual to assess his or her own capability and related strengths and weaknesses, and to shape aspirations for personal growth.

Increased knowledge about the role, and self-awareness of capability in it, may positively impact self-efficacy, help frame a developmental agenda, and assist in making career choices by provoking questions about the configuration of capability of the individual, and its fit with the context the individual is in. Individuals often bring their coping strategies from one context to another, and hold on to what they know for too long, and risk becoming dysfunctional in the process. This research emphasizes the need for individuals to let go of their adherence to the old context, and review their capability and coping strategies in the light of their perception of the new context.

In terms of development, the individual may need a change of perspective on what constitutes development. For example, an individual may need to be open to mentoring, and may need to take a proactive approach to deliberate job rotation involving stretch and challenge. Career choices about roles and assignments may need to be evaluated not just in task terms, but developmentally as well, and a degree of discomfort in the choice may well be healthy. Equally, individuals who enrol onto a formal learning process may need to appreciate that there is no "silver bullet" for their development, and that a range of learning processes needs to be engaged with. Most of all, individuals may need to develop the ability to access different modes of learning – in other words, they must learn how to learn (Honey and Mumford, 2000).

This research highlights the need for individuals to recognize that performance outcomes are dynamic, and shaped by the interaction between capability and self-efficacy. Capability may be rendered inappropriate as contexts evolve, and individuals may need a high degree of external awareness and self-awareness in order to sense change in their environment, and to adapt their capability accordingly. Similarly, self-efficacy can be eroded by a significant setback, and individuals may need to make accurate causal attributions and seek support in doing so if necessary.

### The organization

The link between strategic leader capability and the long-term competitive advantage of the organization has been emphasized previously in this study. Organizations therefore need to attend to the tasks of identifying, developing, and retaining strategic leader talent.

The dimensions of strategic leader capability serve to integrate leadership into strategy, and strategy into leadership. The framework underlines the need to change the notion of strategy from the widely-held view of strategy as an analytical plan (e.g. Porter, 1980; Ansoff, 1987), to one in which strategy is a seamless, day-to-day activity which is a crucial part of the work of leaders (Mintzberg, 1973; Pascale, 1996). While a plan serves many useful purposes, it must be held lightly, and strategy must also embrace creative approaches and emergent events. Equally, the framework prompts a shift from a focus on leader behaviours and styles alone, to one that embraces the leader's role in the organization's strategic choices.

The dimensions of strategic leader capability also contribute to the selection or appointment process for such roles, and help to clarify what organizations should look for. The dimensions can also assist in the assessment of the talent pool and succession pipeline. In the process a debate on the following questions may be provoked: who is best positioned to take this high level overview of individuals and their capability? How can greater objectivity be introduced into the "stock-taking" process? Which contexts within the organization require more of which ability?

In developing the talent pool, some organizations may make a different choice in the "make" (i.e. develop) or "buy" (i.e. recruit) decision. In the recruitment strategy, organizations need to consider the fit between the capability of the potential leader joining the organization from outside, and the context to which they are being appointed. Organizations also need careful induction programmes for new entrants, so that individuals can adapt their coping strategies to the new context, while retaining the ability to introduce fresh approaches into this context.

This research suggests that in the process of evaluating individuals, an important – and relatively novel – variable to focus on is the range of development processes the individual has been through. Exposure to a set of mastery experiences, and effective mentoring relationships, may be indicative of the acquisition of capability and self-efficacy.

Another key issue raised by the framework of the dimensions of strategic leader capability concerns the ways and means in which gaps in capability can be mitigated. Although this research has not made any observations in this regard, it seems plausible that appropriate team composition may be one way of dealing with the gaps (Child, 1972; Hambrick and Mason, 1984; Ireland and Hitt, 1999). Another way would be to intervene developmentally. Since much potent development happens on the job, work assignments and relationships need to be considered not just from a task perspective, but also from a developmental perspective.

If individuals are to benefit from high impact development opportunities and experiences that occur on the job, then organizations may need to shift the burden and responsibility for development from external vendors to in-house facilitators. For example, those entrusted with leader development in organizations need well thought through strategies for providing mentors, and the right degree of job challenge. Both these processes are likely to be very resource intensive, implying that the number of individuals who can benefit from available development will be limited. Development takes time, and mastery requires repeated experience, reflection, and practice. As a result, the higher the level of the focal individual in the organization, the higher the likely cost of failure. Thus, which individuals should be targeted for development, and at what point in their career, becomes an important selection decision. Additionally, recognizing that real learning is not about a "one week fix", both individuals and organizations need a commitment to lifelong learning. In turn, this is likely to require a culture of supportive and developmental relationships, perhaps one in which seeking help is seen as a sign of maturity rather than weakness, and leaders are also assessed on how well they have developed others.

There is a general tendency in development discussions in organizations to focus on capability. This research emphasizes that organizations must also focus on self-efficacy. In particular, the interaction between capability and self-efficacy may help organizations in developing an overall talent deployment strategy, by helping individuals to develop accurate perceptions of their performance, and working out performance and development mechanisms to deal with individuals in each category.

It may be conjectured that the first priority would be to re-assign the Non-Starters into different roles better suited to their capability and self-efficacy. The second priority would be to deal with the Misplaced Faith category, which has the potential to damage the organization. A way forward here would be to enhance the accuracy of the individual's self-perceptions, perhaps through a 360-degree feedback process accompanied by coaching designed to help the individual face reality in a supportive way. Attention would also need to be paid to diagnosis of gaps in capability, and the best way of mitigating these. The third priority would be to focus on Wasted Talent, a category that is benign but represents cost. Individuals in this category could achieve more, and they may need self-efficacy enhancements through social persuasion by mentors, who by definition believe in the individual, as well as developmental assignments. Lastly, the organization needs to recognize the High Performers, and create the space and opportunity for them to deliver to their full potential.

### The developers

The leader development industry – typically made up of business schools, training organizations, and consulting firms – attracts significant client expenditure. However, the focus of the industry has traditionally been on formal training programmes, which have often been criticized for inadequate effectiveness and impact in terms of both content and learning process. This study stimulates new thinking about the what, how, and why of strategic leader development.

In this research, the dimensions of strategic leader capability have provided a new focus on what needs to be developed. At the same time, an integrated perspective of development has highlighted the value as well as limitations of both informal and formal learning processes. Taken together, these findings have significant implications for the leader development industry.

This research suggests that strategic leader capability is multidisciplinary, and that strategy and leadership are best viewed as two sides of the same coin. However, formal learning, for the most part, tends to be linear and functionally packaged. There is therefore a pressing need to tackle capability holistically, and this means there is a greater need for developers to work together on a cross-disciplinary basis. The strategy and leadership communities – often at arm's length from each other in a traditional business school setting – must engage more with each other.

Developers must also let go of the assumption of context neutrality that underpins many current leader development interventions, and pay special attention to the distinctive context for each individual and organization. For example, developers need to do more to understand the capability gaps in individuals and client organizations and focus the intervention appropriately.

In addition, developers must focus not only on the strategic leader capability in question, but also on the development of the self-efficacy of individuals.

Currently, specialist leadership programmes often focus on developing self-awareness and provide a safe environment in which to explore effective relationships, the individual's motivations and behaviours, and their impact on others. Similarly, a one week programme on strategy may improve the individual's ability to conduct strategic analysis, visualize different scenarios, and think through strategic options and choices. Such programmes have a value which should not be denied. However, it must be acknowledged that while such interventions may develop some aspects of capability – behavioural complexity and strategic conversation respectively in the examples cited – this type of learning does not necessarily make the individual a strategic leader. If the task is to develop strategic leaders, then developers must think beyond the mould of structured programmes. A significant proportion of the capability required cannot be acquired cognitively and tidy classroom abstractions are but one – and arguably a small – part of the puzzle.

If it is assumed that much of the development industry is anchored in formal learning, then it is in the arena of development processes that the challenges for developers become even more profound.

Firstly, developers can improve the effectiveness of formal learning, and mitigate some of the inefficiencies of informal learning, by embracing multiple development processes, and managing them deliberately and better. In effect, perhaps there is a "golden mean" between a haphazard accumulation of experience, and an overly planned training and development regime. Managed experiences, rather than programmes, are called for. For example, developers must find ways and means of simulating mastery experiences, and the mentor-protégé relationship, and encourage individuals to be braver and riskier in their development agendas. A related issue is the need to offer individuals opportunities for repeated practice over time, based on the premise that longer development interventions are likely to be more effective.

Secondly and perhaps more radically, recognizing that much influential learning happens informally on the job, developers must learn to become agents of learning inside organizations, rather than operating from the outside. In other words, developers must find ways and means to support the evolving learning of the individual in the workplace, and become facilitators or architects of learning journeys, rather than teachers or transmitters of knowledge. As a consequence, the leader development industry may need to reconsider the types of "products" it puts into the marketplace. A new value proposition could be to help with the "on-the-job" growth of potential strategic leaders. This could entail, for example, bringing some objectivity to the process of matching the appropriate stretch assignment with individuals in the talent pool, as well as preparing their mentors. Given that individuals learn different things from the same experiences, and the same things from different experiences, this would also result in a much more individualized offering.

Inevitably, such shifts would require new skill sets, and set the scene for new types of developers most likely to make a positive impact.

## Further research: A springboard

The findings, conclusions, and contribution of this research must be accompanied by several caveats.

This study has been limited by its use of a small sample size, which was opportunistic in nature, and determined by considerations of access to individuals in strategic leader roles. However, this has been potentially mitigated by the diversity of geography, organization types, backgrounds, and tenures of individuals in the sample. In addition, a high proportion of the sample offered recurrent issues and themes, giving confidence that common patterns more generally applicable were also in place.

The phenomena under scrutiny did not lend themselves to control or laboratory conditions, and therefore a degree of subjective interpretation by this author was involved. Additionally, the methodology adopted included a process of social interaction with informants, and this in itself may have influenced their perceptions, which may also have been influenced by the issues which were most salient to them at the time of the interaction.

The research also evolved through a process of continuous learning, and the luxury of going back in time to re-examine an issue through a different and newly acquired lens was not available, although such a process of iteration would undoubtedly have enriched this study.

This study also offers promising avenues for further research. Some of the issues identified here – as examples rather than as an exhaustive list – all represent a springboard for further inquiry:

Firstly, more work is needed to determine if all the dimensions of strategic leader capability are equally important in all cases, and if not, to identify the most appropriate configuration of strategic leader capability across a range of contexts. Equally, are there situations in which the abundance of any ability compensates for weaknesses in all the others?

Secondly, there is the interesting possibility of developing diagnostic or assessment instruments for strategic leader capability and self-efficacy based on the frameworks presented here. Such instruments would be valuable from a development as well as talent and performance management perspectives, particularly if they could be used to determine individual trajectories, rather than just snapshots at a moment in time. A related issue is the question of who should make these assessments or diagnostic judgements.

Thirdly, while reference has been made in this research to the need for organizations to select individuals for development, it is not clear at this stage as to how such choices should be made. How can individuals who are most amenable to development, and who have the most potential to succeed in leadership roles in the future be identified?

Fourthly, although some tentative relationships between development processes and dimensions of capability have been identified in this research, a more granular view is needed, especially taking into account individual preferences for different modes of learning.

Fifthly, and in a similar vein, there are some intriguing questions about the relationship, if any, between variables such as individual age and personality type, and optimal development processes, which have remained unaddressed in this research.

Lastly, due to a deliberate focus on the individual, the strategic leadership process at the group or collective level, and related development issues, have been acknowledged but not investigated in this study.

## Conclusion

In conclusion, I believe that this study has served its purpose in terms of enhancing and enriching our understanding of the making of strategic leaders – what they do, how they develop their capability, and how they leverage it – as well as offering some new insights and ways of working in the domain of strategic leader development.

While the constructs that make up the new theoretical frameworks offered here were known previously, I believe that their juxtaposition and synthesis has resulted in new insights. While it would be rash to claim definitive or final answers, the perspective that this research has made available on the dimensions, development, and deployment of strategic leader capability is richer and more sophisticated than that available before. In particular, this research has identified plausible dimensions of strategic leader capability, the nature of influential development processes, and the significance and role of self-efficacy in leader development and performance. The integrated framework that has been developed along the way may also be helpful in interrogating current and proposed practice in strategic leader development. The study has also highlighted some of the weaknesses of current formally managed strategic leader development practices and has suggested possible intervention designs that could enhance ways and means of making strategic leaders.

# 8
# Appendices

## Appendix 1: People

### (a) Phase I: Informal panel of experts

| # | Name | Organization |
|---|---|---|
| 1 | David Butcher | Cranfield University |
| 2 | Philip Hodgson | Ashridge |
| 3 | Robert Kovach | RHR International |
| 4 | Henry Mintzberg | McGill University |
| 5 | James Moncrieff | LMT Consulting |
| 6 | Ralph Stacey | University of Hertfordshire |

### (b) Phase I: Participants in face validity focus groups

| # | Name | Organization |
|---|---|---|
| 1 | Nick Anthony | Royal Marines |
| 2 | Eric Cassells | Creative Problem Solving Inc |
| 3 | Bill Critchley | Ashridge Consulting |
| 4 | Eversley Felix | BBC Training & Development |
| 5 | John Hughes | Organization Development Team, PwC |
| 6 | Maxine Lange | Maxine Lange Consulting |
| 7 | James Moncrieff | LMT Consulting |
| 8 | Neville Osrin | Hewitt Associates |
| 9 | James Rovell | Warwick University |
| 10 | Hamish Scott | Ashridge Business School |
| 11 | David Young | Cable & Wireless |
| 12 | Steve Watson | Ashridge Business School (facilitator) |

## (c) Phase II: Participants in interviews

| # | Name | Role | Industry | Nationality | Gender |
|---|---|---|---|---|---|
| 1 | Steve | Director | Medical devices | British | Male |
| 2 | David | CEO | Media | British | Male |
| 3 | Anthony | MD | Publishing | British | Male |
| 4 | Thomas | MD | Publishing | British | Male |
| 5 | Tom | MD | Media | British | Male |
| 6 | Chris | COO | Telecommunications | American | Male |
| 7 | Pat | MD | Medical devices | American | Male |
| 8 | Ronnie | Director | Chemicals | British | Male |
| 9 | Jonathan | Chairman | Food | British | Male |
| 10 | Reinoud | CEO | Financial services | Dutch | Male |
| 11 | Wilf | MD | Gaming | British | Male |
| 12 | John | MD | Utilities | British | Male |
| 13 | James | MD | Building materials | British | Male |
| 14 | Rodney | MD | Engineering | British | Male |
| 15 | Judith | MD | Aviation | British | Female |
| 16 | Sue | CEO | Performing arts | British | Female |
| 17 | Rupert | MD | Media | British | Male |
| 18 | Jan | Director | Packaging | Swedish | Male |
| 19 | Jed | MD | Food | British | Male |
| 20 | Brian | MD | Pharmaceuticals | British | Male |
| 21 | Heather | CEO | Charity | British | Female |
| 22 | Tim | MD | Retailing | British | Male |
| 23 | Udo | MD | Pharmaceuticals | Belgian | Male |
| 24 | Nick | President | Chemicals | British | Male |
| 25 | Robert | MD | Financial services | British | Male |

## (d) Phase III: Leadership circle participants

| # | Name | Division | Role |
|---|---|---|---|
| 1 | David | Consumer Media | MD, Magazine |
| 2 | Mark | Consumer Media | Publishing Director, Magazine |
| 3 | Darren | Consumer Media | TV Sales Director |
| 4 | Louise | Business Media | Group Event Director |
| 5 | Fraser | Business Media | Commercial Director |
| 6 | Dan | Business Media | Publishing Director, Magazine |
| 7 | Adrian | Radio | MD, Regional Station |
| 8 | Tracey | Radio | Commercial Director, Regional Stations |

### (e) Phase III: Top Leader Journey participants and facilitators

| | Name | Role | Organization |
|---|---|---|---|
| 1 | Stefan | Managing Director | Danish pharmaceutical company |
| 2 | Martin | Chief Editor | Major UK broadcaster |
| 3 | Paul | General Manager | Aerospace manufacturer |
| 4 | Mik | Division Head | Bank |
| 5 | John | Deputy CEO | Housing group |
| 6 | Gary | Chief Operating Officer | Software company |
| 7 | Ian | Managing Director | Financial services company |
| 8 | Robin | Chief Executive | New Zealand minerals and forestry products group |
| 9 | Edgar | Head of Division | European Commission |
| 10 | Jon | Divisional Director | Publishing group |
| 11 | Will | Deputy Chief Executive | Ambulance Service |
| 12 | Phil Hodgson | Co-director, Top Leader Journey | Ashridge Business School |
| 13 | Albert Zandvoort | Co-director, Top Leader Journey | Ashridge Business School |

## Appendix 2: Questionnaires

### (a) Phase II: Questionnaire

1. For the record, could we start with a little bit of scene setting? It would be very helpful if you could tell me something about your background as well as your current position and role in the organization.
2. I am particularly interested in your strategic leadership responsibilities. To what extent are you involved with strategy formation and implementation or otherwise shaping the future of the business?
3. What are some of the major or unique challenges and pressures you face in this role?
4. What are the major capabilities needed by someone in a strategic role like yours?
5. Is this your personal view, or a widely shared organizational view?
6. Given these capabilities, how confident do you feel about your ability to discharge this role?
7. I am interested in understanding how you developed your strategic capabilities. To begin with, how were your development needs identified? By whom? When?

8. Could you talk me through the actual development process? Was it a formal or informal development process?
9. Reflecting on the range of development experiences you've cited, what did each of these do for you? What were the outcomes of each? How do you know this?
10. Looking back from your current strategic leadership role, which development experiences worked best for you? Why?
11. What didn't work for you? Why?
12. We talked earlier about the capabilities needed in a strategic role like yours. Are there any that you feel you're not fully on top of or that you need to develop further? Any thoughts on how you might do this most effectively?
13. Do you influence the development of the strategic capabilities of any other individuals in your organization? What kinds of interventions or initiatives do you sponsor and why? What do you shy away from and why?

**(b) Phase III: Post-programme questionnaire for leadership circle participants**

For research purposes, I would like to ask you some questions about the Circle and your learning from the various elements of it. As a reminder, the elements of the Circle are:

- The workshop, covering strategy and team dynamics
- Mentoring
- The live case study which we think of as a stretch assignment
- Networking with peers from across the organization through the Circle process

1. Going back in time, when you enrolled or were nominated onto The Circle, what were you hoping to learn from it?
2. Looking back, what have you actually learned so far?
3. Was there any part of the Circle that made a particular impact on you? If so, what was it, and why and how did it impact you?
4. How did you benefit from the strategy workshop?
5. How did you benefit from the mentoring? Please describe this process. What did it do for you and why?
6. Did you feel stretched by the live case study? What did the stretch do for you?
7. Did you benefit from the interaction and networking with your peers? If so, how?

8. Has the Circle improved your understanding of the capabilities of strategic leaders? What has this improved understanding resulted in?
9. I am investigating four strategic leader capabilities and how they might be developed. For each capability, please could you tell me which element of the Circle was most effective?
   a) ability to conduct a strategic conversation: was it the workshop, mentoring, the stretch case study, or networking with peers?
   b) enhanced understanding of the organization's context as well as ways and means of challenging it: was it the workshop, mentoring, stretch case study, or networking with peers?
   c) ability to exercise judgement over conflicting processes: was it the workshop, mentoring, stretch case study, or networking with peers?
   d) ability to deploy a repertoire of behaviours so as to maximize your effectiveness as a leader in the organization: was it the workshop, mentoring, stretch case study, or networking with peers?
10. How have you changed as a result of the Circle? Please give specific examples. What has brought about this change?

### (c) Phase III: Pre-programme questionnaire for Top Leader Journey participants

My colleagues and I look forward to working with you at Ashridge on the Top Leader Journey. In advance of the programme, we will be very grateful if you could take a few minutes to respond to the questions given below. These will (a) enable us to advise you on the leadership capabilities and development processes most likely to be effective in your case, and (b) contribute to our ongoing research on the development of strategic leaders. Your responses will be kept strictly confidential and will not be shared without your prior permission. Thank you.

Part 1: General

1. The most significant personal challenges you face as a leader in your work environment are:
2. What you most need to learn is:
3. The learning process that usually works best for you is:
4. What attracted you to the Top Leader Journey is:
5. May I disclose your responses to the previous questions 1–4 to the executive coach who will work with you during the Top Leader Journey?

Part 2: Importance of capabilities in role

Please indicate the extent to which each of the following statements reflects your views by assigning a score on a scale of 1 to 10 in which 1 = "not at all" and 10 = "totally".

| # | **Statement** | **Score** |
|---|---|---|
| 1 | My work requires me to manage several conflicting processes (e.g. short term versus long term, growth versus profit) | |
| 2 | In my role I am often required to operate in situations of high ambiguity and incomplete information | |
| 3 | A detailed understanding of the drivers of business performance in the industry and the organization are vital in a role like mine | |
| 4 | It is important in my role to be able to stand back from the detail of my company and industry and challenge the "way we've always done things" | |
| 5 | In my role, shaping the organization's strategic direction is a continuously evolving process rather than a one-off event | |
| 6 | In my role I find that both analytical and non-analytical skills (e.g. trial and error, creative thinking) are crucial in making strategy | |
| 7 | Effectiveness in my role requires adapting my behaviour to suit a given situation or context, and the person I am interacting with | |
| 8 | In my position you have to take in and integrate many types of data from many sources | |

Part 3: Self-Assessment of Competence

Please indicate the extent to which each of the following statements reflects your views by assigning a score on a scale of 1 to 10 in which 1 = "not at all" and 10 = "totally".

| # | Statement | Score |
|---|---|---|
| 1 | I am comfortable and confident in situations in which I have to synthesize apparently contradictory process | |
| 2 | I am effective in situations of ambiguity and incomplete information | |
| 3 | I understand the drivers of performance in my industry and my organization well | |
| 4 | I'm good at challenging the "way we've always done things around here" | |
| 5 | I have a strategic plan, but I hold it lightly and adapt to emerging events and circumstances | |
| 6 | When making strategy, I bring both analytical and non-analytical perspectives (e.g. trial and error, creative thinking) to the situation | |
| 7 | I am able to adapt my behaviour to the situation or person I am facing while retaining credibility | |
| 8 | I am good at synthesizing different types of data from different sources | |

### (d) Phase III: Post-programme questionnaire for Top Leader Journey participants

*Thank you for your continued participation in the Top Leader Journey research. In today's discussion, I'd like you to reflect on your development during and after the TLJ. Your responses will be kept strictly confidential.*

1. Going back in time, when you enrolled on the Top Leader Journey, what were you hoping to learn from it?
2. What did you actually learn?
3. Was there any part of the Top Leader Journey that made a particular impact on you? If so, what was it, and why and how did it impact you?

4. Did you undertake any "stretch assignment" during or after the Top Leader Journey? What was it? Why do you consider it a stretch? What did it do for you?
5. Did you undertake any "co-mentoring" during or after the Top Leader Journey? What were the main elements of this process and what did it do for you?
6. Did you benefit from the "reflective time and space" that the TLJ offered? If yes, why and how?
7. How have you changed as a result of the Top Leader Journey? Please give specific examples. What has brought about this change?
8. Has the Top Leader Journey improved your understanding of the capabilities of strategic leaders? What has this improved understanding resulted in?
9. What have you learnt about the effective development of strategic leaders?
10. How do you intend to continue your own development?

I'd now like to take you through a brief questionnaire that you may recall responding to before the Top Leader Journey programme. The purpose of asking you these questions once again is to make meaningful "before" and "after" comparisons. (See part 3 of questionnaire c).

# References


Akin, G. (1987), "Varieties of Managerial Learning", *Organizational Dynamics*, Vol. 16, No. 2, pp. 36–48.

Alexander, L.D., O'Neill, H.M., Snyder, N.H. and Townsend, J.B. (1986), "How Academy Members Teach the Business Policy/Strategic Management Case Course", *Journal of Management Case Studies*, Vol. 2, No. 4, pp. 334–344.

Allio, R.J. (2005), "Leadership Development: Teaching Versus Learning", *Management Decision*, Vol. 43, No. 7/8, pp. 1071–1077.

Amabile, T.M. (1998), "How to Kill Creativity", *Harvard Business Review*, Vol. 76, No. 5, pp. 77–87.

Ansoff, I.H. (1979), *Strategic Management*, Macmillan, London.

Ansoff, I.H. (1987), "The Emerging Paradigm of Strategic Behaviour", *Strategic Management Journal*, Vol. 8, No. 6, pp. 501–515.

Appelbaum, S.H., Ritchie, S. and Shapiro, B.T. (1994), "Mentoring Revisited: an Organizational Behaviour Construct", *Journal of Management Development*, Vol. 13, No. 4, pp. 62–72.

Argyris, C. (1993), *Knowledge for Action: a Guide to Overcoming Barriers to Organizational Change*, Jossey-Bass, San Francisco.

Argyris, C. and Schön, D. (1978), *Organizational Learning: a Theory of Action Perspective*, Addison-Wesley, Reading.

Argyris, C. and Schön, D. (1996), *Organizational Life II: Theory, Methods and Practice*, Addison-Wesley, Reading.

Arnold, J. and Johnson, K. (1997), "Mentoring in Early Career", *Human Resource Management Journal*, Vol. 7, No. 4, pp. 61–70.

Ashby, W.R. (1952), *Design for a Brain*, Wiley, New York.

Bandarowski, J.F. (1985), *Creative Planning Throughout the Organization*, AMA Publications Division, New York.

Bandura, A. (1994), "Self-Efficacy", in Ramachandran, V.S. (ed.), *Encyclopaedia of Human Behavior*, Academic Press, New York, pp. 71–81.

Bandura, A. (1997), *Self-Efficacy: the Exercise of Control*, W. H. Freeman, New York.

Barney, J.B. (1991), "Firm Resources and Sustained Competitive Advantage", *Journal of Management*, Vol. 17, No. 1, pp. 99–120.

Barr, P.S., Stimpert, J.L. and Huff, A.S. (1992), "Cognitive Change, Strategic Action, and Organizational Renewal", *Strategic Management Journal*, Vol. 13, Special issue, pp. 15–35.

Bartlett, C.A. and Ghoshal, S. (1989), *Managing Across Borders: the Transnational Solution*, Hutchinson Business Books, London.

Bartunek, J.M. and Louis, M.R. (1988), "The Design of Work Environments to Stretch Managers' Capacities for Complex Thinking", *Human Resources Planning*, Vol. 11, No. 1, pp. 13–22.

Bass, B. (1981), *Stogdill's Handbook of Leadership*, Free Press, New York.

Bennis, W. (1992), *On Becoming a Leader*, Century Business, London.

Bennis, W. (1998), "Speed and Complexity", *Executive Excellence*, Vol. 15, No. 6, pp. 3–4.

Bennis, W. and Nanus, B. (1985), *Leaders*, Harper and Row, New York.
Bennis, W.G. and Thomas, R.J. (2002), "Crucibles of Leadership", *Harvard Business Review*, Vol. 80, No. 9, pp. 39–45.
Blaikie, N. (2000), *Designing Social Research*, Polity Press, Cambridge.
Blake, R.R. and Mouton, J.S. (1964), *The Managerial Grid*, Gulf, Houston.
Block, P. (1987), *The Empowered Manager*, Jossey-Bass, San Francisco.
Bongiorno, L. (1993), "Raise Your Hand If You're Sure Strategy is Being Taught in American Business Schools", *Journal of Business Strategy*, Vol. 14, No. 5, pp. 36–41.
Bonn, I. (2001), "Developing Strategic Thinking as a Core Competency", *Management Decision*, Vol. 39, No. 1, pp. 63–71.
Boud, D., Keogh, R. and Walker, D. (1985), *Reflection: Turning Experience into Action*, Kogan Page, London.
Boud, D. and Middleton, H. (2003), "Learning From Others at Work: Communities of Practice and Informal Learning", *Journal of Workplace Learning*, Vol. 15, No. 5, pp. 194–202.
Bourgeois, L.J. and Brodwin, D.R. (1984), "Strategic Implementation: Five Approaches to an Elusive Phenomenon", *Strategic Management Journal*, Vol. 5, No. 3, pp. 241–264.
Bourgeois, L.J. and Eisenhardt, K.M. (1988), "Strategic Decision Processes in High Velocity Environments", *Management Science*, Vol. 34, No. 7, pp. 816–835.
Bower, J.L. (1970), *Managing the Resource Allocation Process*, Harvard Business School Publishing, Cambridge.
Bowman, C. (1994), "Stuck in the Old Routines", *European Management Journal*, Vol. 12, No. 1, pp. 76–82.
Bowman, C. and Daniels, K. (1995), "The Influence of Functional Experience on Perceptions of Strategic Priorities", *British Journal of Management*, Vol. 6, No. 3, pp. 157–167.
Brews, P.J. and Hunt, M.R. (1999), "Learning to Plan and Planning to Learn: Resolving the Planning School/Learning School Debate", *Strategic Management Journal*, Vol. 20, No. 10, pp. 889–913.
Brocklesby, J. and Cummings, S. (2003), "Strategy as Systems Thinking", in Cummings, S. and Wilson, D. (eds), *Images of Strategy*, Blackwell Publishing, Oxford.
Brookfield, S.D. (1995), *Becoming a Critically Reflective Teacher*, Jossey-Bass, San Francisco.
Bunker, K.A. and Webb, A.D. (1992), *Learning How to Learn From Experience: Impact of Stress and Coping*, Report no. 154, Center for Creative Leadership, Greensboro.
Burgelman, R. (1991), "Interorganizational Ecology of Strategy Making and Organizational Adaptation: Theory and Field Research", *Organizational Science*, Vol. 2, No. 3, pp. 239–262.
Burgelman, R.A. (1983a), "A Model of the Interaction of Strategic Behavior, Corporate Context, and the Concept of Strategy", *Academy of Management Review*, Vol. 8, No. 1, pp. 61–70.
Burgelman, R.A. (1983b), "A Process Model of Internal Corporate Venturing in the Diversified Major Firm", *Administrative Science Quarterly*, Vol. 28, No. 2, pp. 223–244.
Burke, R.J. (1984), "Mentors in Organizations", *Group and Organization Studies*, Vol. 9, No. 3, pp. 353–372.

Burns, J.L. (1978), *Leadership*, Harper and Row, New York.

Burrell, G. and Morgan, G. (1979), *Sociological Paradigms and Organizational Analysis*, Heinemann, Portsmouth.

Butcher, D. and Clarke, M. (2001), *Smart Management: Using Politics in Organisations*, Palgrave, Basingstoke.

Castanias, R.P. and Helfat, C.E. (1991), "Managerial Resources and Rents", *Journal of Management*, Vol. 17, No. 1, pp. 155–171.

Chaffee, E.E. (1985), "Three Models of Strategy", *Academy of Management Review*, Vol. 10, No. 1, pp. 89–98.

Chakravarthy, B.S. (1982), "Adaptation: a Promising Metaphor for Strategic Management", *Academy of Management Review*, Vol. 7, No. 1, pp. 35–44.

Chakravarthy, B.S. and White, R.E. (2002), "Strategy Process: Forming, Implementing, and Changing Strategies", in Pettigrew, A., Thomas, H. and Whittington, R. (eds), *Handbook of Strategy and Management*, Sage, London, pp. 182–205.

Chandler, A. (1962), *Strategy and Structure*, MIT Press, Cambridge.

Chao, G.T., Walz, P.M. and Gardner, P.D. (1992), "Formal and Informal Mentorships: a Comparison of Mentoring Functions and Contrast With Nonmentored Counterparts", *Personnel Psychology*, Vol. 45, No. 3, pp. 619–636.

Chia, R. (2002), "The Production of Management Knowledge: Philosophical Underpinnings of Research Design", in Partington, D. (ed.), *Essential Skills for Management Research*, Sage, London, pp. 1–18.

Child, J. (1972), "Organization Structure, Environment, and Performance: the Role of Strategic Choice", *Sociology*, Vol. 6, pp. 1–22.

Christensen, C.M. and Donovan, T. (1999), "Putting your Finger on Capability", *Teaching Note*, Harvard Business School, Cambridge.

Clarke, M. (1999), "Management Development as a Game of Meaningless Outcomes", *Human Resource Management Journal*, Vol. 9, No. 2, pp. 38–49.

Clutterbuck, D. (2004), *Everyone Needs a Mentor: Fostering Talent in Your Organisation*, CIPD, London.

Cohen, M.D., March, J.G. and Olsen, J.P. (1972), "A Garbage Can Model of Organisational Choice", *Administrative Science Quarterly*, Vol. 17, No. 1, pp. 1–25.

Colley, H., Hodkinson, P. and Malcolm, J. (2003), *Informality and Formality in Learning*, Report no. 1492, Learning Skills and Research Center, London.

Collins, J.C. and Porras, J.I. (1998), *Built to Last*, Century Business, London.

Collins, E.G.C. and Scott, P. (1978), "Everyone Who Makes It Has a Mentor", *Harvard Business Review*, Vol. 56, pp. 89–101.

Conger, J. (1990), "The Dark Side of Leadership", in Hickman, G.R. (ed.), *Leading Organizations: Perspectives for a New Era*, Sage, London.

Conger, J. and Fulmer, R.M. (2003), "Developing Your Leadership Pipeline", *Harvard Business Review*, Vol. 81, No. 12, p. 76.

Conger, J. and Kanungo, N. (1987), "Toward a Behavioural Theory of Charismatic Leadership in Organizational Settings", *Academy of Management Review*, Vol. 12, pp. 637–647.

Conger, J. and Kanungo, N. (1988), *Charismatic Leadership*, Jossey-Bass, San Francisco.

Conlon, T.J. (2004), "A Review of Informal Learning Literature, Theory and Implications for Practice in Developing Global Professional Competence", *Journal of European Industrial Training*, Vol. 28, No. 2–4, pp. 283–295.

Covey, S. (1991), *Principle-Centred Leadership*, Fireside, New York.

Cox, C. and Jennings, R. (1995), "The Foundations of Success: the Development and Characteristics of British Entrepreneurs and Intrapreneurs", *Leadership and Organization Development Journal*, Vol. 16, No. 7, pp. 4–9.
Cox, C.J. and Cooper, C.L. (1989), "The Making of the British CEO: Childhood, Work Experience, Personality, and Management Style", *Academy of Management Executive*, Vol. 3, No. 3, pp. 241–245.
Croom, S. and Batchelor, J. (1997), "The Development of Strategic Capabilities – An Interaction View", *Integrated Manufacturing Systems*, Vol. 8, No. 5, pp. 299–312.
Cseh, M., Watkins, K. and Marsick, V. (1999), "Reconceptualizing Marsick and Watkins' Model of Informal and Incidental Learning in the Workplace", *Proceedings of the Academy of Human Resource Development Conference*, Vol. 1, Academy of Human Resource Development, Baton Rouge.
Cummings, S. (1995), "Pericles of Athens – Drawing From the Essence of Strategic Leadership", *Business Horizons*, Vol. 28, No. 1, pp. 22–29.
Cummings, S. and Wilson, D. (2003), "Images of Strategy", in Cummings, S. and Wilson, D. (eds), *Images of Strategy*, Blackwell, Oxford, pp. 1–40.
Daft, R.L. and Weick, K.E. (1984), "Toward a Model of Organizations as Interpretive Systems", *Academy of Management Review*, Vol. 9, No. 2, pp. 284–295.
Davids, M. (1995), "Where Style Meets Substance", *Journal of Business Strategy*, Vol. 16, No. 1, pp. 48–60.
Davies, J. and Easterby-Smith, M. (1984), "Learning and Developing from Managerial Work Experiences", *Journal of Management Studies*, Vol. 21, No. 2, pp. 169–183.
Davis, N.J. (2001), "Building Muscle: Developing Leaders with Follower Weight", *Organization Development Journal*, Vol. 19, No. 3, pp. 27–35.
de Bono, E. (1984), *Tactics: The Art and Science of Success*, Little, Brown, Boston.
de Bono, E. (1996), *Serious Creativity*, Harper Collins Business, London.
Dean, J.W. and Sharfman, M.P. (1996), "Does Decision Process Matter? A Study of Strategic Decision-Making Effectiveness", *Academy of Management Journal*, Vol. 39, No. 2, pp. 368–396.
Dechant, K. (1994), "Making the Most of Job Assignments: An Exercise in Planning for Learning", *Journal of Management Education*, Vol. 18, pp. 198–211.
DeKluyver, C. (2000), *Strategic Thinking: an Executive Perspective*, Prentice-Hall, Englewood Cliffs.
Denison, D.R., Hooijberg, R. and Quinn, R.E. (1995), "Paradox and Performance: a Theory of Behavioural Complexity in Managerial Leadership", *Organization Science*, Vol. 65, No. 5, pp. 524–540.
Densten, I.L. and Gray, J.H. (2001), "Leadership Development and Reflection: What's the Connection?", *The International Journal of Educational Management*, Vol. 15, No. 3, pp. 119–124.
Dollinger, M.J. (1984), "Environmental Boundary Spanning and Information-Processing Effects on Organizational Performance", *Academy of Management Review*, Vol. 27, No. 2, pp. 351–368.
Drucker, P.F. (1974), *Management: Tasks, Responsibilities*, Practices, William Heinemann, London.
Duhaime, I.M. and Schwenk, C.R. (1985), "Conjectures on Cognitive Simplification in Acquisition and Divestment Decision Making", *Academy of Management Review*, Vol. 10, No. 2, pp. 287–295.
Dutton, J.E. and Ashford, S.J. (1993), "Selling Issues to Top Management", *Academy of Management Review*, Vol. 18, No. 3, pp. 397–424.

Dutton, J.E. and Jackson, S.E. (1987), "Categorizing Strategic Issues: Links to Organizational Action", *Academy of Management Review*, Vol. 12, No. 1, pp. 76–91.

Easterby-Smith, M.P.V. and Davies, J. (1983), "Developing Strategic Thinking", *Long Range Planning*, Vol. 16, No. 4, p. 389.

Eden, D. (1992), "Leadership and Expectations: Pygmalion Effects and Other Self-Fulfilling Prophecies in Organizations", *Leadership Quarterly*, Vol. 3, No. 4, pp. 271–305.

Egelhoff, W.G. (1982), "Strategy and Structure in Multinational Corporations: an Information-Processing Approach", *Administrative Science Quarterly*, Vol. 27, No. 3, pp. 435–458.

Eiseman, J. (1978), "Reconciling 'Incompatible' Positions", *Journal of Applied Behavioral Science*, Vol. 14, No. 2, pp. 133–150.

Eisenhardt, K.M. (1989), "Making Fast Strategic Decisions in High-Velocity Environments", *Academy of Management Journal*, Vol. 32, No. 3, pp. 543–576.

Eisenhardt, K.M. and Martin, J.A. (2000), "Dynamic Capabilities: What Are They?", *Strategic Management Journal*, Vol. 21, No. 10/11, pp. 1105–1121.

Eisenhardt, K.M. and Zbaracki, M.J. (1992), "Strategic Decision Making", Strategic Management Journal, Vol. 13, Special issue, Winter, pp. 17–37.

Emmerik, I.J.H.V. (2004), "The More You Can Get the Better: Mentoring Constellations and Intrinsic Career Success", *Career Development International*, Vol. 9, No. 6, pp. 578–594.

Engestrom, Y. (2001), "Expansive Learning at Work: Towards an Activity-Theoretical Conception", *Journal of Education and Work*, Vol. 14, No. 1, pp. 133–156.

Ericson, T., Melander, A. and Melin, L. (2001), "The Role of the Strategist", in Volberda, H.W. and Elfring, T. (eds), *Rethinking Strategy*, Sage, London, pp. 57–68.

Fernandez, J.E. and Hogan, R.T. (2002), "Values-Based Leadership", *Journal for Quality and Participation*, Vol. 25, No. 4, pp. 25–27.

Floyd, S.W. and Lane, P. (2000), "Strategizing Throughout the Organization: Managing Role Conflict in Strategic Renewal", *Academy of Management Review*, Vol. 25, No. 1, pp. 154–177.

Floyd, S.W. and Wooldridge, B. (1992), "Managing Strategic Consensus: The Foundation of Effective Implementation", *Academy of Management Executive*, Vol. 6, No. 4, pp. 27–39.

Floyd, S.W. and Wooldridge, B. (1994), "Dinosaurs or Dynamos? Recognizing Middle Management's Strategic Role", *Academy of Management Executive*, Vol. 8, No. 4, pp. 47–57.

Frederickson, J.W. (1983), "Strategic Process Research: Questions and Recommendations", *Academy of Management Review*, Vol. 8, No. 4, pp. 565–575.

Frederickson, J.W. (1984), "The Comprehensiveness of Strategic Decision Processes: Extension, Observations, Future Directions", *Academy of Management Review*, Vol. 27, No. 3, pp. 445–466.

Frederickson, J.W. (1986), "The Strategic Decision Process and Organizational Structure", *Academy of Management Review*, Vol. 11, No. 2, pp. 197–280.

Frederickson, J.W. and Iaquinto, A.L. (1989), "Inertia and Creeping Rationality in Strategic Decision Processes", *Academy of Management Journal*, Vol. 32, No. 3, pp. 516–542.

Friday, E., Friday, S.S. and Green, A.L. (2004), "A Reconceptualization of Mentoring and Sponsorship", *Management Decision*, Vol. 42, No. 5, pp. 628–644.

Frost, P.J. and Fukami, C.V. (1997), "Teaching Effectiveness in the Organizational Sciences: Recognizing and Enhancing the Scholarship", *Academy of Management Journal*, Vol. 40, No. 6, pp. 1271–1282.

Gardiner, C.S. (1972), "Complexity Training and Prejudice Reduction", *Journal of Applied Social Psychology*, Vol. 2, No. 4, pp. 325–342.

Gardner, R. and Schoen, R.A. (1962), "Differentiation and Abstraction in Concept Formation", *Psychological Monographs*, Vol. 66, No. 560.

Glaser, B.G. and Strauss, A.L. (1967), *The Discovery of Grounded Theory: Strategies for Qualitative Research*, Aldine, Chicago.

Goleman, D. (2000), "Leadership That Gets Results", *Harvard Business Review*, Vol. 78, No. 2, pp. 79–88.

Grundy, T. and Wensley, R. (1999), "Strategic Behaviour: the Driving Force of Strategic Management", *European Management Journal*, Vol. 17, No. 3, pp. 326–334.

Guba, E.G. and Lincoln, Y.S. (1998), "Competing Paradigms in Qualitative Research", in Denzin, N.K. and Lincoln, Y.S. (eds), *The Landscape of Qualitative Research*, Sage, Thousand Oaks, pp. 195–220.

Gundlach, M.J., Martinko, M.J. and Douglas, S.C. (2003), "Emotional Intelligence, Causal Reasoning, and the Self-Efficacy Development Process", *International Journal of Organizational Analysis*, Vol. 11, No. 3, pp. 229–246.

Hall, R.I. (1984), "The Natural Logic of Management Policy Making: its Implications for the Survival of an Organization", *Management Science*, Vol. 30, No. 8, pp. 905–927.

Hambrick, D.C. (1984), "Taxonomic Approaches to Studying Strategy: Some Conceptual and Methodological Issues", *Journal of Management*, Vol. 10, No. 1, pp. 27–41.

Hambrick, D.C., Geletkanycz, M.A. and Frederickson, J.W. (1993), "Top Executive Commitment to the Status Quo: Some Tests of its Determinants", *Strategic Management Journal*, Vol. 14, No. 6, pp. 401–418.

Hambrick, D.C. and Mason, P.A. (1984), "Upper Echelons: the Organization as a Reflection of its Top Managers", *Academy of Management Review*, Vol. 9, No. 2, pp. 193–206.

Hamel, G. and Prahalad, C.K. (1989), "Strategic Intent", *Harvard Business Review*, Vol. 67, No. 3, pp. 63–77.

Handfield-Jones, H. (2000), "How Executives Grow", *McKinsey Quarterly*, Vol. 1, pp. 116–123.

Handy, C. (1989), *The Age of Unreason*, Harvard Business School Press, Cambridge.

Handy, C. (1994), *The Age of Paradox*, Harvard Business School Press, Cambridge.

Hannan, M.T. and Freeman, J. (1989), "The Population Ecology of Organisations", *American Journal of Sociology*, Vol. 82, No. 5, pp. 929–964.

Hardy, C. (1994), *Managing Strategic Action*, Sage, London.

Hart, S.L. (1992), "An Integrative Framework for Strategy-Making Processes", *Academy of Management Review*, Vol. 17, No. 2, pp. 327–351.

Hart, S.L. and Banbury, C. (1994), "How Strategy-Making Processes Can Make a Difference", *Strategic Management Journal*, Vol. 15, No. 4, pp. 251–269.

Hart, S.L. and Quinn, R.E. (1993), "Roles Executives Play: CEOs, Behavioral Complexity, and Firm Performance", *Human Relations*, Vol. 46, No. 5, pp. 543–575.

Higgins, M.C. (2000), "The More the Merrier? Multiple Developmental Relationships and Work Satisfaction", *Journal of Management Development*, Vol. 19, No. 4, pp. 277–296.

Higgins, M.C. and Kram, K.E. (2001), "Reconceptualizing Mentoring at Work: A Developmental Network Perspective", *Academy of Management Review*, Vol. 26, No. 2, pp. 264–288.

Hjelle, L.A. and Ziegler, D.J. (1981), *Personality Theories: Basic Assumptions, Research, and Applications*, McGraw-Hill, Singapore.

Holbeche, L. (1996), "Peer Mentoring: the Challenges and Opportunities", *Career Development International*, Vol. 1, No. 7, p. 24.

Hollenbeck, G.P. and Hall, D.T. (2004), "Self-Confidence and Leader Performance", *Organizational Dynamics*, Vol. 33, No. 3, pp. 254–269.

Honey, P. and Mumford, A. (2000), *The Learning Styles Questionnair*e, Peter Honey Publications, Maidenhead.

Hooijberg, R. (1996), "A Multidirectional Approach Toward Leadership: an Extension of the Concept of Behavioral Complexity", *Human Relations*, Vol. 49, No. 7, pp. 917–946.

Hooijberg, R. and Quinn, R.E. (1992), "Behavioural Complexity and the Development of Effective Managers", in Phillips, R.L. and Hunt, J.G. (eds), *Strategic Management: a Multi-organizational Level Perspective*, Quorum, New York.

House, R.J. and Shamir, B. (1993), "Toward the Integration of Transformational, Charismatic, and Visionary Theories", in Chemmers, M.M. and Ayman, R. (eds), *Leadership Theory and Research: Perspectives and Directions,* Academic Press, San Diego, pp. 81–103.

Hult, M. and Lennung, S.A. (1980), "Towards a Definition of Action Research: a Note and Bibliography", *Journal of Management Studies*, Vol. 17, No. 2, pp. 241–250.

Hunt, D. and Michael, C. (1983), "Mentorship – A Career Training and Development Tool", *Academy of Management Review*, Vol. 8, No. 3, pp. 475–485.

Inkeles, A. (1964), *What Is Sociology?,* Prentice-Hall, Englewood Cliffs.

Ireland, D.R. and Hitt, M.A. (1999), "Achieving and Maintaining Strategic Competitiveness in the 21st Century: the Role of Strategic Leadership", *Academy of Management Executive*, Vol. 13, No. 1, pp. 43–57.

Itami, H. (1987), *Mobilizing Invisible Assets*, Harvard University Press, Cambridge.

Johnson, G. (1988), "Rethinking Incrementalism", *Strategic Management Journal*, Vol. 9, No. 1, pp. 75–91.

Johnson, G. (1993), "Managing Strategic Change: Strategy, Culture, and Action", *Long Range Planning*, Vol. 25, No. 1, pp. 28–36.

Johnson, P. and Duberley, J. (2000), "Understanding Management Research: An Introduction to Epistemology", Sage, London.

Johnson, P. and Harris, D. (2002), "Qualitative and Quantitative Issues in Research Design", in Partington, D. (ed.), *Essential Skills for Management Research*, Sage, London, pp. 99–116.

Jonas, H., Fry, R. and Srivastava, S. (1990), "The Office of the CEO: Understanding the Executive Experience", *Academy of Management Executive*, Vol. 4, No. 3, pp. 36–48.

Katz, R. (1974), "Skills of an Effective Administrator", *Harvard Business Review*, Vol. 64, No. 2, pp. 90–102.

Keele, R.L., Buckner, K. and Bushnell, S.J. (1987), "Formal Mentoring Programs are No Panacea", *Management Review*, Vol. 76, No. 2, pp. 67–68.

Kenny, D.A. and Zaccaro, S.J. (1983), "An Estimate of Variance Due to Traits in Leadership", *Journal of Applied Psychology*, Vol. 68, No. 4, pp. 678–685.

Kiesler, S. and Sproull, L. (1982), "Managerial Response to Changing Environments: Perspectives on Problem Sensing From Social Cognition", *Administrative Science Quarterly*, Vol. 27, No. 4, pp. 548–570.
Kirkpatrick, S.A. and Locke, E.A. (1991), "Leadership: Do Traits Matter?", *The Executive*, Vol. 5, No. 2, pp. 248–260.
Kisfalvi, V. (2000), "The Threat of Failure, the Perils of Success and CEO Character: Sources of Strategic Persistence", *Organization Studies*, Vol. 21, No. 3, pp. 611–639.
Kohlberg, L. (1969), "Stage and Sequence: The Cognitive Development Approach to Socialization", in Goslin, D. (ed.), *Handbook of Socialization Theory and Research*, Rand McNally, Chicago, pp. 347–389.
Kolb, D. (1984), *Experiential Learning: Experience As the Source of Learning and Development*, Prentice-Hall, Englewood Cliffs.
Korn Ferry (1989), *Twenty-First Century CEO*, Korn Ferry, New York.
Kotter, J. (1982), "What Effective General Managers Really Do", *Harvard Business Review*, Vol. 60, No. 6, pp. 156–167.
Kotter, P. (1988), *The Leadership Factor*, Free Press, New York.
Kouzes, J. and Posner, B. (1995), *The Leadership Challenge*, Jossey-Bass, San Francisco.
Kram, K.E. (1983), "Phases of the Mentor Relationship", *Academy of Management Journal*, Vol. 26, No. 3, pp. 353–372.
Kram, K.E. (1985), *Mentoring at Work: Developmental Relationships in Organizational Life*, Scott Foresman, Glenview.
Langley, A. (1990), "Patterns in the Use of Formal Analysis in Strategic Decisions", *Organization Studies*, Vol. 11, No. 1, pp. 17–45.
Langley, A. (1995), "Between 'Paralysis by Analysis' and 'Extinction by Instinct'", *Sloan Management Review*, Vol. 36, No. 3, p. 76.
Larson, L.L. and Rowland, K.M. (1974), "Leadership Style and Cognitive Complexity", *Academy of Management Review*, Vol. 17, No. 1, pp. 37–45.
Lawrence, P.R. and Lorsch, J.W. (1986), *Organization and Environment: Managing Differentiation and Integration*, Harvard Business School Press, Cambridge.
Legge, K. (2003), "Strategy as Organizing", in Cummings, S. and Wilson, D. (eds), *Images of Strategy*, Blackwell, Oxford, pp. 75–104.
Leslie, B., Aring, M.K. and Brand, B. (1998), "Informal Learning: the New Frontier of Employee and Organizational Development", *Economic Development Review*, Vol. 15, No. 4, pp. 12–18.
Levinson, H. (1979), "Mentoring: Socializing for Leadership", *Annual Meeting of the Academy of Management*, Atlanta.
Levinson, H. and Rosenthal, S. (1984), *CEO: Corporate Leadership in Action*, Basic Books, New York.
Lewin, K. (1947), "Frontiers in Group Dynamics", *Human Relations*, Vol. 1, pp. 5–41.
Lewis, M.W. (2000), "Exploring Paradox: Toward a More Comprehensive Guide", *Academy of Management Review*, Vol. 25, No. 4, pp. 760–776.
Liedtka, J.M. and Rosenblum, J.W. (1996), "Sharing Conversations: Making Strategy, Managing Change", *California Management Review*, Vol. 39, No. 1, pp. 141–157.
Liedtka, J.M. and Rosenblum, J.W. (1998), "Teaching Strategy As Design: A Note From the Field", *Journal of Management Education*, Vol. 22, No. 3, pp. 285–303.

Likert, R. (1967), *The Human Organization*, McGraw-Hill, New York.

Lippert, R.J. (2001), *Whither Executive Education? A Working Paper*, University of South Carolina.

Mahler, W.R. and Drotter, S.J. (1986), *The Succession Planning Handbook for the Chief Executive*, Mahler Publishing, Midland Park.

Malone, J.W. (2001), "Shining a New Light on Organizational Change: Improving Self-Efficacy Through Coaching", *Organization Development Journal*, Vol. 19, No. 2, pp. 27–36.

Manning, T. (2002), "Strategic Conversation as a Tool for Change", *Strategy and Leadership*, Vol. 30, No. 5, pp. 35–38.

Marsick, V. and Volpe, F. (1999), "Informal Learning on the Job", in Marsick, V. and Volpe, F. (eds), *Advances in Developing Human Resources*, Berrett-Koehler, San Francisco.

McCall, M.W. (1988), "Developing Executives Through Work Experiences", *HR, Human Resource Planning*, Vol. 11, No. 1, pp. 1–11.

McCall, M.W. (2004), "Leadership Development Through Experience", *Academy of Management Executive*, Vol. 18, No. 3, pp. 127–130.

McCall, M.W. and Kaplan, R. (1985), *Whatever It Takes: Decision Makers at Work*, Prentice-Hall, Englewood Cliffs.

McCall, M.W., Lombardo, M.M. and Morrison, A.M. (1988), *The Lessons of Experience, Lexington Books*, Lexington.

McCauley, C.D. (1986), *Developmental Experiences in Managerial Work: a Literature Review*, Report no. 26, Center for Creative Leadership, Greensboro.

McCauley, C.D. and Douglas, C.A. (2004), "Developmental Relationships", in McCauley, C.D. and Velso, E.V. (eds), *Handbook of Leadership Development*, Jossey-Bass, San Francisco, pp. 85–115.

McCauley, C.D., Eastman, L.J. and Ohlott, P.J. (1995), "Linking Management Selection and Development Through Stretch Assignments", *Human Resource Management*, Vol. 34, No. 1, pp. 93–115.

McDaniel, E. and Lawrence, C. (1990), *Cognitive Complexity: An Approach to the Measure of Thinking*, Springer-Verlag, New York.

McGregor, D. (1966), *The Human Side of Enterprise*, McGraw-Hill, New York.

Merriam, S. and Caffarella, R. (1991), *Learning in Adulthood*, Jossey-Bass, San Francisco.

Mezirow, J. (1990), *Fostering Critical Reflection*, Jossey-Bass, San Francisco.

Miles, R.E. and Snow, C.C. (1978), *Organization Strategy, Structure, and Process*, McGraw-Hill, New York.

Miller, D. (1989), "Matching Strategies and Strategy Making: Process, Content, and Performance", *Human Relations*, Vol. 42, No. 3, pp. 241–260.

Miller, D. (1990), *The Icarus Paradox*, Harper Business, New York.

Miller, D., Eisenstat, R. and Foote, N. (2002), "Strategy from the Inside Out: Building Capability-Creating Organizations", *California Management Review*, Vol. 44, No. 3, pp. 37–54.

Miller, L.M. (1989), *Barbarians to Bureaucrats: Corporate Life Cycle Strategies*, Clarkson N Potter, New York.

Mintzberg, H. (1973), *The Nature of Managerial Work*, Harper and Row, New York.

Mintzberg, H. (1978), "Patterns in Strategy Formation", *Management Science*, Vol. 24, No. 9, pp. 934–948.

Mintzberg, H. (1979), *The Structuring of Organizations*, Prentice-Hall, Englewood Cliffs.
Mintzberg, H. (1981), "Organization Design: Fashion or Fit?", *Harvard Business Review*, Vol. 59, No. 1, p. 103.
Mintzberg, H. (1983), "Crafting Strategy", *Harvard Business Review*, Vol. 65, No. 4, pp. 66–75.
Mintzberg, H. (1989), *Mintzberg on Management: Inside Our Strange World of Organizations*, Free Press, New York.
Mintzberg, H., Ahlstrand, B. and Lampel, J. (1998), *Strategy Safari*, Prentice-Hall Europe, Hemel Hempstead.
Mintzberg, H. and Lampel, J. (1999), "Reflecting on the Strategy Process", *Sloan Management Review*, Vol. 40, No. 3, pp. 21–30.
Mintzberg, H. and Lampel, J. (2001), *MBAs as CEOs*, available at: www.henrymintzberg.com
Mintzberg, H. and Quinn, J.B. (1996), *The Strategy Process: Concepts, Contexts, Cases* (3rd edition), Prentice-Hall, Englewood Cliffs.
Mintzberg, H. and Waters, J.A. (1985), "Of Strategies, Deliberate and Emergent", *Strategic Management Journal*, Vol. 6, No. 3, pp. 257–272.
Mitroff, I. (1983), "Archetypal Social Systems Analysis: On the Deeper Structure of Human Systems", *Academy of Management Review*, Vol. 8, No. 3, pp. 387–397.
Moncrieff, J. (1999), "Is Strategy Making a Difference?", *Long Range Planning*, Vol. 32, No. 2, pp. 273–276.
Moxley, R.S. and Pulley, M.L. (2003), "Tough Going: Learning From Experience the Hard Way", *Leadership in Action*, Vol. 23, No. 2, pp. 14–18.
Mumford, A. (1992), "Accidental Learning Opportunities", *Training and Management Development*, Vol. 2, No. 1, pp. 301–305.
Mumford, A. (1995), "How Managers Help With Development", *Industrial and Commercial Training*, Vol. 27, No. 8, pp. 8–12.
Mumford, A. (1996), "Four Approaches to Learning From Experience", *Employee Counselling Today*, Vol. 8, No. 5, pp. 22–31.
Nonaka, I. (1988), "Toward Middle-Up-Down Management: Accelerating Information Creation", *Sloan Management Review*, Vol. 29, No. 3, pp. 9–18.
Nulty, P. (1989), "America's Toughest Bosses", *Fortune*, February 27, pp. 40–54.
Nutt, P.C. (1984), "Types of Organizational Decision Processes", *Administrative Science Quarterly*, Vol. 29, No. 3, pp. 414–450.
Nutt, P.C. (1987), "Identifying and Appraising How Managers Install Strategy", *Strategic Management Journal*, Vol. 8, No. 1, pp. 1–14.
O'Shannassy, T. (2002), "Modern Strategic Management: Balancing Strategic Thinking and Strategic Planning for Internal and External Stakeholders", *Singapore Management Review*, Vol. 25, No. 1, pp. 53–67.
Ohmae, K. (1982), *The Mind of the Strategist*, Penguin Books, New York.
Orndoff, K. (2002), "Developing Strategic Competencies: a Starting Point", *Information Management Journal*, Vol. 36, No. 4, pp. 57–61.
Paglis, L.L. and Green, S.G. (2002), "Leadership Self-Efficacy and Managers' Motivation for Leading Change", *Journal of Organizational Behavior*, Vol. 23, No. 2, pp. 215–229.
Pascale, R. (1990), *Managing on the Edge*, Simon and Schuster, New York.
Pascale, R.T. (1996), "The Honda Effect", *California Management Review*, Vol. 38, No. 4, pp. 80–91.

Pascale, R.T. (1999), "Surfing the Edge of Chaos", *Sloan Management Review*, Vol. 40, No. 3, pp. 83–94.

Patton, M.Q. (1987), *How to Use Qualitative Methods in Evaluation*, Sage, Beverly Hills.

Pellegrino, K.C. and Carbo, J.A. (2001), "Behind the Mind of the Strategist", *TQM Magazine*, Vol. 13, No. 6, pp. 375–380.

Peters, T.J. and Waterman, R.H. (1982), In *Search of Excellence: Lessons From America's Best Run Companies*, Harper and Row, London.

Peterson, T.O. and Arnn, R.B. (2005), "Self-Efficacy: The Foundation of Human Performance", *Performance Improvement Quarterly*, Vol. 18, No. 2, pp. 5–18.

Pettigrew, A. (2003), "Strategy as Process, Power and Change", in Cummings, S. and Wilson, D. (eds), *Images of Strategy*, Blackwell, Oxford, pp. 301–330.

Podsakoff, P.M., MacKenzie, S.B., Moorman, S.B. and Fetter, R. (1990), "Transformational Leader Behaviours and Substitutes for Leadership as Determinants of Employee Satisfaction, Commitment, Trust, and Organizational Citizenship Behaviors", *Leadership Quarterly*, Vol. 1, No. 2, pp. 107–142.

Popper, M. (2005), "Main Principles and Practices in Leader Development", *Leadership and Organization Development Journal*, Vol. 26, No. 1, pp. 62–75.

Porter, M.E. (1980), *Competitive Strategy: Techniques for Analyzing Industries and Competitors*, Free Press, New York.

Porter, S.S. and Inks, L.W. (2000), "Cognitive Complexity and Salesperson Adaptability: an Exploratory Investigation", *Journal of Personal Selling and Sales Management*, Vol. 20, No. 1, pp. 15–21.

Quinn, J.B. (1980), "Managing Strategic Change", *Sloan Management Review*, Vol. 21, No. 4, pp. 3–20.

Quinn, R. (1988), *Beyond Rational Management*, Jossey-Bass, San Francisco.

Quinn, R. and Cameron, K. (1988), *Paradox and Transformation*, Ballinger, Cambridge.

Quinn, R., Denison, D. and Hooijberg, R. (1990), "An Empirical Assessment of the Competing Values Leadership Instrument", in Quinn, R., Faerman, S., Thompson, M. and McGrath, M. (eds), *Becoming a Master Manager*, Wiley, New York.

Quinn, R.E., Spreitzer, G.M. and Hart, S. (1991), "Challenging the Assumptions of Bipolarity: Interpenetration and Managerial Effectiveness", in Srivasta, S. and Fry, R. (eds), *Executive Continuity*, Jossey-Bass, San Francisco.

Quinn, R.E., Faerman, S.R., Thompson, M.P. and McGrath, M.R. (1996), *Becoming a Master Manager*, John Wiley & Sons, New York.

Raelin, J. (2000), *Work-Based Learning: the New Frontier of Management Development*, Prentice-Hall, Englewood Cliffs.

Ragins, B.R. and Cotton, J.L. (1999), "Mentor Functions and Outcomes: a Comparison of Men and Women in Formal and Informal Mentoring Relationships", *Journal of Applied Psychology*, Vol. 84, No. 4, pp. 529–550.

Redmond, M.R., Mumford, M.D. and Teach, R. (1993), "Putting Creativity to Work: Effects of Leader Behavior on Subordinate Creativity", *Organizational Behavior and Human Decision Processes*, Vol. 55, No. 1, pp. 120–151.

Rowe, G.W. (2001), "Creating Wealth in Organizations: The Role of Strategic Leadership", *Academy of Management Executive*, Vol. 15, No. 1, pp. 81–94.

Scandura, T.A., Tejeda, M.J., Werther, W.B. and Lankau, M.J. (1996), "Perspectives on Mentoring", *Leadership and Organization Development Journal*, Vol. 17, No. 3, p. 50.

Schendel, D.E. and Hofer, C.W. (1979), *Strategic Management: a New View of Business Policy and Planning*, Little, Brown, Boston.
Schleede, J. (2002), "The Future of Management Education", *Mid-American Journal of Business*, Vol. 17, No. 1, pp. 5–8.
Schön, D. (1983), *The Reflective Practitioner: How Professionals Think in Action*, Maurice Temple Smith, London.
Schön, D. (1987), *Educating the Reflective Practitioner: Toward a New Design for Teaching and Learning in the Professions*, Jossey-Bass, San Francisco.
Schroeder, H.M. (1971), "Conceptual Complexity and Personality Organization", in Schroeder, H.M. and Suedfeld, P. (eds), *Personality Theory and Information Processing*, Ronald, New York, pp. 240–273.
Schwenk, C.R. (1988), "The Cognitive Perspective on Strategic Decision Making", *Journal of Management Studies*, Vol. 25, No. 1, pp. 41–55.
Seijts, G.H. and Latham, G.P. (2006), "Learning Goals or Performance Goals: is it the Journey or the Destination?", *Ivey Business Journal*, Vol. May/June, pp. 1–6.
Seiling, J. and Hinrichs, G. (2005), "Mindfulness and Constructive Accountability as Critical Elements of Effective Sensemaking", *Organization Development Journal*, Vol. 23, No. 3, pp. 82–88.
Senge, P. (1990), *The Fifth Discipline: The Art and Practice of the Learning Organization*, Doubleday, New York.
Senge, P. (1992), "Mental Models", *Planning Review*, Vol. 20, No. 2, pp. 4–12.
Shaw, P. (2002), *Changing Conversations in Organizations: A Complexity Approach to Change*, Routledge, London.
Shetty, Y. and Perry, S. (1976), "Are Top Executives Transferable Across Companies?", *Business Horizons*, Vol. 19, No. 3, pp. 23–28.
Shrivastava, P. and Grant, J.H. (1985), "Empirically Derived Models of Strategic Decision Making Processes", *Strategic Management Journal*, Vol. 6, No. 2, pp. 97–113.
Shrivastava, P. and Schneider, S. (1984), "Organizational Frames of Reference", *Human Relations*, Vol. 37, No. 10, pp. 795–809.
Simon, H.A. (1993), "Strategy and Organizational Evolution", *Strategic Management Journal*, Vol. 14, Special issue, pp. 131–142.
Smith, B. and Morphey, G. (1994), "Tough Challenges: How Big a Learning Gap?", *Journal of Management Development*, Vol. 13, No. 9, pp. 3–5.
Smith, J.A. and Foti, R.J. (1998), "A Pattern Approach to the Study of Leader Emergence", *Leadership Quarterly*, Vol. 9, No. 2, pp. 928–936.
Smith, P.A.C. (2001), "Action Learning and Reflective Practice in Phase Environments that are Related to Leadership Developments", *Management Learning*, Vol. 32, No. 1, pp. 31–48.
Snell, R. (1989), "Graduating From the School of Hard Knocks", *Journal of Management Development*, Vol. 8, No. 5, pp. 23–30.
Snell, R. (1992), "Experiential Learning at Work: Why Can't it be Painless?", *Management Decision*, Vol. 30, No. 6, pp. 133–142.
Sonsino, S. (2002), "Leadership Perspective", in Jenkins, M. and Ambrosini, V. (eds), *Strategic Management: a Multi-Perspective Approach*, Palgrave, Basingstoke, pp. 222–249.
Sorohan, E.G. (1993), "We Do; Therefore, We Learn", *Training and Development*, Vol. 47, No. 10, pp. 47–55.

Sosik, J.J., Lee, D. and Bouquillon, E.A. (2005), "Context and Mentoring: Examining Formal and Informal Relationships in High Tech Firms and K-12 Schools", *Journal of Leadership and Organizational Studies*, Vol. 12, No. 2, pp. 94–108.

Spender, J.C. (1989), *Industry Recipes: the Nature and Sources of Managerial Judgement*, Blackwell, Oxford.

Spreitzer, G.M. (2006), "Leading to Grow and Growing to Lead: Leadership Development Lessons From Positive Organizational Studies", *Organizational Dynamics*, Vol. 35, No. 4, pp. 305–313.

Stacey, R.D. (1996), *Strategic Management of Organisational Dynamics*, Pitman, London.

Stajkovic, A. and Luthans, F. (1998), "Social Cognitive Theory and Self-Efficacy: Going Beyond Traditional Motivational and Behavioral Approaches", *Organizational Dynamics*, Vol. 26, No. 4, pp. 62–74.

Starbuck, W.H. (1983), "Organisations as Action Generators", *American Sociological Review*, Vol. 48, No. 1, pp. 91–102.

Starkey, K. (2002), "Andrew Pettigrew on Executives and Strategy: An Interview", *European Management Journal*, Vol. 20, No. 1, pp. 20–34.

Streufert, S. and Driver, M.J. (1965), "Conceptual Structure, Information Load and Perceptual Complexity", *Psychological Science*, Vol. 3, No. 5, pp. 249–250.

Streufert, S., Streufert, S.C. and Castore, C.H. (1968), "Leadership in Negotiations and the Complexity of Conceptual Structure", *Journal of Applied Psychology*, Vol. 52, No. 3, pp. 218–223.

Streufert, S. and Swezey, R. (1986), *Complexity, Managers, and Organizations*, Academic Press, Orlando.

Stumpf, S.A. (1989), "Work Experiences That Stretch Managers' Capacities for Strategic Thinking", *Journal of Management Development*, Vol. 8, No. 5, pp. 31–40.

Stumpf, S.A. and Mullen, T.P. (1991), "Strategic Leadership: Concepts, Skills, Style and Process", *Journal of Management Development*, Vol. 10, No. 1, pp. 42–53.

Tait, R. (1996), "The Attributes of Leadership", *Leadership and Organization Development Journal*, Vol. 17, No. 1, pp. 27–31.

Teece, D.J., Pisano, G. and Shuen, A. (1997), "Dynamic Capabilities and Strategic Management", *Strategic Management Journal*, Vol. 18, No. 7, pp. 509–533.

*The Economist* (2002), "The $100,000 Question: Do You Really Need That MBA?", *The Economist*, July 25, p. 64.

Thomas, R.J. and Cheese, P. (2005), "Leadership: Experience is the Best Teacher", *Strategy and Leadership*, Vol. 33, No. 3, pp. 24–29.

Thompson, J.L. (1996), "Strategic Effectiveness and Success: The Learning Challenge", *Management Decision*, Vol. 34, No. 7, pp. 14–22.

Tichy, N. (1983), *Managing Strategic Change: Technical, Political and Cultural Dynamics*, Wiley, New York.

Tichy, N. (2002), *The Cycle of Leadership*, Harper Business, New York.

Tichy, N. and Devanna, M. (1986), *The Transformational Leader*, Wiley, New York.

Toit, A.D. (2003), "Knowledge: A Sense Making Process Shared Through Narrative", *Journal of Knowledge Management*, Vol. 7, No. 3, pp. 27–37.

Triandis, H. (1977), *Interpersonal Behaviour*, Brooks/Cole, Monterey.

Tuckman, B. (1967), "Personality Structure, Group Composition and Group Functioning", *Sociometry*, Vol. 27, No. 4, pp. 469–487.

Vandermerwe, S. and Vandermerwe, A. (1991), "Making Strategic Change Happen", *European Management Journal*, Vol. 9, No. 2, pp. 174–181.

Vicere, A.A. (1988), "University-Based Executive Education: Impacts and Implications", *Journal of Management Development*, Vol. 7, No. 4, pp. 5–13.

Vickers, G. (1965), *The Art of Judgement: a Study of Policy Making*, Chapman and Hall, London.

Vilkinas, T. and Cartan, G. (2001), "The Behavioural Control Room for Managers: the Integrator Role", *Leadership and Organization Development Journal*, Vol. 22, No. 4, pp. 175–185.

Wagner, J.A. and Gooding, R.Z. (1997), "Equivocal Information and Attribution: An Investigation of Patterns of Managerial Sensemaking", *Strategic Management Journal*, Vol. 18, No. 4, pp. 275–286.

Wall, S.J. and Wall, S.R. (1995), "The Evolution (Not the Death) of Strategy", *Organizational Dynamics*, Vol. 24, No. 2, pp. 6–19.

Walsh, J.P. (1995), "Managerial and Organizational Cognition: Notes from a Trip Down Memory Lane", *Organization Science*, Vol. 6, No. 3, pp. 280–321.

Wang, P. and Chan, P.S. (1995), "Top Management Perception of Strategic Information Processing in a Turbulent Environment", *Leadership and Organization Development Journal*, Vol. 16, No. 7, pp. 33–43.

Wasburn, M.H. and Crispo, A.W. (2006), "Strategic Collaboration: Developing a More Effective Mentoring Model", *Review of Business*, Vol. 27, No. 1, pp. 18–25.

Weick, K.E. (1979), *The Social Psychology of Organizing*, Addison-Wesley, Reading.

Weick, K.E. (2001), *Making Sense of the Organization*, Blackwell, Oxford.

Weick, K.E., Sutcliffe, K.M. and Obstfeld, D. (2005), "Organizing and the Process of Sensemaking", *Organization Science*, Vol. 16, No. 4, pp. 409–421.

Weick, K. and Westley, F. (1996), "Organizational Learning: Affirming an Oxymoron", in Clegg, S.R., Hardy, C. and Nord, W.R. (eds), *Handbook of Organization Studies*, Sage, London.

Westfall, B. (1992), "Leaders Care for the Spirit", *Executive Excellence*, Vol. 9, No. 9, pp. 11–12.

Whittington, R. (2003), "The Work of Strategizing and Organizing: for a Practice Perspective", *Strategic Organization*, Vol. 1, No. 1, pp. 117–125.

Wildavsky, A.B. (1979), Speaking *Truth to Power: the Art and Craft of Policy Analysis*, Little, Brown, Boston.

Williams, S. (1996), *A Balloon Waiting to be Burst? Pseudo-management Training*, Research Report no. 22, Social Affairs Unit, London.

Wilmott, H. (1994), "Management Education: Provocation to a Debate", *Management Learning*, Vol. 25, No. 1, pp. 105–136.

Wilson, I. (1998), "Strategic Planning for the Millennium: Resolving the Dilemma", *Long Range Planning*, Vol. 31, No. 4, pp. 507–513.

Wilson, J.A. and Elman, N.S. (1990), "Organizational Benefits of Mentoring", *Academy of Management Executive*, Vol. 4, No. 4, pp. 88–94.

Wooldridge, B. and Floyd, S.W. (1990), "The Strategy Process, Middle Management Involvement, and Organizational Performance", *Strategic Management Journal*, Vol. 11, No. 3, pp. 231–242.

Yost, D.S., Sentner, S.M. and Forlenza-Bailey, A. (2000), "An Examination of Construct of Critical Reflection: Implications for Teacher Education Programming in the Twenty-First Century", *Journal of Teacher Education*, Vol. 5, No. 1, pp. 39–48.

Yukl, G.A. (1989), *Leadership in Organizations*, Prentice-Hall, Englewood Cliffs.
Zabriskie, N.B. and Huellmantel, A.B. (1991), "Developing Strategic Thinking in Senior Management", *Long Range Planning*, Vol. 24, No. 6, pp. 25–33.
Zaleznik, A. (1977), "Managers and Leaders: Are They Different?", *Harvard Business Review*, Vol. 55, No. 3, pp. 67–78.

# Index